MOLECULAR PHYSICS

MOLECULAR PHYSICS

By

Dr. Ajit Kumar Sharma

M.Sc., Ph.D.

Head

Department of Physics

D.A.V. (P.G.) College, Bulandshahr (U.P.)

(India)

DPH

DISCOVERY PUBLISHING HOUSE PVT. LTD.

NEW DELHI-110 002

Published by:
Tilak Wasan
DISCOVERY PUBLISHING HOUSE PVT. LTD.
4383/4B, Ansari Road, Darya Ganj
New Delhi-110 002 (India)
Phone : +91-11-23279245, 43596064-65
Fax : +91-11-23253475
E-mail : discoverypublishinghouse@gmail.com
sales@discoverypublishinggroup.com
parul.wasan@gmail.com
web : www.discoverypublishinggroup.com

First Edition: **2014**

ISBN: 978-93-5056-430-1

Molecular Physics

Printed at:
Dynamic Printers
Delhi

Preface

Molecular physics is the development of fast computers and sophisticated software, which allow the calculation of molecular structures and potential energy surfaces in molecular ground states and even in excited states with an astonishing accuracy. Also, the dynamics of excited molecular states can be today visualized on a computer screen in slow motion to give a vivid and detailed picture of the way molecular processes occur on a femtosecond scale. This allows a much better understanding of chemical and biological reaction paths. Quantum chemistry, working in this field, has therefore received more attention in chemistry and biology. The success of molecular biology is partly based both on the new experimental techniques and on such computer simulations.

Molecular dynamics (MD) is a computer simulation of physical movements of atoms and molecules. The atoms and molecules are allowed to interact for a period of time, giving a view of the motion of the atoms. In the most common version, the trajectories of molecules and atoms are determined by numerically solving the Newton's equations of motion for a system of interacting particles, where forces between the particles and potential energy are defined by molecular mechanics force fields. The method was originally conceived within theoretical physics in the late 1950s and early 1960s, but is applied today mostly in materials science and the modeling of biomolecules.

Molecular spectra have a complex structure. Typical molecular spectra are band spectra, which are observed in emission, absorption, and Raman scattering in the form of the aggregate of more or less narrow bands in the ultra-violet, visible, and near-infrared regions and break down into a set of closely positioned lines when the spectral instruments used have sufficient resolving power.

A molecular orbital differs from the atomic case only in that the orbital must describe the motion of an electron in the field of more than one nucleus, as well as in the average field of the other electrons. A molecular orbital will in general, therefore, encompass all the nuclei in the molecule, rather than being centred on a single nucleus as in the atomic case. Once the forms and properties of the molecular orbitals are known, the electronic configuration and properties of the molecule are again determined by assigning electrons to the molecular orbitals in the order of increasing energy and in accordance with the Pauli exclusion principle.

Molecular scale electronics, also called single molecule electronics, is a branch of nanotechnology that uses single molecules, or nanoscale collections of single molecules, as electronic components. Because single molecules constitute the smallest stable structures imaginable, this miniaturisation is the ultimate goal for shrinking electrical circuits.

The language of the book is simple and self explanatory, this will help the students to grasp the fundamentals of the subject easily.

—Author

Contents

1

Introduction

Molecular physics is the study of the physical properties of molecules, the chemical bonds between atoms as well as the molecular dynamics. Its most important experimental techniques are the various types of spectroscopy. The field is closely related to atomic physics and overlaps greatly with theoretical chemistry, physical chemistry and chemical physics.

Additionally to the electronic excitation states which are known from atoms, molecules are able to rotate and to vibrate. These rotations and vibrations are quantised, there are discrete energy levels. The smallest energy differences exist between different rotational states, therefore pure rotational spectra are in the far infrared region (about 30–150 μm wavelength) of the electromagnetic spectrum. Vibrational spectra are in the near infrared (about 1–5 μm) and spectra resulting from electronic transitions are mostly in the visible and ultraviolet regions. From measuring rotational and vibrational spectra properties of molecules like the distance between the nuclei can be calculated. One important aspect of molecular physics is that the essential atomic orbital theory in the field of atomic physics expands to the molecular orbital theory.

THE PHYSICAL PROPERTIES OF MOLECULAR SUBSTANCES

Molecules are made of fixed numbers of atoms joined together by covalent bonds, and can range from the very small (even down to single atoms, as in the noble gases) to the very large (as in polymers, proteins or even DNA). The covalent bonds holding the molecules together are very strong, but these are largely irrelevant to the physical properties of the substance. Physical properties are governed by the intermolecular forces attracting one molecule to its neighbours van der Waals attractions or hydrogen bonds.

MELTING AND BOILING POINTS

Molecular substances tend to be gases, liquids or low melting point solids, because the intermolecular forces of attraction are comparatively weak. You don't have to break any covalent bonds in order to melt or boil a molecular substance.

The size of the melting or boiling point will depend on the strength of the intermolecular forces. The presence of hydrogen bonding will lift the melting and boiling points. The larger the molecule the more van der Waals attractions are possible - and those will also need more energy to break.

SOLUBILITY IN WATER

Most molecular substances are insoluble (or only very sparingly soluble) in water. Those which do dissolve often react with the water, or else are capable of forming hydrogen bonds with the water.

Methane, CH_4, Dissolve in Water

The methane itself isn't the problem. Methane is a gas, and so its molecules are already separate - the water doesn't need to pull them apart from one another.

The problem is the hydrogen bonds between the water molecules. If methane were to dissolve, it would have to force its way between water molecules and so break hydrogen bonds. That costs a reasonable amount of energy.

The only attractions possible between methane and water molecules are the much weaker van der Waals forces - and not much energy is released when these are set up. It simply isn't energetically profitable for the methane and water to mix.

Ammonia, NH_3, Dissolve in Water

Ammonia has the ability to form hydrogen bonds. When the hydrogen bonds between water molecules are broken, they can be replaced by equivalent bonds between water and ammonia molecules.

Some of the ammonia also reacts with the water to produce ammonium ions and hydroxide ions.

$$NH_3 + H_2O \rightleftharpoons NH_4^+ + OH^-$$

The reversible arrows show that the reaction doesn't go to completion. At any one time only about 1 per cent of the ammonia has actually reacted to form ammonium ions. The solubility of ammonia is mainly due to the hydrogen bonding and not the reaction. Other common substances which are freely soluble in water because they can hydrogen bond with water molecules include ethanol (alcohol) and sucrose (sugar).

SOLUBILITY IN ORGANIC SOLVENTS

Molecular substances are often soluble in organic solvents which are themselves molecular. Both the solute (the substance which is dissolving) and the solvent are likely to have molecules attracted to each other by van der Waals forces. Although these attractions will be disrupted when they mix, they are replaced by similar ones between the two different sorts of molecules.

ELECTRICAL CONDUCTIVITY

Molecular substances won't conduct electricity. Even in cases where electrons may be delocalised within a particular molecule, there isn't sufficient contact between the molecules to allow the electrons to move through the whole solid or liquid.

SOME INDIVIDUAL EXAMPLES

Iodine, I_2

Iodine is a dark grey crystalline solid with a purple vapour. M.Pt: 114°C. B.Pt: 184°C. It is very, very slightly soluble in water, but dissolves freely in organic solvents. Iodine is therefore a low melting point solid. The crystallinity suggests a regular packing of the molecules.

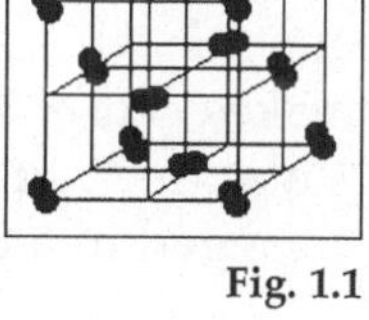

Fig. 1.1

The structure is described as face centred cubic - it is a cube of iodine molecules with another molecule at the centre of each face. The orientation of the iodine molecules within this structure is quite difficult to draw (let alone remember!). If your syllabus and past exam papers suggests that you need to remember it, look carefully at the next sequence of diagrams showing the layers.

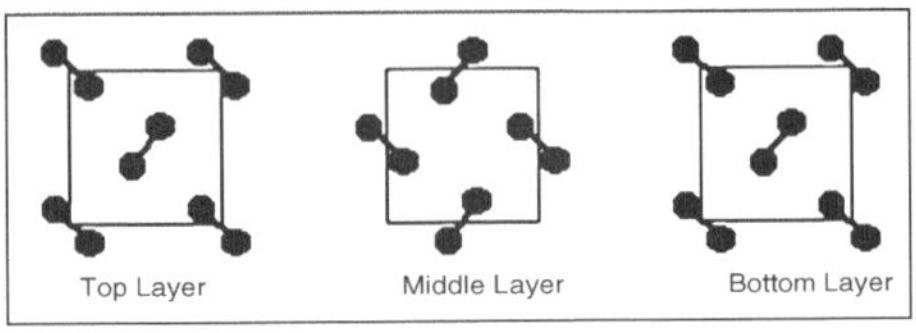

Fig. 1.2

Notice that as you look down on the cube, all the molecules on the left and right hand sides are aligned the same way. The ones in the middle are aligned in the opposite way.

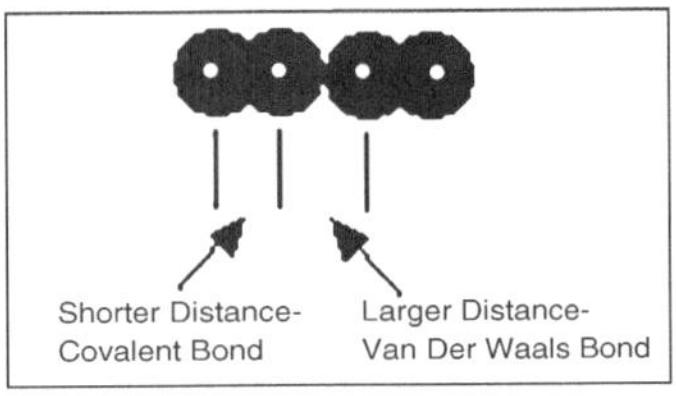

Fig. 1.3

All these diagrams show an 'exploded' view of the crystal. The iodine molecules are, of course, touching each other. Measurements of the distances between the centres of the atoms in the crystal show two different values:

The iodine atoms within each molecule are pulled closely together by the covalent bond. The van der Waals attraction between the molecules is much weaker, and you can think of the atoms in two separate molecules as just loosely touching each other.

Ice

Ice is a good example of a hydrogen bonded solid.

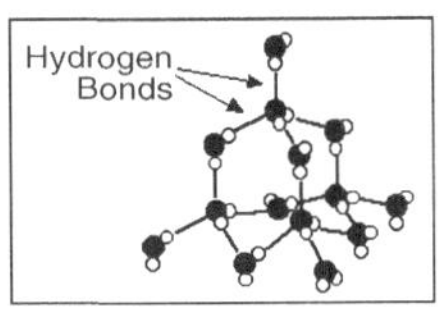

Fig. 1.4

There are lots of different ways that the water molecules can be arranged in ice. This is one of them, but NOT the common one - I can't draw that in any way that makes sense! The one below is known as 'cubic ice', or 'ice Ic'. It is based on the water molecules arranged in a diamond structure.

This is just a small part of a structure which extends over huge numbers of molecules in three dimensions. In the diagram, the lines represent hydrogen bonds. The lone pairs that the hydrogen atoms are attracted to are left out for clarity.

Cubic ice is only stable at temperatures below -80°C. The ice you are familiar with has a different, hexagonal structure. It is called 'ice Ih'.

The Unusual Density Behaviour of Water

The hydrogen bonding forces a rather open structure on the ice if you made a model of it, you would find a significant amount of wasted space. When ice melts, the structure breaks down and the molecules tend to fill up this wasted space.

This means that the water formed takes up less space than the original ice. Ice is a very unusual solid in this respect most solids show an increase in volume on melting. When water freezes, the opposite happens - there is an expansion as the hydrogen bonded structure establishes. Most liquids contract on freesing. Remnants of the rigid hydrogen bonded structure are still present in very cold liquid water, and don't finally disappear until 4°C. From 0°C to 4°C, the density of water increases as the molecules free themselves from the open structure and take up less space. After 4°C, the thermal motion of the molecules causes them to move apart and the density falls. That's the normal behaviour with liquids on heating.

POLYMERS

Bonding in Polymers

Polymers like poly(ethene) commonly called polythene consist of very long molecules. Poly(ethene) molecules are made by joining up lots of ethene molecules into chains of covalently bound carbon atoms with hydrogens attached. There may be short branches along the main chain, also consisting of carbon chains with attached hydrogens. The molecules are attracted to each other in the solid by van der Waals dispersion forces.

By controlling the conditions under which ethene is polymerised, it is possible to control the amount of branching to give two distinct types of polythene.

High Density Polythene

High density polythene has virtually unbranched chains. The lack of branching allows molecules to lie close together in a regular way which is almost crystalline.

Because the molecules lie close together, dispersion forces are more effective, and so the plastic is relatively strong and has a somewhat higher melting point than low density polythene. High density polythene is used for containers for household chemicals like washing-up liquid, for example, or for bowls or buckets.

Low Density Polythene

Low density polythene has lots of short branches along the chain. These branches prevent the chains from lying close together in a tidy arrangement. As a result dispersion forces are less and the plastic is weaker and has a lower melting point. Its density is lower, of course, because of the wasted space within the unevenly packed structure. Low density polythene is used for things like plastic bags.

ISOLATED ATOMS AND MOLECULES

Atomic, Molecular and Optical physics frequently considers atoms and molecules in isolation. Atomic models will consist of a single nucleus that may be surrounded by one or more bound electrons, whilst molecular models are typically concerned with Molecular Hydrogen and it's Molecular hydrogen ion. It is not concerned with the formation of molecules (although much of the physics is identical) nor does it examine atoms in a solid state as condensed matter. It is concerned with processes such as ionisation, Above threshold ionisation and excitation by photons or collisions with atomic particles.

While modelling atoms in isolation may not seem realistic, if one considers molecules in a gas or plasma then the timescales for molecule-molecule interactions are huge in comparison to the atomic and molecular processes that we are concerned with. This means that the individual molecules can be treated as if each were in isolation for the vast majority of the time they are. By this consideration atomic and molecular physics provides the underlying theory in plasma physics and atmospheric physics even though both deal with huge numbers of molecules.

ELECTRONIC CONFIGURATION

Electrons form notional shells around the nucleus. These are naturally in a ground state but can be excited by the absorption of energy from light (photons), magnetic fields, or interaction with a colliding particle (typically other electrons).

Electrons that populate a shell are said to be in a bound state. The energy necessary to remove an electron from its shell (taking it to infinity) is called the binding energy. Any quantity of energy absorbed by the electron in excess of this amount is converted to kinetic energy according to the conservation of energy. The atom is said to have undergone the process of ionisation.

In the event that the electron absorbs a quantity of energy less than the binding energy, it may transition to an excited state or to a Virtual state. After a statistically sufficient quantity of time, an electron in an excited state will undergo a transition to a lower state via spontaneous emission. The change in energy between the two energy levels must be accounted for (conservation of energy). In a neutral atom, the system will emit a photon of the difference in energy. However, if one of its inner shell electrons has been removed, a phenomenon-known as the Auger effect may take place where the quantity of energy is transferred to one of the bound electrons causing it to go into the continuum. This allows one to multiply ionise an atom with a single photon.

There are strict selection rules as to the electronic configurations that can be reached by excitation by light– however there are no such rules for excitation by collision processes.

MOLECULAR DYNAMICS APPLET

This applet simulates the dynamics of simple atoms and molecules in a two-dimensional universe. The force between the molecules is weakly attractive at short distances, but strongly repulsive when they touch. Use the applet to explore phases of matter, emergent behaviour, irreversibility, and thermal effects at the nanoscale.

THE PHYSICS

- The force between the atoms is calculated from the Lennard-Jones formula (truncated at a distance of 3 molecular diameters). This is a reasonably accurate model of the interactions between noble gas atoms.
- The simulation uses a natural system of units, with the atomic diameter, the atomic mass, the depth of the Lennard-Jones potential, and Boltzmann's constant all set equal to 1. For argon (for example), the unit of distance is 3.4 angstroms, the unit of mass is 40 atomic mass units, and the unit of energy is 0.01 electron-volts; the corresponding unit of time is then 2.2 picoseconds, the unit of velocity is 160 meters per second, and the unit of temperature is 120 kelvin. The Molecular size scrollbar determines the scale of the image, in screen pixels per unit of distance.
- The motion of the atoms is governed by Newton's laws, approximated using the Verlet algorithm with the indicated Time step. For sufficiently small time steps, the system's total energy should be approximately conserved.
- Atoms drawn in light gray are artifically fixed in space, as if they have infinite mass.
- Atoms can also be connected by a bond, drawn as a thin gray line, which creates an attractive spring-like force between them (in addition to the Lennard-Jones force). The spring constant is 5 in natural units. Although this feature allows some interesting

qualitative demonstrations, it is not realistic: Actual covalent bonds are thousands of times stiffer.

- The walls exert a linear (spring) force on the molecules, with a spring constant of 50 in natural units.
- There's also an optional uniform downward force, controlled by the Gravity scrollbar. The magnitude of this force, however, is not meant to be realistic. Earth's gravitational constant is utterly negligible in the units used here (a little over 10^{-13} for argon).
- That's all the physics! Everything else you see is a consequence of these basic laws (applied repeatedly as the atoms move), plus the initial configuration of the atoms. The simulation code knows nothing about phase transformations or crystal structure or irreversibility.

MOLECULAR DYNAMICS

Molecular dynamics (MD) is a computer simulation of physical movements of atoms and molecules. The atoms and molecules are allowed to interact for a period of time, giving a view of the motion of the atoms. In the most common version, the trajectories of molecules and atoms are determined by numerically solving the Newton's equations of motion for a system of interacting particles, where forces between the particles and potential energy are defined by molecular mechanics force fields. The method was originally conceived within theoretical physics in the late 1950s and early 1960s, but is applied today mostly in materials science and the modeling of biomolecules.

Because molecular systems consist of a vast number of particles, it is impossible to find the properties of such complex systems analytically; MD simulation circumvents this problem by using numerical methods. However, long MD simulations are mathematically ill-conditioned, generating cumulative errors in numerical integration that can be minimized with proper selection of algorithms and parameters, but not eliminated entirely.

The results of molecular dynamics simulations may be used to determine macroscopic thermodynamic properties of the system based on the ergodic hypothesis: the statistical ensemble averages are equal to time averages of the system. MD has also been termed 'statistical mechanics by numbers' and 'Laplace's vision of Newtonian mechanics' of predicting the future by animating nature's forces and allowing insight into molecular motion on an atomic scale.

AREAS OF APPLICATION

There is a significant difference between the focus and methods used by chemists and physicists, and this is reflected in differences in the jargon used by the different fields. In chemistry and biophysics, the interaction between the particles is either described by a 'force field' (classical MD), a quantum chemical model, or a mix between the two.

These terms are not used in physics, where the interactions are usually described by the name of the theory or approximation being used and called the potential energy, or just the 'potential'. Beginning in theoretical physics, the method of MD gained popularity in materials science and since the 1970s also in biochemistry and biophysics. In chemistry, MD serves as an important tool in protein structure determination and refinement using experimental tools such as X-ray crystallography and NMR. It has also been applied with limited success as a method of refining protein structure predictions. In physics, MD is used to examine the dynamics of atomic-level phenomena that cannot be observed directly, such as thin film growth and ion-subplantation. It is also used to examine the physical properties of nanotechnological devices that have not or cannot yet be created.

In applied mathematics and theoretical physics, molecular dynamics is a part of the research realm of dynamical systems, ergodic theory, Atomic, molecular, and optical physics and statistical mechanics in general. The concepts of energy conservation and molecular entropy come from thermodynamics. Some techniques to calculate conformational entropy such as principal components analysis come from information theory.

Mathematical techniques such as the transfer operator become applicable when MD is seen as a Markov chain. Also, there is a large community of mathematicians working on volume preserving, symplectic integrators for more computationally efficient MD simulations.

MD can also be seen as a special case of the discrete element method (DEM) in which the particles have spherical shape (*e.g.* with the size of their van der Waals radii.) Some authors in the DEM community employ the term MD rather loosely, even when their simulations do not model actual molecules.

STEERED MOLECULAR DYNAMICS (SMD)

Steered molecular dynamics (SMD) simulations, or force probe simulations, apply forces to a protein in order to manipulate its structure by pulling it along desired degrees of freedom. These experiments can be used to reveal structural changes in a protein at the atomic level. SMD is often used to simulate events such as mechanical unfolding or stretching.

There are two typical protocols of SMD: one in which pulling velocity is held constant and one in which applied force is constant. Typically, part of the studied system (*e.g.* an atom in a protein) is restrained by a harmonic potential. Forces are then applied to specific atoms at either a constant velocity or a constant force.

Umbrella Sampling is used to move the system along the desired reaction coordinate by varying, for example, the forces, distances, and angles manipulated in the simulation. Through umbrella sampling, all of the system's configurations—both high-energy and low-energy—are adequately sampled. Then, each configuration's change in free energy can be calculated as the potential mean force. A popular method of computing PMF is through the weighted histogram analysis method (WHAM), which analyses a series of umbrella sampling simulations.

MOLECULAR SPECTRA

Optical emission and absorption spectra, as well as Raman scattering spectra, that belong to free or weakly bound molecules. Molecular spectra have a complex structure. Typical molecular spectra are band spectra, which are observed in emission, absorption, and Raman scattering in the form of the aggregate of more or less narrow bands in the ultra-violet, visible, and near-infrared regions and break down into a set of closely positioned lines when the spectral instruments used have sufficient resolving power.

The specific structure of molecular spectra differs for different molecules and, generally speaking, grows more complex as the number of atoms in the molecule increases. For extremely complex molecules the visible and ultraviolet spectra consist of a few broad continuous bands; the spectra of such molecules are similar. Molecular spectra arise during quantum transitions between the energy levels ε' and ε'' of molecules according to the relation,

$$h\nu = \varepsilon' - \varepsilon'' \qquad (1)$$

where $h\nu$ is the energy of the emitted or absorbed photon of frequency ν (h is Planck's constant). During Raman scattering, $h\nu$ is equal to the energy difference between the incident and scattered photons. Molecular spectra are much more complex than atomic line spectra because of the greater complexity of internal motion in molecules. In addition to the motion of electrons with respect to two or more nuclei, vibrational motion of the nuclei (together with the inner electrons that surround them) about equilibrium positions and rotational motion of the molecule as a whole take place in molecules. Three types of energy levels and three types of spectra—electronic, vibrational, and rotational—correspond to these three types of motion.

According to quantum mechanics, the energy of all types of motion in a molecule can assume only discrete values—that is, the energy is quantised. The total energy S> of a molecule may be represented approximately as the sum of the quantised values of the energy of all three types of its motion:

$$\varepsilon = \varepsilon_{el} + \varepsilon_{vib} + \varepsilon_{rot} \qquad (2)$$

In order of magnitude,

$$\varepsilon_{el} : \varepsilon_{vib} : \varepsilon_{rot} = 1 : \sqrt{m/M} : m/M \qquad (3)$$

where m is the mass of the electron, and the quantity M is of the order of the mass of atomic nuclei in a molecule—that is, m/M ∞ 10^{-3}– 10^{-5}. Consequently,

$$\varepsilon_{e1} \approx \varepsilon_{vib} \approx \varepsilon_{rot} \qquad (4)$$

The quantity ε_{ei} is usually of the order of a few electron volts (eV), or a few hundred kilojoules per mole (kJ/mol), ε_{vib}Vib ∞ 10–2– 10^{-1} eV, and ε_{rot} ∞ 10^{-5}–10^{-3} eV.

According to (4), the system of energy levels of a molecule is characterised by the aggregate of widely separated electron levels (the various values of ε_{el} when $\varepsilon_{vib} = \varepsilon_{rot} = 0$), much more closely situated vibrational levels (various values of ε_{Vib} for a given ε_{ei} and for ε_{rot} = 0), and still more closely situated rotational levels (various values of εrot for given ε^{ei} and ε_{Vib}).

The electron energy levels ε_{ei} in (Eq. 2) corresponds to the equilibrium configurations of the molecule (in the case of a diatomic molecule characterised by the equilibrium values ro of the internuclear distance r). A certain equilibrium configuration and a certain value of E_{ei} correspond to each electron state. The lowest value corresponds to the ground energy level.

The set of the electron states of a molecule is determined by the properties of its electron shell. In principle the values of ε_{ei} may be calculated by the methods of quantum chemistry, but this task can be carried out only by approximate methods and for comparatively simple molecules. The most important information regarding the electron levels of a molecule (the position and characteristics of the electron energy levels), which is determined by its chemical structure, can be obtained by studying its molecular spectrum. The value of the quantum number S, which characterises the absolute value of the total spin moment of all electrons in the molecule, is an extremely important characteristic of a given electron energy level. Chemically stable molecules usually have an even number of electrons, and for them S = 0,1, 2 . . . (the value S = 0 is typical of the ground electron level, whereas 5 — 0 and S = 1 are typical of excited levels). Levels with S = 0 are called singlets, and those with S = 1 are called triplets (since the interaction in the molecule leads to splitting into K = 2S + 1 = 3 sublevels). Free radicals usually have an odd number of electrons; for them S = 1/2, 3/2 . . ., and the value 5=1/2 (doublet levels that split into K = 2 sublevels) is typical of both the ground and excited levels.

For molecules whose equilibrium configurations are symmetrical, the electron levels may be classified in another way. In the case of diatomic and linear triatomic molecules that have an axis of symmetry (of infinite order) that passes through the nuclei of all atoms, the electron levels are characterised by values of the quantum number λ, which defines the absolute value of the projection of the total orbital moment of all electrons onto the axis of the molecule. Levels with λ = 0, 1, 2... are correspondingly designated as Σ, Π, Δ..., and the quantity K: is indicated by a superscript on the left (for example, $^3\Sigma.^2\Pi$ ...) For molecules that have a center of symmetry, such as CO_2 and C_6H_6, all electron levels are divided into even and odd levels, which are designated by the indices g and u (depending on whether the wave function retains its sign or changes it upon reversal at the center of symmetry).

The vibrational energy levels (the values of ε_{Vib}) can be found by quantising the vibrational motion, which may be considered to be approximately harmonic. In the simplest case of a diatomic molecule (one vibrational degree of freedom, corresponding to a change in the internuclear distance r) it is considered as a harmonic oscillator; quantisation gives the equidistant energy levels:

$$\varepsilon_{vib} = hn_e\ (\nu + 1/2) \tag{5}$$

where ν^e is the fundamental frequency of the harmonic vibrations of the molecule, and ν is the vibrational quantum number, which assumes the values 0, 1, 2, ... The vibrational levels for two electron states.

A total of f "normal oscillations", with frequences νi (i = 1, 2, 3, ..., f) and a complex system of vibrational levels,

$$\varepsilon_{vib} = \sum_{i=1}^{f} h\nu_i \left(v_i + 1/2\right) \qquad (6)$$

where $v_i = 0, 1, 2, \ldots$ are the corresponding vibrational quantum numbers, can be obtained for every electron state of a polyatomic molecule consisting of N atoms ($N \geq 3$) with f vibrational degrees of freedom ($f = 3N - 5$ and $f = 3N - 6$ for linear and non-linear molecules, respectively). The set of frequencies of normal vibrations in the ground electron state is a very important characteristic of a molecule and depends on its chemical structure. All or part of the atoms of a molecule participate in a certain normal vibration; in the process, the atoms perform harmonic vibrations with the same frequency v_i but with different amplitudes that determine the shape of the vibration.

Normal vibrations are divided according to shape into stretching vibrations (in which the lengths of the bond lines change) and deformational vibrations (in which the angles between chemical bonds—the valence angles—change). The number of vibration frequencies is 2 for molecules of low symmetry (molecules that do not have axes of symmetry of an order greater than 2), and all vibrations are non-degenerate; for more symmetrical molecules there are doubly or triply degenerate oscillations (pairs and triplets of frequency-coincident vibrations).

For example, for the non-linear triatomic molecule H_2O f = 3, and three non-degenerate oscillations (two stretching vibrations and one deformational vibration) are possible. The more highly symmetrical linear triatomic molecule CO_2 has f = A —two non-degenerate (stretching) vibrations and one doubly degenerate (deformational) vibration. For the plane high-symmetry molecule C_6H_6 we obtain f = 30—ten non-degenerate and ten doubly degenerate vibrations; of these, 14 take place in the plane of the molecule (eight stretching and six deformational vibrations) and six non-planar deformational vibrations take place perpendicular to the plane. The still more highly symmetric tetrahedral molecule CH_4 has f = 9—one non-degenerate (stretching) vibration, one doubly degenerate (deformational) vibration, and two triply degenerate vibrations (one stretching and one deformational).

The rotational energy levels may be found by quantising the rotational motion of the molecule if it is considered as a solid with well-defined moments of inertia. In the simplest case, a diatomic or linear multiatomic molecule, its energy of rotation is,

$$\varepsilon_{rot} = 1/2(M^2/1)$$

where *I* is the molecule's moment of inertia with respect to the axis perpendicular to the axis of the molecule, and M is the angular momentum. According to the rules of quantisation,

$$M^2 \frac{h^2}{4\pi^2} J(J+1)$$

where the rotational quantum number J = 0, 1, 2, . . . and, consequently, the following is obtained for $\varepsilon_{rot,}$

$$\varepsilon_{rot} \frac{h^2}{8\pi^2 I} J(J+1) = hBJ(J+1) \qquad (7)$$

where the rotational constant $B = h/8\pi^2 I$ defines the scale of the distances between energy levels, which decreases as the masses of the nuclei and the internuclear distances increase.

Various types of molecular spectra arise during different types of transitions between the energy levels of molecules. According to Eq. (1) and Eq. (2),

$$\Delta\varepsilon = \varepsilon' - \varepsilon'' = \Delta\varepsilon_{vib} + \Delta\varepsilon_{rot} \triangleright \qquad (8)$$

where changes in $\Delta\varepsilon_{ei}$, $\Delta\varepsilon_{vib}$, and $\Delta\varepsilon_{rot}$ (the electronic, vibrational, and rotational energies, respectively) satisfy the condition,

$$\Delta\varepsilon_{el} \gg \Delta\varepsilon_{vib} \gg \Delta\varepsilon_{rot} \qquad (9)$$

The distances between levels are of the same order as the energies Eei, Evib, and Erot themselves, which satisfy condition Eq. (4).

When $\Delta\varepsilon_{el} \neq 0$, electron molecular spectra that can be seen in the visible and ultraviolet (UV) regions are produced. When $\Delta\varepsilon_{el} \neq 0$, usually $\Delta\varepsilon_{vib} \neq 0$ and $\Delta\varepsilon_{rot} \neq 0$; different vibrational bands correspond to different $\Delta\varepsilon_{vib}$ for a given $\Delta\varepsilon_{ei}$, and the different rotational lines into which the given band breaks down correspond to different $\Delta\varepsilon_{rot}$ for given $\Delta\varepsilon_{ei}$ and $\Delta\varepsilon_{vib}$. The characteristic band structure is obtained. The aggregate of bands with a given ASei (which corresponds to a purely electron transition of frequency $v_{ei} = \Delta\varepsilon_{ei}/h$) is called a system of bands; the individual bands have different intensities that depend on the relative probabilities of the transitions, which can be calculated approximately by quantum-mechanical methods.

For complex molecules, the bands of one system that correspond to a given electron transition usually merge into one broad continuous band, and several such broad bands may be superimposed on one another. Characteristic discrete electron spectra are observed in frozen solutions of organic compounds. Electron (or, more accurately, electron-vibrational-rotational) spectra are studied experimentally with spectrographs and spectrometers that use glass optics (for the visible region) and quartz optics (for the UV region), in which prisms or diffraction gratings are used to split the light into a spectrum.

When $\Delta\varepsilon_{ei} = 0$ and $\Delta\varepsilon_{vib} \neq 0$, vibrational molecular spectra are obtained that can be observed in the near infrared region (up to a few microns) and the central infrared region (up to a few dozen microns), usually in absorption but also in Raman scattering of light. When $\Delta\varepsilon_{rot} \neq 0$ and for a given ε_{vib}, a vibrational band that breaks down into individual rotational lines is usually obtained. Bands that correspond to

$$\Delta vi = v\,i - v''i = I \text{ when } \Delta v_k = v'k - v''\,k = 0$$

where $k \neq i$

These selection rules, which forbid other transitions, are strictly satisfied for purely harmonic vibrations. For anharmonic vibrations, bands for which $\Delta v > 1$ (overtones) appear. Their intensity is usually small and decreases as Δv increases.

Vibrational (or, more accurately, vibrational-rotational) spectra are studied experimentally in absorption in the infrared region by means of infrared spectrometers with prisms that are transparent to infrared radiation or with diffraction gratings, and also by means of Fourier spectrometers, and, in Raman scattering, by means of high-transmission spectrographs (for the visible region) using laser excitation.

When $\Delta\varepsilon_{ei} = 0$ and $\Delta\varepsilon_{vib} = 0$, purely rotational molecular spectra that consist of individual lines are produced. They are observed in absorption in the remote infrared region (hundreds of microns) and especially in the microwave region, and also in Raman spectra. For diatomic and linear polyatomic molecules (and also for sufficiently symmetric non-linear polyatomic molecules), the lines are equidistant (in the frequency scale) at intervals of $\Delta\nu = 2B$ in absorption spectra and $\Delta\nu = 4\,B$ in Raman spectra.

Purely rotational spectra are studied in absorption in the remote infrared region by means of infrared spectrometers with special diffraction gratings (echelette gratings) and Fourier spectrometers, whereas microwave (SHF) spectrometers are used in the microwave region and high-transmission spectrographs are used in Raman scattering. Methods of molecular spectroscopy, which are based on the study of molecular spectra, make it possible to solve various problems of chemistry, biology, and other sciences (for example, to determine the composition of petroleum products and polymers).

In chemistry, molecular structure is studied on the basis of molecular spectra. Electron molecular spectra make it possible to obtain information on the electron shells of molecules, to determine excited levels and their characteristics, and to find the dissociation energies of molecules (from the convergence of the vibrational levels of the molecule towards the dissociation boundaries). The study of vibrational molecular spectra makes it possible to find the characteristic frequencies of vibrations that correspond to certain types of chemical bonds in a molecule (for example, simple double and triple C—C bonds and C—H, N—H, and O—H bonds for organic molecules) of various groups of atoms (such as CH_2, CH_3, and NH_2), to determine the three-dimensional structure of molecules, and to distinguish between cis- and trans- isomers.

Both infrared absorption spectra and Raman scattering spectra are used for this purpose. The infrared absorption spectrum method has come into particularly wide use as one of the most effective optical methods of studying molecular structure. It provides the most complete information when combined with the study of Raman scattering spectra. The study of rotational molecular spectra and the rotational structure of electron and vibrational spectra makes it possible to find the parameters of the equilibrium configuration of a molecule (the bond length and valence angles) with high precision (for simpler molecules such as H_2O) from experimentally determined values of the moments of inertia of molecules, which are obtained from the values of the rotational constants.

The spectra of isotopic molecules (in particular, molecules in which hydrogen is replaced by deuterium), which have identical parameters of their equilibrium configurations but different moments of inertia, are studied to increase the number of parameters that can be determined.

Let us examine the benzene molecule, C_eH_e, as an example of the use of molecular spectra to determine the chemical structure of molecules. The study of its molecular spectrum confirms the correctness of the model of a planar molecule in which all six C—C bonds in the benzene ring are equivalent and form a regular hexagon, which has a sixth-order axis of symmetry that passes through the center of symmetry of the molecule perpendicular to its plane. The molecular electron absorption spectrum of C_6H_6 consists of several systems of bands that correspond to transitions from the ground, even singlet level to excited odd levels, the first of which is a triplet and the higher levels are singlets. The system of bands is most intensive in the region of 1840 angstroms (Å), where $\varepsilon_5 - \varepsilon^1 = 7.0$ eV, and the system of bands in the region of 3400 Å ($\varepsilon_2 - \varepsilon_1 = 3.8$ eV), which corresponds to a singlet-triplet transition prohibited by the approximate selection rules for total spin, is the weakest. The transitions correspond to the excitation of π-electrons, which are delocalised over the entire benzene ring.

The pattern of the levels obtained from the electron molecular spectra is in agreement with approximate quantum-mechanical calculations. The vibrational molecular spectra of C_6H_6 correspond to the presence in the molecule of a center of symmetry: vibration frequencies that are manifested in the infrared absorption spectrum (active frequencies) are absent (inactive) in the Raman scattering spectrum, and *vice-versa* (called alternative prohibition). Of the 20 normal oscillations of C_6H_6, four are active in the infrared absorption spectrum and seven are active in the Raman scattering spectrum; the other 11 are inactive in both.

The values of the measured frequencies (in cm^{-1}) are 673, 1038, 1486, and 3080 in the infrared absorption spectrum and 607, 850, 992, 1178, 1596, 3047, and 3062 in the Raman scattering spectrum. The frequencies 673 and 850 correspond to non-planar vibrations, and all other frequencies correspond to planar vibrations. The frequencies 992 (which corresponds to stretching vibration of the C—C bonds, which consists in periodic compression and expansion of the benzene ring), 3062 and 3080 (which correspond to stretching vibrations of the C—H bonds), and 607 (which corresponds to deformational vibration of the benzene ring) are especially characteristic of planar vibrations.

The observed vibrational spectra of C_6H_6 (and the analogous vibrational spectra of C_6D_6) are in very good agreement with the theoretical calculations that made it possible completely to interpret the spectra and to find the forms of all normal vibrations.

The structure of various classes of organic and inorganic molecules, including extremely complex molecules such as those of polymers, may be determined in the same manner by using the molecular spectra.

CALCULATING MOLECULAR SPECTRA

High resolution molecular spectroscopy probes both the basic physics of a molecule and gives information on its environment.

The calculation of molecular spectra can be used to:

- Test potential energy surfaces;
- Predict and assign spectra;
- Calculate transition intensities which are needed to obtain physical data from observed spectra such as number density, temperature, ortho/para ratios;
- Generate bulk data like specific heats, opacities;
- Establish links with reaction dynamics;
- Quantum 'chaology', classical dynamics of highly excited molecules is chaotic.

Conventionally vibration-rotation spectra are described using the following model. Vibrational motions of the molecule are modelled with simple harmonic oscillations about the equilibrium position. Rotational energy levels are much more difficult to model. A standard treatment is the rigid-rotor model with a perturbative expansion. The molecule changes in response to the rotational motion via a centrifugal distortion. This is for example a second order perturbation calculation.

An alternative method for reproducing molecular spectra is by direct solution of the underlying quantum mechanical equations of the problem. To do this completely from first principles it is necessary to consider both how the electrons and the nuclei move. A standard step in such a treatment is the Born-Oppenheimer approximation, *i.e.,* it is assumed that the light electrons can relax instantaneously to any movement by the heavy and slow nuclei. Within these approximation the two motions can be treated separately.

For high accuracy it is usual to use procedures based on the Variational Principle. It gives much to high values for the absolute electronic energy of the system, but this energy is not important. The important question is how the bond lengths and bond angles of the molecule vary. Such calculations define a potenial (hyper-) surface on which the nuclei move. In water this potential energy surface has 3 dimensions corresponding to the 3 vibrational degrees of motion.

The method favoured by us to get accurate energy levels and wavefunctions for the vibrational and rotational motion of a triatomic molecule on a given potential energy surface is the Discrete Variable Representation (c.f.DVR3D, a programme for the fully pointwise calculation of rotational-vibrational spectra of triatomic molecules by J.Tennyson, J.R. Henderson, N.G. Fulton. Since variational methods treat vibrational and rotational motion using the same potential an improvement derived from studying vibrational motions can lead to greatly improved estimates of rotational levels.

2

Spectra of Diatomic Molecules

EVALUATION OF THE SPECTRAL DATA

The evaluation involved the selection of the best sets of transition frequencies and molecular constants which were consistent with the measured transitions and their uncertainties. The selection of the most reliable transition frequencies posed few problems since there were relatively few cases where a variety of measurements were reported for the same transition. In cases where this did occur, the selection was based on both the overall consistency of the measurement in question with the other spectral data available, and on the reported uncertainty in the measurements. In nearly all cases the measurements with the smallest reported uncertainties were found to be the most reliable.

The determination of the most reliable molecular constants posed more severe difficulties. Inconsistencies arose in cases where data were reported by several independent workers who studied quite different regions of the spectrum, *e.g.*, molecular beam measurements vs. microwave measurements or centimeter vs. millimetre wave measurements. Since all of the available data had not been analysed simultaneously in these instances, a complete reanalysis was carried out to eliminate the discrepancies. A second source of difficulty involved the number of parameters determinable from the spectral data available. Many recalculations were carried out to determine the minimum set of molecular constants necessary to fit the observed spectra with the result that in a few cases a set of molecular constants, consisting of fewer parameters than were reported in the original work, was sufficient for the analysis. Such recalculations were performed on all of the Group IV/VI diatomic molecules from CO through PbTe, on most of the Group III/VII molecules, and a number of the heavy alkali halides.

These recalculations allowed the detection of a number of misprints in the literature which had not been detectable by simple inspection of the data set. In addition, several misassignments in quantum numbers were corrected. This was primarily a problem in hyperfine structure assignments on the species AlCl, GaC1, GaBr, GaI, InCl, InBr, and InI where the hyperfine structure was only partially resolved. In these cases accurate calculation of the relative intensities was necessary to determine the spectral assignments.

THE BORN-OPPENHEIMER APPROXIMATION

The difference in mass between the electrons and the ions in the systems to be calculated is so great (or, equivalently, the electrons have a relaxation time so much shorter than the ions) that the electrons respond almost instantaneously to changes in the position of the ions. This leads to the Born-Oppenheimer approximation, which states that the degrees of freedom of the electrons and the ions can be uncoupled. Another way of looking at this is to say that for each position of the nuclei, the electrons can be assumed to be in the ground state.

This is tremendously important for almost all calculations in materials science and condensed matter physics, as it means that for each atomic configuration, the electronic degrees of freedom can be relaxed to the ground state, and the energy for that configuration calculated. This removes the extremely difficult problem of calculating the interactions between moving electrons and ions.

However, the assumption that the electrons and ions can be treated separately is not always a good one, particularly when an electron is excited into a long-lived state, or performs a transition non-adiabatically. This kind of reaction has been studied by the researchers, and has been successfully applied in the tight binding formalism to studies of H2 in water and photodissociation of I2 in Ar clusters. Researchers have also studied non-adiabatic molecular dynamics for other systems, but have not yet published results of this formalism, presenting it at meetings only.

THE ROTATION/ VIBRATION SPECTRUM OF HCL

A diatomic molecule differs from an atom in having additional degrees of freedom caused by the ability of the molecule to rotate and vibrate about its center of mass. These motions can be, in first approximation, considered separately and lead to sets of energy levels, $\in$, but with relatively small values of $\Delta\in$.

Since $\Delta\in = h\nu$, the frequencies of electromagnetic radiation absorbed or emitted by a transition between two of these levels will lie in the infrared (frequency (nu)$\nu > 10^{13}$Hz, wavelength (lambda) < 20 μm) or microwave regions ($\nu < 10^{11}$Hz, lambda > 20μm) of the electromagnetic spectrum.

The simplest models for the motion of a diatomic molecule in its electronic ground state are the harmonic oscillator which describes the vibrations of the two atoms along the bond direction and the rigid rotor which approximates the rotation of the molecule in space.

Since a diatomic molecule is under investigation, only one bond can vibrate and the rotation of the molecule occurs only about an axis perpendicular to the bond direction and through the center of mass.

QUANTUM MECHANICAL RESULTS RELATED TO MOLECULAR MOTION

Vibration

Application of Quantum Mechanics to the Simple Harmonic Oscillator (SHO) leads to the energy levels for the vibration of the chemical bond:

$$\in(v) = h\nu\left(v + \tfrac{1}{2}\right) \qquad (1)$$

where v is a quantum number having only the values $v = 0,1,2$ . . ., and h is Planck's constant.

ν is the vibrational frequency (in Hz) given by,

$$\nu = \frac{1}{2\pi}\sqrt{\frac{k}{\mu}} \qquad (2)$$

where μ is the reduced mass of the diatomic molecule, equal to $(m_1m_2)/(m_1+m_2)$ (of the order of 10^{-27} kg for HCl), and k is the force constant of the bond in units of Nm^{-1} or dynes cm^{-1}. Note that the heavier the molecule and/or the weaker the bond, the smaller the vibrational frequency. The vibrational frequency is often expressed in units of cm^{-1}, rather than Hz, through the relation,

$$\tilde{\nu} c = \nu$$

where c is the velocity of light (3×10^{10} cm s^{-1}). This scaling makes the vibrational frequency of most molecules a convenient number in units of cm^{-1}, or wavenumbers, *i.e.,* $\tilde{\nu}$ varies from about 100 to 4,000 cm^{-1}. (The molecule of concern here, HCl, has $\tilde{\nu}$ ca. 3000 cm^{-1}.) Note from Equation. (1) that the lowest energy level of a harmonic oscillator has $\in_\circ = h\nu/2$ (the zero point energy) and adjacent levels are equally spaced with $\Delta\in = hc\tilde{\nu}$.

Rotation

Quantum Mechanics also provides the rotational eigen-energies of a rigid linear rotor,

$$\in(J) = \frac{h^2}{8\pi^2 I} J(J+1) \tag{3}$$

where J is a quantum numbercan take only the values 0, 1, 2 . . ., and I is the moment of inertia of the dumb-bell.

Here $I = m_1 r_1{}^2 = \mu R^2$ where μ is again the reduced mass, and R is the interatomic distance ($\mu = r_1 + r_2$). If the rotational constant is defined by,

$$\mathbf{B = h/(8\pi 2I)}$$

for the diatomic molecule. The rotational constant can be expressed in wavenumber units,

$$\tilde{B} = \mathbf{B/c \text{ in } cm^{-1}}$$

and varies from about 0.05 to 20 cm^{-1} among diatomics (for HCl, $\tilde{B}$ ca. $11 cm^{-1}$). From Eq. (3), one sees that the spacing between adjacent levels for a rigid rotor is,

$$\Delta \in (J) = 2\tilde{B} J'$$

where J' designates the upper rotational level. Thus, the rotational levels are not equally spaced, and they are much closer together than the vibrational levels of the same molecule because of the relatively small values of $2\tilde{B}$ relative to that of $\tilde{v}$.

Infra-Red Transitions

Since both rotational and vibrational motions are simultaneously occurring in the diatomic, the energy level scheme for two adjacent vibration levels (spaced, say, 3000 cm^{-1} apart) where $\tilde{B}$ ca. 10 cm^{-1} in the two states. Each vibrational state has a set of rotational levels.

These rotational levels are not exactly the same since $\tilde{B}$ varies slightly with v, the quantum number labeling the vibrational state. (This latter effect is called vibration-rotation coupling).

However, these are only a first approximation to the true Term Values since there are small additional terms to be added to account for departures from our simplest models of vibration and rotation:

$$T(v,J)=\tilde{v}_e\left(v+\frac{1}{2}\right)-\tilde{v}_e x_e\left(v+\frac{1}{2}\right)^2+\tilde{B}_e J(J+1)$$

$$-D_e J^2(J+1)^2-\alpha_e\left(v+\frac{1}{2}\right)J(J+1) \qquad (4)$$

Equations (1) and (3) may be combined and if expressed as Term Values of a given state and level of the molecule as labelled by v and J, T(v,J) [in units of cm^{-1} then,

$$T(v,J)=\frac{\in(v,J)}{hc}=\tilde{v}\left(v+\frac{1}{2}\right)+\tilde{B}J(J+1)$$

However, these are only a first approximation of the true term values since there are small additional terms to be added to account for departures from our simplest models of vibration and rotation:

$$T(v,J)=\tilde{v}_e\left(v+\frac{1}{2}\right)-\tilde{v}_e x_e\left(v+\frac{1}{2}\right)^2+\tilde{B}_e J(J+1$$

$$-D_e J^2(J+1)^2 . \alpha_e\left(v+\frac{1}{2}\right)J(J+1) \qquad (4)$$

Here:

- The term D_e corrects for the non-rigidity of the bond which can be expected to stretch as the molecules rotates, moreso at the high J values (*i.e.*, centrifugal distortion)
- The term α_e is due to the interaction between rotation and vibration; since R changes during the vibrational motion, so does I and therefore $\tilde{B}$.

Quantum mechanics also stipulates that only the certain transitions are 'allowed' via electric dipole radiation. The selection rules for this process are such that both v and J change by 1 quantum in allowed transitions. ($\Delta v = +/-1$, $\Delta J=+/-1$) Only molecules with permanent electric dipole moments may exhibit infrared absorption, $\Delta v= +1$,or emission, $\Delta v = -1$. $\Delta J = 0$ is allowed only for electronic transitions in some diatomic molecules and non-linear polyatomic molecules. Traditionally, the ΔJ transitions are grouped together as branches:

ΔJ = + 1, R branch

ΔJ = - 1, P branch

ΔJ = 0, Q branch (forbidden here)

To a first approximation the length of the arrow (proportional to the frequency $\tilde{v}$ of the transition) differ by $2\tilde{B}$ among the P branch transitions and among the R branch transitions, but with $4\tilde{B}$ between the central P(1) and R(0) lines. If the forbidden Q branch transition v = 0, J′ = 0 to v =1, J′=0 (call it v_0) were included in the Figure then all spacings would be $2\tilde{B}$. If the very small term involving D_e is neglected, the combined rotation-vibration transitions can be written,

$$\tilde{v}_R\left(J''\right)=\tilde{v}_\circ+\left(2\tilde{B}_e-3\alpha_e\right)+\left(2\tilde{B}_e-4\alpha_e\right)J''-\alpha J''^2$$

where $J''=0,1,2..$

$$\tilde{v}_p\left(J''\right)=\tilde{v}_\circ+\left(2\tilde{B}_e-2\alpha_e\right).J''-\alpha_e J''^2 \qquad (5)$$

where $J''=1,2,3,\ldots$

$$\tilde{v}_\circ=\tilde{v}_e-2\tilde{v}_e x_e \; for\, v'=1 \,\text{and}\, v''=0. \qquad (6)$$

For least squares fitting the P and R equations can be conveniently combined by letting m = (J"+1) in the R branch and (m = –J′) in the P branch, yielding,

$$\tilde{\upsilon}_R(m) = \tilde{\upsilon}_\circ + 2(\tilde{B}_e - \alpha_e - \alpha_e)m - \alpha_e m^2$$

$$\text{so that } \Delta\tilde{\upsilon}(m) = \tilde{\upsilon}(m+1) - \tilde{\upsilon}(m) \text{ is} \tag{7}$$

$$\Delta\tilde{\upsilon}(m) = (2\tilde{B}_e - 3\alpha_e) - 2\alpha_e m \tag{8}$$

(Note that there is no value corresponding to $\nu_\circ$ (m=0) for this molecule.) For example, the transitions in Fig. below can be assigned values of m from –5 to +5 (with 0 missing) and a plot of $\Delta\tilde{\upsilon}$ (m) versus m will yield $\tilde{B}$e and α_e. Then by use of Equation (7) one can also find $\tilde{\upsilon}_0$. A typical spectrum is given in Fig. below.

RELATIVE INTENSITIES OF ABORPTION LINES

All absorption lines are not expected to have the same intensity. The relative intensities are governed largely by the populations of molecules occupying the various rotational levels in the ground v=0 vibrational state (where the rotational levels are designated by J′):

$$I_{J''} \alpha \frac{N_{J''}}{N_{total}} = (2J''+1)e^{-e''Rot/kT}$$

where,

$$\in''_{Rot} = hc\tilde{B}_e J''(J''+1).$$

This is the Boltzmann distribution, where the factor 2J"+1 corresponds to the degeneracy $g_{J''}$ of a given rotational level. One can see that there would be an exponential decrease in intensity with increasing J′except for the partially compensating factor of $g_{J''}$ causing a maximum in the relative intensities.

Isotopic Substitution

Both the vibrational frequency $\tilde{\nu}$, [Eq. (2)], and the rotational constant $\tilde{B}$ (through the moment of inertia, I) are affected by a change in the reduced mass μ of the molecule.

Changing the mass by the introduction of an isotope, such as D for H in HCl, will not change the force constant k or the equilibrium bond distance R_e since the character of the chemical bond is unaffected. Then from Eq. (2).

$$\frac{V_{DCI}}{V_{HCI}} = \left(\frac{\mu_{HCI}}{\mu_{DCI}}\right)^{\frac{1}{2}} \tag{9}$$

and from the definition of B

$$\frac{B_{DCI}}{B_{HCI}} = \frac{\mu_{HCI}}{\mu_{DCI}} \tag{10}$$

Note that Eq. (9) is a first approximation, anharmonicity will change the calculated ratio slightly. HCl (or DCl) prepared in the laboratory already contains two kinds of isotopomers, $H^{35}Cl$ and $H^{37}Cl$, since the natural abundance of isotopes of chlorine is 75.5 per cent ^{35}Cl and 24.5 per cent ^{37}Cl, but the isotope shift between the chlorine isotopes is much smaller than that induced by deuteration as can be seen by the much smaller reduced mass ratio of $\mu(H^{37}Cl)/\ \mu\ (H^{35}Cl)$ relative to $\mu(D^{35}Cl)/\mu(H^{35}Cl)$.

Since the two dominant parameters, $\tilde{B}$ and $\tilde{v}$ are different for the different isotopes, one can expect a different spectrum for each isotopomer. One can, in first approximation, calculate the shifts involved.

In the case of a mixture of $H^{35}Cl$ and $H^{37}Cl$ (or $D^{35}Cl$ and $D^{37}Cl$), the chlorine isotope effect is small and the spectrometer used in the measurements may have insufficient resolution to detect the small splittings ($<1 cm^{-1}$) in the absorption lines.

VIBRATIONAL SPECTROSCOPY

If the vibrational spectrum of a gas-phase heteronuclear diatomic molecule is obtained at high enough resolution, it is found that each line of the spectrum actually consists of a large number of closely spaced components.

These components arise from the rotational transitions that accompany vibrational transitions - since the gaps between vibrational levels are so much greater than those between rotational levels, the lines representing rotational transitions are much more closely spaced than those representing vibrational transitions. Thus the rotational lines are only observable as components within the broader lines representing vibrational transitions. The appearance of a vibration-rotation spectrum is as follows:

Analysis of the quantum mechanics of this situation shows that for a diatomic molecule undergoing a vibrational transition with $\Delta v = 1$, the rotational quantum number J can change by ±1. For molecules with an angular momentum about their axis, $\Delta v = 0$ is also allowed. (*e.g.*, NO, which has an electronic angular momentum about its axis, arising from an unpaired electron in the molecule.)

The appearance of the spectrum can best be discussed using the combined rotation-vibration terms, S, which depend upon both quantum numbers J and v. The simplest expression that can be obtained, ignoring both anharmonicity and centrifugal distortion, is as follows:

$$S(J,v) = \left(v + \frac{1}{2}\right)\tilde{v} + BJ(J+1)$$

When we consider the vibrational transition $v+1 \leftarrow v$, we can see that the rotational transitions will lead to the formation of two or three branches within the vibrational line.

The transitions for which $\Delta J = -1$ form the P–branch of the spectrum:

$$\tilde{\upsilon}_P = S(\upsilon+1, J-1) - S(\upsilon, J) = \tilde{\upsilon} - 2BJ$$

The P-branch thus consists of lines at lower frequency than $\tilde{\upsilon}$, the fundamental frequency. They are predicted to be equally spaced, with a distance of 2B between them.

The transitions for which $\Delta J = -1$ form the R-branch of the spectrum:

$$\tilde{\upsilon}_R = S(\upsilon+1, J+1) - S(\upsilon, J) = \tilde{\upsilon} + 2B(J+1)$$

The R-branch thus consists of lines at higher frequency than the fundamental frequency, again predicted to be equally spaced by 2B, but again this is not true in practice.

The transitions for which $\Delta J = 0$, if they are permitted, form the Q-branch of the spectrum:

$$\tilde{\upsilon}_Q = S(\upsilon + 1, J) - S(\upsilon, J) = \tilde{\upsilon}$$

This is predicted to be a single line at the fundamental frequency (the frequency corresponding to the pure vibrational transition). However, the effects of anharmonicity and centrifugal distortion mean that it actually consists of a cluster of very closely spaced lines around $\tilde{\upsilon}$.

ELECTRONIC TRANSITIONS

Like atoms, due to different configurations of electrons, molecules display several energy levels. They are characterised by spin (singlet, doublet, triplet...) and by an angular moment, or, more precisely, by **L**z which is the projection of this moment parallel to the axis of the molecule which represents a special direction. The respective eigenvalues Λ are denoted with greek letters:

Λ	± 1	± 2	± 3	± 4	± 5	...
Term symbol	Σ	Π	Δ	ϕ	Γ	...

in analogy with S, P, D, F, G... to quantum numbers $l = 0, 1, 2, 3, 4...$ for atoms. As a first approximation, we describe the energy of a diatomic molecule as a sum of electronic, vibrational and rotational energies,

$$E = E_{el} + E_{vib} + E_{rot}$$

$$E = T_e + \omega_e(v + ½) + BJ(J+1),$$

where E_{el} is the minimum of the potential curve. With an electronic transition taking place, all three addends may change. Note that ω_e and B for the initial and final electronic state differ. The state of lower energy is doubly primed (v'', J''), the one of higher energy primed (v',J'). A transition corresponds with a difference in energy ΔE.

$$\Delta E = E_{el} + \Delta E_{vib} + \Delta E_{rot} - \Delta E_{el} \;=\; E'_{el} - E''_{el} = T'_e - T''_e$$

$$\Delta E_{vib} = \omega'_e(v' + ½) - \omega''_e(v'' + ½)$$

$$\Delta E_{rot} = B'J'(J'+1) - B''J''(J''+1)$$

Selection rules for transitions have been established. The

table below contains the criteria for transitions and lists examples.

Allowed, $\Delta\Lambda = 0, \pm 1$ and $\Delta S = 0$	*forbidden*
Example	
$^1\Pi \leftarrow {}^1\Sigma$	$^3\Pi \leftarrow 1\Sigma$, since $\Delta S = 1$
$^1\Pi \leftarrow {}^1\Pi$	$^1\Pi \leftarrow$ 1ϕ, since $\Delta\Lambda = -2$
$^3\Delta \leftarrow {}^3\Delta$	$^3\Delta \leftarrow {}^1\Sigma$, since $\Delta S = 1$ and $\Delta\Lambda = 2$

If we consider the rotational states as well, it is required that the total angular momentum of photon and molecule remains constant. The selection rules depend on whether there are solely sigma states or whether an initial, a final state or both states have an electronic angular momentum J. The second case is referred to as 'general' in the table below.

for $\Sigma \leftrightarrow$	$\Delta J = -1$	P branch
	$\Delta J = +1$	R branch
in general	$\Delta J = -1$	P branch
	$\Delta J = 0$	Q branch
	$\Delta J = +1$	R branch

i.e., $\Delta J = 0$ is allowed since, within the system, there is at least one state with an electronic angular momentum that increases or decreases during transition.

No selection rules exist for changes of the vibrational state. This is attributed to remarkable differences in equilibrium distance between r_e' versus r_e'' and frequency ω_e' versus ω_e''. In terms of quantum mechanics, the initial and final potential curves differ.

As a consequence, we deal with two wavefunctions ψ_v and obtain different series of vibrational states v' and v'' and the respective eigenvalues. Apart from this, the Franck-Condon-principle allows to calculate the probability of a transistion to some vibrational level of an excited state, *i.e.* the intensity of lines that reflect such transitions. An overlap of the following kind is the base to determine the probability as a function of v' and v''.

$$\left|\int \psi_{v'}{}^* . \psi_{v''} . d\tau\right|^2$$

The obtained values have been named Franck-Condon-Factors.

$$\nu_0 = E_{el}' - E_{el}'' + \omega_e'(v' + ½) - \omega_e''(v'' + ½)$$

If we choose a transition v'← v'', we expect the wavenumbers for the peaks within the P-, R- und Q-branch as given in the table below. The ratio of intensities for the three branches are decribed by the Hoenl-London-Factors.

$\Delta J = +1$	R branch	$\nu_R = \nu_0 + 2B_{v'} + (3B_{v'} - B_{v''})J'' - (B_{v''} - B_{v'})J''^2$	$J'' = 0, 1, 2...$
$\Delta J = -1$	P branch	$\nu_P = \nu_0 - (B_{v'} + B_{v''})J'' - (B_{v''} - Bv')J''^2$	$J'' = 1, 2...$
$\Delta J = 0$	Q branch	$\nu_Q = \nu_0 - (B_{v''} - B_{v'})J'' - (Bv'' - B_{v'})J''^2$	$J'' = 1, 2...$

Branch	Substitution	Range
R	$J'' = z-1$	for $J'' \geq 0$
P	$J'' = -z$	for $J'' > 1$

Now we want to find out in which way an increase in the rotational quantum number J′ affects the position of lines. To get a comprehensive picture that is founded on data from all three branches of the transition, we modify the equations above.

A substitution of quantum number J′ by some counting variable z yields one equation that expresses the dependency between changes of the rotational state and the wavenumber ω for the transistion.

This substitution and rearrangement of the addends yield the equations,

$\nu_R = \nu_0 + (B_{v'} + B_{v''})z - (B_{v''} - B_{v'})z^2$	$z = 1, 2, 3, ...$
$\nu_P = \nu_0 + (B_{v'} + B_{v''})z - (B_{v''} - B_{v'})z^2$	$z = -1, -2, -3, ...$

Note that we recieved one equation ν(z). We further introduce $\Delta B = B_{v''} - Bv'$ and $B = ½ (B_{v''} + B_{v'})$ as abbreviations and get one expression for the spectral position of transitions with $\Delta J = \pm 1$.

$$\nu = \nu_0 + 2Bz - \Delta Bz^2$$

An analogous derivation with a quasi-substitition J'' = z yields a second equation $\nu = \nu_0 - \Delta Bz^{-2}$ for lines of the Q branch. Usually we have $|\Delta B| < B$, thus the lines of this branch accumulate close to ν_0.

MOLECULAR ELECTRONIC TRANSITION

Molecular electronic transitions occur when electrons in a molecule are excited from one energy level to a higher energy level. The energy change associated with this transition provides information on the structure of a molecule and determines many molecular properties such as colour. Planck's law gives the relationship between the energy involved in the electronic transition and the frequency of radiation.

ORGANIC MOLECULES AND OTHER MOLECULES

The electronic transitions in organic compounds and some other compounds can be determined by ultraviolet-visible spectroscopy, provided that transitions in the ultraviolet (UV) or visible range of the electromagnetic spectrum exist for this compound. Electrons occupying a HOMO of a sigma bond can get excited to the LUMO of that bond. This process is denoted as a $\sigma \leftarrow \sigma^*$ transition. Likewise promotion of an electron from a p-bonding orbital to an antibonding p orbital* is denoted as a $\pi \rightarrow \pi^*$ transition.

Auxochromes with free electron pairs denoted as n have their own transitions, as do aromatic pi bond transitions. Sections of molecules which can undergo such detectable electron transitions can be referred to as chromophores since such transitions absorb electromagnetic radiation (light), which may be hypothetically perceived as colour somewhere in the electromagnetic spectrum. The following molecular electronic transitions exist:

$\sigma \rightarrow \sigma^*$

$\pi \rightarrow \pi^*$

$n \rightarrow \sigma^*$

$n \rightarrow \pi^*$

aromatic p $\rightarrow$ aromatic π^*

In addition to these assignments, electronic transitions also have so-called bands associated with them. The following bands are defined: the R-band from the German radikalartig or radical-like, the K-band from the German Konjugierte or conjugated, B-band from benzoic and the E-band from ethylenic (system devised by A. Burawoy in 1930). For example, the absorption spectrum for ethane shows a $\sigma \rightarrow \sigma^*$ transition at 135 nm and that of water a $n \rightarrow \sigma^*$ transition at 167 nm with an extinction coefficient of 7,000. Benzene has three aromatic $\pi \rightarrow \pi^*$ transitions; two E-bands at 180 and 200 nm and one B-band at 255 nm with extinction coefficients respectively 60,000, 8,000 and 215. These absorptions are not narrow bands but are generally broad because the electronic transitions are superimposed on the other molecular energy states.

Franck-Condon Principle

Classically, the Franck-Condon principle is the approximation that an electronic transition is most likely to occur without changes in the positions of the nuclei in the molecular entity and its environment. The resulting state is called a Franck–Condon state, and the transition involved, a vertical transition. The quantum mechanical formulation of this principle is that the intensity of a vibronic transition is proportional to the square of the overlap integral between the vibrational wavefunctions of the two states that are involved in the transition.

The Franck-Condon principle is closely related to the Born-Oppenheimer approximation, in which the various motions (electronic, nuclear vibrations and rotations) are considered to be separable, and in which the electrons respond to the instantaneous vibrations of the system whereas the system responds only to the average position of the electrons. The principle, proposed by J. Franck in 1925 and developed quantum-mechanically by E. U. Condon in 1928, is important in discussing systems of more than one atom. It is therefore valuable in molecular spectroscopy and in the interpretation of the optical properties of liquids and solids.

The Franck-Condon Principle describes the intensities of vibronic transitions, or the absorption or emission of a photon. It states that when a molecule is undergoing an electronic transition, such as ionisation, the nuclear configuration of the molecule experiences no significant change. This is due in fact that nuclei are much more massive than electrons and the electronic transition takes place faster than the nuclei can respond. When

QUANTUM MECHANICAL INTERPRETATIONS

The position operator usually has a continuous spectrum, much like the momentum operator in an infinite space. But the momentum in a compact space, the angular momentum, and the Hamiltonian of various physical systems, specially bound states, tend to have a discrete (quantised) spectrum -- that is where the name quantum mechanics comes from. However computing the spectra or cross sections associated with scattering experiments (like for instance high resolution electron energy loss spectroscopy) usually requires the computation of the non-quantised or continuous spectrum (density of states) of the Hamiltonian.

This is particularly true when broad resonances or strong background scattering is observed. The branch of quantum mechanics concerned with these scattering events is referred to as scattering theory. The formal scattering theory has a strong overlap with the theory of continuous spectra.

The quantum harmonic oscillator and the hydrogen atom are examples of physical systems in which the Hamiltonian has a discrete spectrum. In the case of the hydrogen atom, it has both continuous as well as discrete part of the spectrum; the continuous part represents the ionised atom.

CHARACTERISATION OF THE LINE PROFILE

Some astrophysical parameters can be extracted from a spectrum by the measurement of the spectral line profile. For example the measurement of the profile gives access to the temperature of surface of a star, at its disk speed, at the speed of expansion of gases, at the pressure, etc. Many quantities are often given: the equivalent width of the line, the line FWHM, the FWZI, the V/R ratio and the peak intensity.

Equivalent Width (W) is defined as the section of a surface counted between the level of the continuum, normalised to unity, and reference zero, having a surface identical to the profile of line. The equivalent width is thus measured in wavelength unit (in angstroms for example). Sometimes the normalised equivalent width $W\lambda$ is used, which is the equivalent width W divided by the wavelength of the line, which is useful to compare the shape of lines located at different wavelengths.

Mathematically we have:

$$W = \sum \frac{Fe - F\lambda}{Fe} d\lambda$$

with F_c=1 the continuum level unit normalised, F_λ the line profile level, and d_λ the sampling in wavelength unit.

A problem is when for example an emission line is superimposed on a large photospheric absorption line. If W is the measured total equivalent width (emission + absorption) and if Wph is the equivalent width of the photospheric line, the true equivalent width We of the emission line is:

$$We = W - Wph$$

The true difficulty is here to know W_{ph} which is often deduced starting from a theoretical profile of photospheric line or from interpolation of observational data.

Full Width at Half Maximum (FWHM) is the width measured at half level between the continuum and the peak of the line. The FWHM is expressed either in wavelength unit or in speed unit when the objective is to measure expansion or disk speeds (if FWHM is in unit of wavelength, the width in km/sec is given by c. FWHM/l, with c is the speed of the light = 3.10^5 km/s). Example, suppose that the FWHM is of 2A at 6563A, the equivalent resolved velocity is about 90 km/s.

Notice that the FWHM measured had to be corrected for instrumental width according to the equation:

$$FWHM_{Corrscted} = \sqrt{FWHM^2\ obasrved - FWHM^2{}_{instrument}}$$

$FWHM_{instrument}$ is the width that one measured on a very fine line. It is also the theoretical spectral resolution of the spectrograph.

Some time the FWZI is defined: the Full Width at Zero Intensity. It is the base width (at continuum level) of broad emission or absorption component lines.

The V/R is useful for the study of Be-stars. Often for these stars a central intensity minima divide emission into a Violet (V, at shorter wavelength) and a Red (R, at the long wavelength side) component. Relative intensities of these two components, V/R, measured from the continuum, check the asymmetries of the observed profile. Asymmetries are sometime also observed in single emission lines. In this case if V>R the violet flank is steeper than the red one and if R>V the reverse is found. Note that R>V is produced by expanding motion and V>R by contracting motion.

The peak intensity (P) is the ratio between the intensity at the center of the line I and the intensity of the continuum Ic:

$$P = \frac{I}{Ic}$$

It should be noticed that these definitions remain valid if the line is in emission or absorption compared to the continuum. It will be still noted also that the precision of the estimation of these parameters requires a good accuracy on the level of continuum, that implies the photometric procedures of calibration that we saw previously.

In the case of double pic Be stars, an useful parameters often given, is the peak separation ΔV_{peak} (in km/sec).

It is also possible to derive the projected rotational velocity (V.sin i) of Be stars using the FWHM value of an isolated and relatively quiet nearly photospheric line, *i.e.*, a line less affected by the emission and/or absorption produced by the circumstellar enveloppes (He I at 6678 angstroms is some time a good line in the case of my survey). Under the assumption of a Gaussian profiles for this line the V.sin i valeur is computed using the following formula:

$$V.\mathrm{Sin}\,i = c.\frac{FWHM}{2.\lambda.(\mathrm{In}2)^{1/2}}$$

where λ is the laboratory wavelength of the line, c is the velocity of light and FWHM given in unit of wavelength.

A derived parameter from the preceding informations is the radii of the emission disk in the case of Be stars studies (Keplerian rotation of the disk hypothesis):

$$\frac{R_s}{R_*} = \left(\frac{2.V.\sin i}{\Delta Vpeok}\right)^z$$

where R_e is the radius of the emission disk and R* is the photospheric radius of the star.

For the situation of a weak emission feature into an absorption photospheric line it is useful to subtract this photospheric profile before equivalent width calculation. We use the following empirical formulae for fitting the photospheric profile P(λ):

$$P(\lambda) = \exp\left(-\left[\left(\alpha.(\lambda - \lambda_e)^b + c\right)^{-1}\right]\right)$$

where λ_c is the central wavelength of the observed profile and where a, b, c are constants which are determined interactively and graphically under VisualSpec. For the example below (17 Tau star) the computed parameter values are:

$$a = 0.042, \quad b = 2.30, \quad c = 2.80, \quad \lambda_c = 6563.4 \text{ A}$$

DOPPLER BROADENING

In atomic physics, Doppler broadening is the broadening of spectral lines due to the Doppler effect caused by a distribution of velocities of atoms or molecules. Different velocities of the emitting particles result in different (Doppler) shifts, the cumulative effect of which is the line broadening. The resulting line profile is known as a Doppler profile. A particular and perhaps the most important case is the thermal Doppler broadening due to the thermal motion of the particles. Then, the broadening depends only on the frequency of the spectral line, the mass of the emitting particles, and their temperature, and therefore can be used for inferring the temperature of an emitting body. Saturated absorption spectroscopy, also known as Doppler-free spectroscopy, can be used to find the true frequency of an atomic transition without cooling a sample down to temperatures at which the Doppler broadening is minimal.

DERIVATION

When thermal motion causes a particle to move towards the observer, the emitted radiation will be shifted to a higher frequency. Likewise, when the emitter moves away, the frequency will be lowered. For non-relativistic thermal velocities, the Doppler shift in frequency will be:

$$f = f_o\left(1 + \frac{\upsilon}{c}\right)$$

where f is the observed frequency, f_o is the rest frequency, is the velocity of the emitter towards the observer, and c is the speed of light.

Since there is a distribution of speeds both towards and away from the observer in any volume element of the radiating body, the net effect will be to broaden the observed line. If $P\upsilon$ $(\upsilon)d\upsilon$ is the fraction of particles with velocity component $\upsilon$to $\upsilon + d\upsilon$ along a line of sight, then the corresponding distribution of the frequencies is,

$$P_f(f)df = P_\upsilon(\upsilon_f)\frac{d\upsilon}{df}df,$$

where $\upsilon_f = c\left(\frac{f}{f_o} - 1\right)$ is the velocity towards the observer corresponding to the shift of the rest frequency fto f. Therefore,

$$P_f(f)df = \frac{c}{f_o}P_\upsilon\left(c\left(\frac{f}{f_o} - 1\right)\right)df.$$

We can also express the broadening in terms of the wavelength λ. Recalling that in the non-relativistic limit $\frac{\lambda - \lambda_0}{\lambda_0} \approx \frac{f - f_0}{f_0}$, we obtain

$$P_\lambda(\lambda)d\lambda = \frac{c}{\lambda_0}P_\upsilon\left(c\left(1 - \frac{\lambda}{\lambda_0}\right)\right)d\lambda.$$

In the case of the thermal Doppler broadening, the velocity distribution is given by the Maxwell distribution,

$$P_\upsilon(\upsilon)d\upsilon = \sqrt{\frac{m}{2\pi\kappa T}}\exp\left(-\frac{m\upsilon^2}{2\kappa T}\right)d\upsilon,$$

where m is the mass of the emitting particle, T is the temperature and κ is the Boltzmann constant.

Then,

$$P_f(f)df\left(\frac{c}{f_0}\right)\sqrt{\frac{m}{2\pi\kappa T}}\exp\left(-\frac{m\left[c\left(\frac{f}{f_0}-1\right)\right]^2}{2\kappa T}\right)df.$$

We can simplify this expression as,

$$P_f(f)df\sqrt{\frac{mc^2}{2\pi\kappa T\,f_0{}^2}}\exp\left(-\frac{mc^2(f-f_0)^2}{2\kappa T\,f_0{}^2}\right)df$$

which we immediately recognise as a Gaussian profile with the standard deviation,

$$\sigma_f=\sqrt{\frac{kT}{mc^2}}f_0$$

and full width at half maximum (FWHM)

$$\Delta f_{FWHM}=\sqrt{\frac{8\kappa T\,\text{In}2}{mc^2}}f_0\,.$$

Similarly,

$$P_\lambda(\lambda)d\lambda=\sqrt{\frac{mc^2}{2\pi\kappa T\lambda_0^2}}\exp\left(-\frac{mc^2(\lambda-\lambda_0)^2}{2\kappa T\lambda_0^2}\right)d\lambda$$

with the standard deviation,

$$\sigma_\lambda=\sqrt{\frac{\kappa T}{mc^2}}\lambda_0$$

and FWHM,

$$\Delta\lambda_{FWHM}=\sqrt{\frac{8\kappa T\,\text{In}2}{mc^2}}\lambda_0$$

APPLICATIONS AND CAVEATS

In astronomy and plasma physics, the thermal Doppler broadening is one of the explanations for the broadening of spectral lines, and as such gives an indication for the temperature of observed material. It should be noted, though, that other causes of velocity distributions may exist, *e.g.*, due to turbulent motion. For a fully developed turbulence, the resulting line profile is generally very difficult to distinguish from the thermal one. Another cause could be a large range of macroscopic velocities resulting, *e.g.*, from the receding and approaching portions of a rapidly spinning accretion disk. Finally, there are many other factors which can also broaden the lines. For example, a sufficiently high particle number density may lead to significant Stark broadening.

VOIGT PROFILE

In spectroscopy, the Voigt profile (named after Woldemar Voigt) is a line profile resulting from the convolution of two broadening mechanisms, one of which alone would produce a Gaussian profile (usually, as a result of the Doppler broadening), and the other would produce a Lorentzian profile. Voigt profiles are common in many branches of spectroscopy and diffraction. Due to the computational expense of the convolution operation, the Voigt profile is often approximated using a pseudo-Voigt profile.

All normalised line profiles can be considered to be probability distributions. The Gaussian profile is equivalent to a Gaussian or normal distribution and a Lorentzian profile is equivalent to a Lorentz or Cauchy distribution. Without loss of generality, we can consider only centered profiles which peak at zero. The Voigt profile is then a convolution of a Lorentz profile and a Gaussian profile:

$$V(x;\sigma,\gamma)=\int_{-\infty}^{\infty} G(x';\sigma)L(x-x';\gamma)dx'$$

where x is frequency from line center, G (x; σ) is the centered Gaussian profile:

$$G(x;\sigma)\equiv\frac{e^{-x2}/\left(2\sigma^2\right)}{\sigma\sqrt{2\pi}}$$

and L (x; γ) is the centered Lorentzian profile:

$$L(x;\gamma)\equiv\frac{\gamma}{\pi\left(x^2+\gamma^2\right)}.$$

The defining integral can be evaluated as:

$$V(x;\sigma,\gamma)=\frac{\mathrm{Re}[\omega(z)]}{\sigma\sqrt{2\pi}}$$

where Re[w(z)] is the real part of the complex error function of z and,

$$z=\frac{x+i\gamma}{\sigma\sqrt{2}}.$$

PROPERTIES

The Voigt profile is normalised:

$$\int_{-\infty}^{\infty}V(x;\sigma,\gamma)dx=1$$

since it is the convolution of normalised profiles. The Lorentzian profile has no moments (other than the zeroth) and so the moment-generating function for the Cauchy distribution is not defined.

It follows that the Voigt profile will not have a moment-generating function either, but the characteristic function for the Cauchy distribution is well defined, as is the characteristic function for the normal distribution. The characteristic function for the (centered) Voigt profile will then be the product of the two:

$$\vartheta f(t;\sigma,\gamma)=E\left(e^{ixt}\right)=e^{-\sigma^2t^2/2-\gamma}|t|.$$

Since both the normal and the Cauchy distribution are stable distributions, they are closed under convolution and it follows that the Voigt distribution will also be closed under convolution.

Cumulative Distribution Function

Using the above definition for z, the CDF can be found as follows:

$$F(x_0;\mu,\sigma)=\int_{-\infty}^{x_0}\frac{\mathrm{Re}(\omega(z))}{\sigma\sqrt{2\pi}}dx=\mathrm{Re}\left(\frac{1}{\sqrt{\pi}}\int_{\approx(-8)}^{\approx(x0)}\omega(z)dz\right)$$

Substituting the definition of the complex error function yields for the indefinite integral:

$$\frac{1}{\sqrt{\pi}}\int \omega(z)dz = \frac{1}{\sqrt{\pi}}\int e^{-\approx 2}\left[1-\text{erf}(-iz)\right]dz$$

Which may be solved to yield:

$$\frac{1}{\sqrt{\pi}}\int \omega(z)dz = \frac{\text{erf}(z)}{2} + \frac{iz^2}{\pi}\,{}_2F_2\left(1,1;\frac{3}{2},2;-z^2\right)$$

where ${}_2F_2$ () is a hypergeometric function. In order for the function to approach zero as x approaches negative infinity (as the CDF must do), an integration constant of 1/2 must be added. This gives for the CDF:

$$F(x;\mu,\sigma) = \text{Re}\left[\frac{1}{2} + \frac{\text{erf}(z)}{2} + \frac{iz^2}{\pi}\,{}_2F_2\left(1,1;\frac{3}{2},2;-z^2\right)\right]$$

The Width of the Voigt Profile

The full width at half maximum (FWHM) of the Voigt profile can be found from the widths of the associated Gaussian and Lorentzian widths. The FWHM of the Gaussian profile is,

$$f_G = 2\sigma\sqrt{2\text{In}(2)}.$$

The FWHM of the Lorentzian profile is just $f_L = 2\gamma$. Define $\phi = f_L / f_G$. Then the FWHM of the Voigt profile (fv) can be estimated as:

$$f_v \approx f_G\left(1 - c_0 c_1 + \sqrt{\phi^2 + 2c_1\phi + c_0^2 c_1^2}\right)$$

where c_0 = 2.0056 and c_1= 1.0593. This estimate will have a standard deviation of error of about 2.4 percent for values of ϕ between 0 and 10. Note that the above equation will be exactly correct in the limit of $\phi = 0$ and $\phi = \infty$, that is for pure Gaussian and Lorentzian profiles.

A better approximation with an accuracy of 0.02 per cent is given by

$$f_v \approx 0.5346 f_L + \sqrt{0.2166 f_L^2 + f_G^2}.$$

Note that this approximation will be exactly correct for a pure Gaussian, but will have an error of about 0.0325 percent for a pure Lorentzian profile.

The Uncentered Voigt Profile

If the Gaussian profile is centered at μ and the Lorentzian profile is centered at μ_L, the convolution will be centered at $\mu_G + \mu_L$ and the characteristic function will then be:

$$\vartheta_f(t;\sigma,\gamma,\mu_G,\mu_L)=e^{i}(\mu_G+\mu_L)t-\sigma^2t^2/2-\gamma|t|.$$

The mode and median will then both be located at $\mu_G + \mu_L$.

VOIGT FUNCTIONS

The Voigt functions U, V, and H (sometimes called the line broadening function) are defined by

$$U(x,t)+iV(x,t)=\sqrt{\frac{\pi}{4^t}}e\approx^2 \operatorname{erfc}(z)$$

$$H(\alpha,u)=\frac{U\left(u/\alpha,1/4\alpha^2\right)}{a\sqrt{\pi}}$$

where,

$$z=(1-ix)/2\sqrt{t}$$

and erfc is the complementary error function.

Relation to Voigt Profile

$$V(x;\sigma,\gamma)=H(\alpha,u)/\left(\sqrt{2}\sqrt{\pi}\sigma\right),$$

with,

$$\alpha=\gamma/\left(\sqrt{2}\sigma\right)$$

and,

$$u=x/\left(\sqrt{2}\sigma\right)$$

MULTI-PHOTON ABSORPTION AND IONISATION

In his famous discovery of the photoelectric effect, Albert Einstein reasoned that photons might ionise an atom only if they had an energy greater than a particular threshold energy corresponding to the ionisation energy of the atom. In 1929,

Maria Göppert-Mayer predicted theoretically that an atom might absorb two or more photons simultaneously, thus allowing an electron to transition to states unreachable by single photon absorption. An atom absorbing multiple photons simultaneously might be ionised by photons with energies less than the threshold energy of which Einstein spoke.

Because any observable effect of this phenomenon could not be possible without a very intense beam of radiation, her prediction could not be investigated in detail until the construction of the first laser in 1960. We examined the phenomenon of two-photon absorption or three-photon ionisation using a Nd-YAG laser and DCM dye laser.

When a single photon collides with a ground state Cesium atom, the atom can absorb the photon via electronic transitions to energy levels higher than the ground state by δ E=h_b ω. Flowing out of the mathematics of quantum mechanical wave functions, selection rules govern these transitions such that the change in angular momentum in single photon transitions is δ l = +1, –1. Thus, an electron in a ground state s-state may transition by one photon only to a higher p-state. When an atom absorbs two photons simultaneously, the electron will change angular momentum by δ l = +2, 0, or –2, since each photon has angular momentum of +1 or –1. This allows an s-state electron to transition to another s-state or to a d-state: states out-of-reach by single photon absorption. If a third photon interacts with the atom soon after the two-photon process, the third photon may ionise the atom. An s-state electron may not transition to a p-state by two photon absorption.

When absorbing multiple photons simultaneously, an atom will proceed to an intermediate state corresponding to a characteristic eigenstate or to a 'virtual state.' These virtual states are not eigenstates; they correspond to no specific n or l state. Instead, they are merely superpositions of waves. No population of electrons transitions to the virtual state. The lifetime of a virtual state is short, relative to eigenstates. Actually, the closer the virtual state is to an actual eigenstate, the longer the lifetime of the virtual state. Think of this as a result of the Werner Heisenburg's Uncertainty Principle: dE $\delta t > h$. These virtual states are discussed further with the topic of Raman Scattering. If the photons corresponding eigenstate energies are incident on the Cesium, the effect of two-photon absorption will be enhanced.

TWO-PHOTON ABSORPTION

Two-photon absorption is a process where two photons are absorbed simultaneously, exciting, *e.g.*, an atom or ion to a higher-lying state, with the energy increase being equal to the sum of the photon energies. This is a non-linear process, occurring with significant rates only at high optical intensities, because the absorption coefficient is proportional to the optical intensity:

$$\alpha = \beta I$$

In an insulator or semiconductor, two-photon absorption can normally occur only if the photon energy is at least half the bandgap energy. Therefore, there are, *e.g.*, no losses via two-photon absorption when ultrashort pulses at 800 nm wavelength propagate in a silica. On the other hand, two-photon absorption at the same wavelength can occur in semiconductors such as GaAs, having a much smaller bandgap. This is used, *e.g.*, in compact autocorrelators for pulse duration measurements: a photodiode which is normally not sensitive at the laser wavelength exhibits a photocurrent only due to TPA.

The phenomenon of two-photon absorption finds applications in various technical areas. For example, it is used in simple autocorrelators for pulse characterisation, where TPA in a photodiode, having a bandgap energy larger than the photon energy, is exploited to obtain a non-linear response. Also, two-photon absorption is often used in fluorescence microscopy (two-photon microscopy) for exciting fluorescence with an infrared laser beam, which can easily penetrate the sample. In other cases, TPA is exploited for optical power limiting or for microfabrication.

Detrimental TPA effects can occur for non-linear frequency conversion of ultrashort pulses in non-linear crystal materials, particularly for conversion of short wavelengths, *e.g.*, in UV sources. The transmission of pulsed pump light (or, *e.g.*, frequency-doubled light) is then significantly lower than for continuous-wave radiation with the same average power. In some materials, the generation of free carriers via TPA can cause photodarkening. TPA can also modify the saturation characteristics of saturable absorbers such as SESAMs, leading to a roll-over of the saturation curve which can help, *e.g.*, to suppress Q-switching instabilities.

MEASUREMENTS

Absorption Rate

The Beer's law for OPA:

$$I(x) = I_0 e^{-acx}$$

changes to,

$$I(x) = I\frac{I_0}{1+\beta cxI_0}$$

for TPA with light intensity as a function of path length or cross section x as a function of concentration c and the initial light intensity I0. The absorption coefficient α now becomes the TPA cross section β.

Units of Cross-section

The molecular two-photon cross-section is usually quoted in the units of Goeppert-Mayer (GM) (after its discoverer, Nobel laureate Maria Goeppert-Mayer), where 1 GM is 10^{-50} cm4 s photon–^{1}. Considering the reason for these units, one can see that it results from the product of two areas (one for each photon, each in cm^2) and a time (within which the two photons must arrive to be able to act together). The large scaling factor is introduced in order that 2-photon absorption cross-sections of common dyes will have convenient values.

TWO-PHOTON EMISSION

The opposite process of TPA is two-photon emission (TPE), which is a single electron transition accompanied by the emission of a photon pair. The energy of each individual photon of the pair is not determined, while the pair as a whole conserves the transition energy.

The spectrum of TPE is therefore very broad and continuous. TPE is important for applications in astrophysics, contributing to the continuum radiation from planetary nebulae (theoretically predicted for them in ref and observed in ref). TPE in condensed matter and specifically in semiconductors was only recently observed, with emission rates nearly 5 orders of magnitude weaker than OPE, with potential applications in quantum information.

DEVELOPMENT OF THE FIELD AND POTENTIAL APPLICATIONS

Until the early 1980s, TPA was used as a spectroscopic tool. Scientists compared the OPA and TPA spectra of different organic molecules and obtained several fundamental structure property relationships. However, in late 1980s, applications were started to be developed. Peter Rentzepis suggested applications in 3D optical data storage. Watt Webb suggested microscopy and imaging. Other applications such as 3D microfabrication, optical logic, autocorrelation, pulse reshaping and optical power limiting were also demonstrated

Microfabrication and Lithography

One of the most distinguishing features of TPA is that the rate of absorption of light by a molecule depends on the square of the light's intensity. This is different than OPA, where the rate of absorption is linear with respect to input intensity. As a result of this dependence, if material is cut with a high power laser beam, the rate of material removal decreases very sharply from the center of the beam to its periphery. Because of this, the 'pit' created is sharper and better resolved than if the same size pit were created using normal absorption.

3D Photopolymerisation

In 3D microfabrication, a block of gel containing monomers and a 2-photon active photoinitiator is prepared as a raw material. Application of a focused laser to the block results in polymerisation only at the focal spot of the laser, where the intensity of the absorbed light is highest. The shape of an object can therefore be traced out by the laser, and then the excess gel can be washed away to leave the traced solid.

Imaging

The human body is not transparent to visible wavelengths. Hence, one photon imaging using fluorescent dyes is not very efficient. If the same dye had good two-photon absorption, then the corresponding excitation would occur at approximately two times the wavelength at which one-photon excitation would have occurred. As a result, it is possible to use excitation in the far infrared region where the human body shows good transparency. It is sometimes said, incorrectly, that Rayleigh scattering is relevant to imaging techniques such as two-photon. According to Rayleigh's scattering law, the amount of scattering is proportional to $1/\lambda^4$, where λ is the wavelength. As a result, if the wavelength is increased by a factor of 2, the Rayleigh scattering is reduced by a factor of 16. However, Rayleigh scattering only takes place when scattering particles are much smaller than the wavelength of light (the sky is blue because air molecules scatter blue light much more than red light).

When particles are larger, scattering increases approximately linearly with wavelength: hence clouds are white since they contain water droplets. This form of scatter is known as Mie scattering and is what occurs in biological tissues. So, although longer wavelengths do scatter less in biological tissues, the difference is not as dramatic as Rayleigh's law would predict.

Optical Power Limiting

Another area of research is optical power limiting. In a material with a strong non-linear effect, the absorption of light increases with intensity such that beyond a certain input intensity the output intensity approaches a constant value. Such a material can be used to limit the amount of optical power entering a system. This can be used to protect expensive or sensitive equipment such as sensors, can be used in protective goggles, or can be used to control noise in laser beams.

Photodynamic Therapy

Photodynamic therapy (PDT) is a method for treating cancer. In this technique, an organic molecule with a good triplet quantum yield is excited so that the triplet state of this molecule interacts with oxygen. The ground state of oxygen has triplet character. This leads to triplet-triplet annihilation, which gives rise to singlet oxygen, which in turn attacks cancerous cells. However, using TPA materials, the window for excitation can be extended into the infrared region, thereby making the process more viable to be used on the human body.

Optical Data Storage

The ability of two-photon excitation to address molecules deep within a sample without affecting other areas makes it possible to store and retrieve information in the volume of a substance rather than only on a surface as is done on the DVD. Therefore, 3D optical data storage has the possibility to provide media that contain terabyte-level data capacities on a single disc.

TPA COMPOUNDS

To some extent, linear and 2-photon absorption strengths are linked. Therefore, the first compounds to be studied (and many that are still studied and used in, *e.g.*, 2-photon microscopy) were standard dyes. In particular, laser dyes were used, since these have good photostability characteristics. However, these dyes tend to have 2-photon cross-sections of the order of 0.1-10 GM, much less than is required to allow simple experiments.

It was not until the 1990s that rational design principles for the construction of two-photon-absorbing molecules began to be developed, in response to a need from imaging and data storage technologies, and aided by the rapid increases in computer power that allowed quantum calculations to be made. The accurate quantum mechanical analysis of two-photon absorbance is orders of magnitude more computationally intensive than that of one-photon absorbance, requiring highly correlated calculations at very high levels of theory.

The most important features of strongly TPA molecules were found to be a long conjugation system (analogous to a large antenna) and substitution by strong donor and acceptor groups (which can be thought of as inducing non-linearity in the system and increasing the potential for charge-transfer). Therefore, many push-pull olefins exhibit high TPA transitions, up to several thousand GM. It is also found that compounds with a real intermediate energy level close to the 'virtual' energy level can have large 2-photon cross-sections as a result of resonance enhancement.

Compounds with interesting TPA properties also include various porphyrin derivatives, conjugated polymers and even dendrimers. In one study a diradical resonance contribution for the compound depicted below was also linked to efficient TPA. The TPA wavelength for this compound is 1425 nanometer with observed TPA cross section of 424 GM.

TPA COEFFICIENTS

The two photon absorption coefficient is defined by the relation,

$$-\frac{dI}{dz} = \alpha I + \beta I^2$$

so that,

$$\beta(\omega) = \frac{2\hbar\omega}{I_2} W_T^{(2)}(\omega)$$

Where β is the two-photon absorption coefficient, α is the absorption coefficient $W_T^{(2)}(\omega)$ is the transition rate for TPA, I is the irradiance, ω is the photon frequency and the thickness of the slice is dz.

The SI units of the coefficient are:

$$\beta(m/W) = (N/E)\sigma^{(2)}$$

Where N is the number density of molecules per cm^3, E is the photon energy (J), $\sigma^{(2)}$ is the two-photon absorption cross section (cm^4s/molecule).

If β (m/W) is multiplied by 10^{-9} it can be converted to the CGS system (cal/cm s/erg).

Due to different laser pulses the TPA coefficients reported has differed as much as a factor 3. With the transition towards shorter laser pulses, from picosecond to subpicosecond durations, noticeably reduced TPA coefficient have been obtained.

TPA in Water

Laser induced TPA in water was discovered in 1980.

Water absorbs UV radiation near 125 nm exiting the 3a1 orbital leading to dissociation into OH^- and H^*. Through TPA this dissociation can be achieved by two photons near 266 nm. Since water and heavy water have different vibration frequencies and inertia they also need different photon energies to achieve dissociation and have different absorption coefficients for a given photon wavelength. A study from Jan 2002 used a femtosecond laser tuned to 0.22 Picoseconds found the coefficient of D2O to be 42±5 10^{-11}(cm/W) whereas H2O was 49 ± 5 10^{-11}(cm/W)

TPA Coefficients for Water

λ (nm)	Pulse Duration τ (ps)	β × 10^{11} (cm/W)
315	29	4
300	29	4.5
289	29	6
282	29	7
282	0.18	19
266	29	10
264	0.22	49±5
216	15	20
213	26	32

VIBRATIONAL LEVELS AND ELECTRONIC ENERGY OF POLYATOMIC TRANSIENT MOLECULES

Most chemical processes including not only laboratory and industrial chemical syntheses but also those which occur in flames, propellant systems, the initiation of energetic materials, atmospheric pollution, chemical vapour deposition, and plasma processing-consist of a complicated sequence of interrelated reactions in which neutral and charged molecular fragments play essential roles. Although these fragments are present in only very small concentration, they are highly chemically reactive.

If a specific molecular fragment is removed from the system, as by introducing a scavenger molecule, the reactions in which that fragment participates stop. Other parts of the overall process continue, resulting in very significant changes in product distribution and yield.

In the early studies of complex chemical processes, it was necessary to postulate mechanisms involving such transient intermediates, present in concentrations too small for direct detection. Conventional end product analysis aids in the selection of suitable mechanisms, but generally does not yield a complete description of the system. Consequently, the improvement of industrial chemical processes often is achieved by semiempirical experimentation. The determination of the detailed chemical mechanism would, in turn, permit the development of rational strategies for removing undesired products and enhancing the yield of the desired species.

In recent years, there has been great progress in the development of techniques suitable for monitoring chemical reaction intermediates. Molecular spectroscopy is especially well suited to this task. Optical detection can be used not only for gas-phase measurements, but also for studies of processes that occur on surfaces or in the condensed phase. It also permits remote sensing, an important advantage. A wide variety of recently developed laser-based spectroscopic detection schemes are not only highly sensitive but also space and time specific. Although the development of spectroscopy-based diagnostics for chemical reaction systems is in its infancy, already the laboratory application of sophisticated sampling and observation techniques has yielded a wealth of vibrational and electronic spectral data for reaction intermediates.

EARLIER DATA COMPILATIONS

For many years, the most important source of vibrational and electronic energy level data for small polyatomic reaction intermediates was the compilation of spectroscopic data for small polyatomic molecules (3-12 atoms) given by Herzberg. To meet the need for an updated, critically evaluated compilation, a series of publications have appeared in the Journal of Physical and Chemical Reference Data, culminating in the publication in 1994 of a monograph (Vibrational and Electronic Energy Levels of Polyatomic Transient Molecules) which presented evaluated spectral data for more than 1550 small polyatomic transient molecules, defined as species that have a lifetime of less than a few minutes in the pressure range (typically 0.1 to 1.0 Torr) encountered in their production. Vibrational fundamentals in the ground and excited electronic states and radiative lifetimes were included. To aid in spectral identification, the principal rotational constants were also given to three decimal places. These tables provide the basis for this database, designed to supplement the published compilation by providing a capability for rapid searches by molecule or wavenumber.

Recent Progress

The rapid growth in the scientific literature concerned with the spectroscopic study of transient molecules and with their detection in chemical reaction systems continues. Since the October 1993 cutoff in the data evaluation for the monograph, substantive new spectroscopic data have been published for many species included in it, and the first data have become available for almost 2000 other molecules. There has been especially great progress in the spectroscopic characterisation of transient species produced by the reaction of metal atoms with oxygen and other small molecules. Despite this rapid progress, many gaps remain in our knowledge of the energy levels of the species represented, and many new and potentially important transient molecules are still to be discovered.

This compilation attempts to provide a comprehensive, critically evaluated summary of vibrational and electronic energy level data for small polyatomic transient molecules, in order to support further research and new technologies such as those of plasma processing and chemical vapour deposition.

SCOPE OF DATABASE

A critical evaluation and summary of experimental vibrational and electronic energy level data for neutral and ionic transient molecules and high temperature species possessing from three to sixteen atoms is presented. By early 2003, evaluated data were available for approximately 3500 molecules, and the published version encompassed non- only the original monograph, but also two supplements. The Chemistry Web Book database brings these results together in an ongoing effort to provide evaluated data to the scientific community. Although radiative lifetimes and principal rotational constants are not presently included in this version of the database, references to the original literature concerned with then are given.

Stable Molecules and High-Temperature Species

Data have been selectively included for some molecules which are important in environmental and industrial chemical reaction systems but which can be studied only with difficulty using conventional sampling techniques because of the ease with which they decompose, rearrange, or polymerise. Also included are data derived from spectra of many high-temperature species, such as metal oxides, studied in molecular beams and in rare-gas matrices.

Unfortunately, with these few exceptions it is not possible to include data for stable molecules. However, the spectra of many of these species are relatively well established, and sources of data such as the tables of Herzberg remain extremely useful. In obtaining spectral identifications with the help of the present data, it is crucial that the possible contribution of the absorptions or emissions by a stable molecule also be considered.

ELECTRONIC SPECTRA

Gas-Phase Electronic Spectra

Gas-phase studies of the electronic spectra of transient molecules were for many years much more readily conducted than were studies of ground-state vibrational spectra. The concentration of transient molecules in flames, chemiluminescent reactions, or various types of discharge may be sufficiently high for spectroscopic study. The photographic plate provides a cumulative detector for visible and ultraviolet radiation.

Much of the electronic spectral data summarised in these tables was obtained using conventional gas-phase ultraviolet absorption or emission spectroscopy, which affords the potential for both a broad spectral survey and very high resolution.

Flash Photolysis

Flash photolysis permits the observation of relatively high concentrations of transient species at short time intervals after the flash. Because the products are generally formed with much less internal energy than is typical of systems with detectable emission spectra, the absorption spectra obtained in flash photolysis studies are more readily analysed. Furthermore, the time-resolved detection used in flash photolysis studies provides information on the rates of formation and disappearance of transient molecules in the system.

Laser-Based Techniques

More recently, a wide variety of laser-based techniques have also been used for electronic spectral observations, often with exceptionally high detection sensitivity. In recent years, very high resolutions have been achieved in laser-based spectroscopic measurements. Since a given laser is tunable over a relatively limited spectral region, laser studies of transient molecules are greatly aided by the availability of survey spectra obtained using other techniques. The spatial configuration of the laser beam makes it an extremely powerful tool for studies of the energy levels of molecules in molecular beams.

If the molecule of interest is present in a supersonic molecular beam, excited rotational and vibrational energy levels can be very effectively depopulated, and the absorption spectrum of the molecule is greatly simplified. The spatial configuration of the laser beam also makes it amenable to the development of probes for chemical reaction intermediates not only in the laboratory but also in the environment and in industrial processes.

Laser studies may be broadly classified according to whether the interaction of the molecule with the laser beam(s) is followed by photon or mass detection. Photon-based observations are amenable to remote sensing applications. Because pulsed lasers offer an exceptionally wide range of time specificity, they are very useful for determining radiative lifetimes and rates of elementary chemical reactions. The coupling of lasers with mass detection can lead to the identification of transient molecules for which survey spectra are not available. Among the mass-based detection schemes are photofragment spectroscopy and resonance-enhanced multiphoton ionisation (REMPI).

REMPI provides a powerful tool for mapping the Rydberg transitions of transient molecules. Whereas laser-excited fluorescence measurements depend upon the presence of electronic energy levels which decay by photon emission, all molecules possess Rydberg energy levels. REMPI measurements depend on multiphoton excitation into a suitable electronic energy level, most often one of Rydberg character.

The selection rules may permit excitation of levels which are not accessible by one-photon excitation from the ground state. The range of tunability of the laser is multiplied by the number of photons required for the excitation of the Rydberg level, significantly broadening the spectral regin which can be probed with a given laser. When the parent molecule is a free radical, almost all of the mass signal is generally found to arise from the parent cation, with very little fragmentation.

Photoelectron Spectroscopy

Much valuable information on the energy levels of molecular cations has been obtained from photoelectron spectroscopy. These tables include selective coverage of the voluminous literature on photoelectron spectroscopic measurements. The number of stable molecules that possess more than six atoms for which photoelectron spectra have been reported is too great to permit the inclusion of low-to-moderate resolution photoelectron spectral data for molecular cations with more than six atoms. Those who need such data for larger molecules may find the reviews by Turner *et al.* Rabalais and Kimura *et al.* helpful. Several criteria are important in determining whether a given reference should be included in the present work. The first of these is resolution. In the few instances in which high resolution photoelectron data are available, these data are heavily weighted.

Where direct spectroscopic observation is possible, the measurements generally are of considerably higher precision than are the photoelectron data, which are then omitted from the tables. A second criterion is the availability of adiabatic ionisation potentials. In order to obtain information on the positions of electronic transitions from photoelectron spectral data, it is necessary to subtract the first ionisation potential from the energy of the photoelectron band. Where there is little change in the molecular geometry in the transition, the difference between the vertical ionisation potentials gives a reasonable approximation to the position of the electronic transition. However, this is not the general case. Therefore, priority is given to papers that include adiabatic ionisation potentials.

For most photoelectron spectroscopic transitions, structure has not been resolved. Many of these states are dissociative. Further information on the dissociation products can be obtained from values of the appearance potentials for various products in photoionisation studies on the parent molecule. Such studies are beyond the scope of this review. The tables of published ionisation and appearance potentials by Lias and co-workers and the on-line version included in the Chemistry WebBook constitute a valuable source of information on the appearance potentials of photofragments.

Matrix Shifts in Electronic Spectra

The range of tunability of visible and ultraviolet lasers, like that of infrared lasers, is limited. Therefore, a preliminary survey using conventional gas-phase and/or matrix-isolation spectroscopic studies is often desirable. A comparison of the positions of the electronic band origins of diatomic molecules in the gas phase and in rare-gas and nitrogen matrices has been published. As in the determination of ground-state vibrational energy levels, neon is the matrix material of choice, with a sharp maximum at 0.0 per cent in the distribution of matrix deviations for valence transitions of covalently bonded molecules. In argon-matrix observations, most such band origins are shifted by less than 2 per cent from the gas-phase values.

At the somewhat higher temperatures often used for electronic spectral observations in matrices of the heavier rare gases or of nitrogen, relatively broad phonon bands become prominent. The blue shift of the phonon maximum from the zero-phonon line in absorption measurements, and the red shift in emission measurements, typically amount to approximately 1 to 1.5 per cent. Rydberg transitions of molecules in matrices often are greatly broadened and experience much larger shifts. Further details of the behaviour of electronic transitions of matrix-isolated molecules.

GROUND- AND EXCITED-STATE VIBRATIONS

Vibration Numbering Conventions

The format of the vibrational tables is similar to that used in the earlier compilations. The vibrational numbering convention is that used by Herzberg. Within a given symmetry species, vibrations are numbered starting with the highest frequency. The same convention is followed for deuterated species.

Therefore, a given type of vibration may be numbered differently for the deuterated than for the unsubstituted molecule. For triatomic molecules, the bending vibration is always designated as ν2. For aromatic molecules, an alternate vibrational numbering scheme developed by Wilson has often been used in the literature.

Where both the Herzberg and the Wilson numbering schemes have been used for the published data, the Herzberg numbering is adopted, and the Wilson numbering is sometimes shown in parentheses. For a few species, only the Wilson numbering has been used. To avoid confusion, this is retained in the present tables, and the use of the Wilson numbering is specifically indicated.

Where possible, the values of $\Delta G(1/2)$, the separation between the $v = 0$ and $v = 1$ levels for the vibration of interest, have been used.

Renner-Teller Interaction

If a bending fundamental is split by Renner-Teller interaction, the position of the unperturbed fundamental is given. Where specific components of such a split fundamental have been studied, they may also be listed, with the transition designated in an explanatory note. For a more complete treatment of the Renner effect and definitions of the associated parameters, see the discussion by Herzberg and the references cited for the molecule of interest.

GROUND-STATE VIBRATIONAL SPECTRA

Gas-Phase Measurements

Studies in the gas phase offer the potential for the most precise, detailed measurements. Because of the high chemical reactivity of transient molecules, it is difficult to obtain gas-phase survey infrared spectra of them. The well known advantages of Fourier transform infrared measurements, coupled with sophisticated digital data handling procedures, have permitted the acquisition of gas-phase survey spectra for a number of transient molecules.

Vibrational Frequencies from Rydberg Transitions

Although vibrational frequencies of ground-state molecular ions have frequently been estimated from structure in Rydberg transitions of the parent neutral species, in this compilation vibrational frequencies of the ions are not inferred from these Rydberg transitions. Many of these transitions have residual valence character, resulting in significant variations in vibrational frequencies from one Rydberg state to another.

MATRIX ISOLATION MEASUREMENTS

As in the earlier compilations, spectral data obtained for molecules trapped in dilute solid solution, with the solvent a rare gas or a small covalent molecule, are included. The application of this sampling technique, known as matrix isolation, for the stabilisation and spectroscopic study of uncharged reaction intermediates has recently been reviewed. Because nitrogen and the rare gases are transparent through the entire infrared spectral region, matrix isolation measurements provide a potentially valuable survey tool.

In these matrices, infrared absorptions are typically sharp, with half band widths between 0.1 and 1 cm^{-1}. Rotational structure is, with few exceptions, quenched. Multiple trapping sites occur, often resulting in the appearance of several absorption maxima-usually one or two of which predominate—over a range of a few cm^{-1}.

Matrix Shifts for Uncharged Covalently Bonded Molecules

Matrix shifts for covalently bonded molecules trapped in solid neon or argon often are quite small. A comparison of the positions of the ground-state vibrational fundamentals of over two hundred diatomic molecules observed in the gas phase and in nitrogen and rare-gas matrices has shown that, typically, the smallest matrix shift occurs for neon matrix observations, with successively greater matrix shifts for the heavier rare gases and for nitrogen. Except for very weakly bonded molecules and for the alkali metal and Group IIIa halides, matrix shifts of most diatomic molecules isolated in solid argon are smaller than 2 per cent. Similar conclusions resulted from a comparison of neon- and argon-matrix shifts for the ground-state vibrational fundamentals of larger molecules.

The generalisation that matrix interactions are minimal for neon and that they increase as the mass of the rare gas is increased and become even more important for nitrogen and most other small molecule matrices is supported both by experimental observations on larger molecules and by ab initio calculations for the weakly bonded CaH_2 and CaF_2 molecules complexed with the rare gases and with nitrogen. The observed matrix shifts for the ground-state fundamental vibrations of transient molecules trapped in solid neon and argon. For neon matrices, the maximum in the distribution lies near 0.0 per cent, and for argon matrices, near 0.2 per cent. For both neon and argon matrices, fewer than one-tenth of the matrix shifts are greater than 1 per cent.

Data are beginning to appear for molecules trapped in a hydrogen matrix. Insufficient information is available for generalisation on the magnitude of matrix shifts in this medium. For the few species heretofore studied, including several transient molecules present in this compilation, the matrix shifts have been comparable to those in a neon matrix.

Many other matrix materials have also been employed for spectroscopic studies. However, complications due to reaction or to relatively strong interaction (*e.g.*, hydrogen bonding) of the transient molecule with the matrix frequently occur. Therefore, observations in such media as solid hydrocarbons and aqueous solutions and studies of condensed reaction products without an inert carrier have been excluded.

Matrix Shifts for Molecular Ions

For molecular ions, neon is the matrix of choice. Polarisation and charge-transfer interactions become successively more important for molecules isolated in the heavier rare gases. Charge delocalisation sometimes also occurs for ionic species trapped in the rare gases. The anomalously large matrix shift for ν_3 of ClHCl- may be attributed to this phenomenon. The data for small cation species trapped in solid neon are consistent with the matrix shift generalisations given above.

Only twelve comparisons are available for molecular cations observed both in the gas phase and trapped in solid argon. The absolute values of five of the observed matrix shifts are greater than 1 per cent. For several other vibrations of molecular ions which have been observed in both neon and argon matrices but not in the gas phase, there are deviations greater than 1 per cent between the neon- and argon-matrix frequencies. Very few comparisons are possible for molecular anions. A number of these species have been generated in rare-gas (usually argon) matrices by charge transfer between a precursor molecule and an alkali metal atom.

Recent studies of such species as CO_2- and SO_2- generated instead by photoionisation and/or Penning ionisation and trapped in solid neon indicate that shifts on the order of 50 cm^{-1} may be attributed to the relatively strong interaction of the anion with the nearby alkali metal cation.

On the other hand, when the uncharged molecule has a relatively large electron affinity, as is true for C_2 and for NO_2, charge transfer occurs at a relatively great separation, and a substantial fraction of the anion population may be trapped in sites in which interaction with the alkali metal cation is minimal.

Matrix Shifts for Ionic Bonds

Matrix shifts for vibrations associated with ionic bonds are often considerably larger than those associated with uncharged molecules or with intramolecular vibrations of molecular ions. Criteria for inclusion of data for species that include an ionic bond are exemplified by the selection process for the heavy-metal oxides.

Often the stable dioxide structures include an $M{+}O_2^-$ species with significant covalent bond character for the attachment of M^+, evidenced by a substantial shift in the O^{2-} stretching fundamental as M^+ is varied. Such species are included in the compilation. On the other hand, there is little evidence for substantial metal-atom participation in the vibrations characteristic of the O_3^- moiety of $M^+O_3^-$. Accordingly, spectral data are given for O_3^-, but not for M^+O_3

MOLECULAR FORMULAS

Molecular formulas are used in this compilation. In order to permit a compact index, an attempt has been made to provide as much structural information as possible in a minimal amount of space. This restriction is especially severe for larger molecules. The following formula abbreviations have been used:

Br	Bridged
cyc	cyclic. If parentheses follow, only the atoms enclosed in them are included in the ring.
c	cis
t	trans

ISOTOPIC SPECIES

Where heavy isotopic peaks are resolved, data are given for the most abundant isotopic species (*e.g.*, ^{7}Li, ^{11}B, ^{35}Cl, ^{79}Br). Data are included for both the normal and the fully deuterium-substituted molecule, except that data are also given for the partially deuterium-substituted species of H_3^+ and H_3.

Units

Except where otherwise indicated, the units of all quantities in these tables are cm^{-1}.

Error Estimates

Error estimates are those of the authors of the original literature. When the uncertainty is not explicitly indicated, the value is given to the estimated number of significant figures. Where vibrational frequencies have been determined with a precision greater than two decimal places, the tabulated values have been rounded off.

EXCITED ELECTRONIC STATES

Symmetry

The heading for each electronic state gives its symmetry, the point group to which the molecule belongs in that electronic state, and, where available, references to the determination of a quantitative molecular structure. For C_{2v} molecules, there is potential ambiguity in the definition of the molecular symmetry axes. The convention in which the x axis is chosen perpendicular to the plane of the molecule, recommended by the Joint Commission for Spectroscopy of IAU and IUPAP has been adopted. Often this has required the interchange of published assignments of energy levels with B_1 and B_2 symmetry.

Assignments Based on Photoelectron Spectroscopy

Most authors of papers on photoelectron spectroscopy have proposed assignments for the various photoelectron bands, using arguments based on molecular orbital theory and often on semiempirical or ab initio calculations. These assignments have been included in the present tables. Where several conflicting assignments have been given in the literature, an attempt has been made to choose the most satisfactory one.

Generally, the assignments of photoelectron spectra have been made with the presumption that the point group to which the molecular cation belongs is the same in all of its excited states. Structural data for these excited states are extremely rare. Therefore, the molecular point group which has been adopted in the analysis of the photoelectron spectrum is given in these tables. In practice, it is likely that there is some variation in excited-state molecular symmetries. Thus, a bent molecular ion may become linear in some of its excited states. For highly symmetric species, Jahn-Teller distortion may reduce the molecular symmetry.

Energy of the Electronic Transition

The energy of the electronic transition follows the state designation and symmetry information. Where possible, T_0, the energy separation between the electronic energy level of interest and the ground electronic, vibrational, and rotational states of the molecule, is given. However, where only low resolution data or photoelectron data are available, often only band maxima have been given in the literature.

With photoelectron data, T_0 is derived by subtracting the value of the first ionisation potential from that of the higher ionisation potential which corresponds to the state of interest. When data for the first adiabatic ionisation potential are available, the subscript 'x' is used to indicate that the first adiabatic ionisation potential is known but that the higher ionisation potential is measured to the peak maximum; the subscript 'xx' implies that the energy difference between the higher and the first absorption maximum was used. If the first photoelectron transition has a gradual onset, a better value of the first ionisation potential may have been obtained from photoionisation data or from the extrapolation of Rydberg series in the spectrum of the parent molecule. Supplementary sources of data for the first ionisation potential are cited in the tables.

However, if the difference between the first adiabatic ionisation potential obtained in the photoelectron spectrum and that obtained in other measurements amounts to only 10 or 20 meV, the photoelectron spectroscopic value is used, because of the advantage of a consistent set of measurements. Where threshold energies differ by one quantum in a vibrational progression, a best value for the ionisation potential is chosen which coincides with the most probable position of the vibrationally unexcited transition. Because of inherent uncertainties in the determination of higher ionisation potentials in many photoelectron spectral measurements, photoelectron peaks above about 18 eV are often omitted.

As in the tables of Herzberg T_0 values are given to the center of multiplet structure. For doublet states, the two components differ by ±A (the spin-orbit splitting constant), and the energy difference is measured from the average of the two bands, whereas for triplet states the three components fall at 0, ±A with respect to the position from which the band energy is measured. This convention is also followed here unless specific states are given. However, in matrix isolation absorption and laser excitation studies only the lowest component is accessible. Except for transitions with relatively small values of A, this is also likely to be true for studies using cooled molecular beams. Often these latter studies give T0 values for the lowest energy component with a precision better than that to which A is known.

Wavelength Range of the Electronic Transition

The wavelength range (nm) in which various electronic transitions have been observed is also tabulated. This range is a composite of the values typical of absorption and emission observations. Laser-excited fluorescence studies often include both excitation and resolved emission measurements. Since the position of the band origin is given, ambiguity should not arise. For information on the range in which the band system is observed for a given type of measurement, see the original literature cited for that measurement technique.

Nuclear Spin Statistics and Overall Parities

We now come to the necessity of imposing Fermi-Dirac or Bose-Einstein statistics, respectively, on the complete molecular wave functions of CH_4 and CD_4. Fermi-Dirac statistics require the complete wave function to be invariant with respect to those proton permutations which can be represented as the product of an even number of binary cycles, and require it to transform into its negative under permutations which can be represented as the product of an odd number of binary cycles. Bose-Einstein statistics require the complete wave function to be invariant with respect to both kinds of deuteron permutations.

Note that neither Fermi-Dirac nor Bose-Einstein statistics place requirements on the behaviour of the complete wave function under the laboratory-fixed inversion operation. As a consequence we need consider complete wave function behaviour only under the proper rotations. Note further, that the C_3 proper rotations and the C_2 proper rotations in methane both correspond to an even number of binary permutation cycles, *i.e.,* that no proper rotations in methane correspond to an odd number of binary permutation cycles.

We conclude from the above statements that complete wave functions of species A_1 or A_2 satisfy Fermi-Dirac statistics, while functions of species E, F_1, and F_2 do not. But, likewise, complete wave functions of species A_1 or A_2 satisfy Bose-Einstein statistics, while functions of species E, F_1, and F_2 do not. One might ask what information has been lost by ignoring the sense-reversing point-group operations when dealing with nuclear spin statistics.

In fact, what is lost is the correlation between the parity of a state and its group-theoretical symmetry species. The σ_d planes, for example, represent permutation-inversion operations of the form (ij)*.

A complete CH_4 wave function should transform into its negative under the permutation (ij) because of Fermi-Dirac statistics. If such a change fails to take place under (ij)*, we must assume that the effects of the permutation (ij) were counteracted by the transformation induced by the laboratory-fixed inversion operation *. These arguments shows that complete wave functions for CH_4 of species A_1 must have negative parity, while those of species A_2 must have positive parity. Complete wave functions for CD_4 of species A1 must have positive parity, while those of species A_2 have negative parity.

3

Raman Effect: NMR and ESR

Raman effect, change in the wavelength of light that occurs when a light beam is deflected by molecules. The phenomenon is named for Sir Chandrasekhara Venkata Raman, who discovered it in 1928. When a beam of light traverses a dust-free, transparent sample of a chemical compound, a small fraction of the light emerges in directions other than that of the incident (incoming) beam. Most of this scattered light is of unchanged wavelength. A small part, however, has wavelengths different from that of the incident light; its presence is a result of the Raman effect.

Raman scattering is perhaps most easily understandable if the incident light is considered as consisting of particles, or photons (with energy proportional to frequency), that strike the molecules of the sample. Most of the encounters are elastic, and the photons are scattered with unchanged energy and frequency. On some occasions, however, the molecule takes up energy from or gives up energy to the photons, which are thereby scattered with diminished or increased energy, hence with lower or higher frequency. The frequency shifts are thus measures of the amounts of energy involved in the transition between initial and final states of the scattering molecule. The Raman effect is feeble; for a liquid compound the intensity of the affected light may be only 1/100,000 of that incident beam. The pattern of the Raman lines is characteristic of the particular molecular species, and its intensity is proportional to the number of scattering molecules in the path of the light. Thus, Raman spectra are used in qualitative and quantitative analysis.

The energies corresponding to the Raman frequency shifts are found to be the energies associated with transitions between different rotational and vibrational states of the scattering molecule. Pure rotational shifts are small and difficult to observe, except for those of simple gaseous molecules. In liquids, rotational motions are hindered, and discrete rotational Raman lines are not found. Most Raman work is concerned with vibrational transitions, which give larger shifts observable for gases, liquids, and solids. Gases have low molecular concentration at ordinary pressures and therefore produce very faint Raman effects; thus liquids and solids are more frequently studied.

DISCOVERY OF THE RAMAN EFFECT

In 1917 Raman resigned from his government service and took up the newly created Palit Professorship in Physics at the University of Calcutta. At the same time, he continued doing research at the Indian Association for the Cultivation of Science, Calcutta, where he became the Honorary Secretary. Raman used to refer to this period as the golden era of his career. Many talented students gathered around him at the IACS and the University of Calcutta.

On February 28, 1928, through his experiments on the scattering of light, he discovered the Raman effect. It was instantly clear that this discovery was an important one. It gave further proof of the quantum nature of light. Raman spectroscopy came to be based on this phenomenon, and Ernest Rutherford referred to it in his presidential address to the Royal Society in 1929. Raman was president of the 16th session of the Indian Science Congress in 1929.

He was conferred a knighthood, and medals and honorary doctorates by various universities. Raman was confident of winning the Nobel Prize in Physics as well, and was disappointed when the Nobel Prize went to Richardson in 1928 and to de Broglie in 1929. He was so confident of winning the prize in 1930 that he booked tickets in July, even though the awards were to be announced in November, and would scan each day's newspaper for announcement of the prize, tossing it away if it did not carry the news. He did eventually win the 1930 Nobel Prize in Physics "for his work on the scattering of light and for the discovery of the effect named after him. He was the first Asian and first non-White to get any Nobel Prize in the sciences. Before him Rabindranath Tagore (also Indian) had received the Nobel Prize for Literature.

Raman scattering: Stokes and anti-Stokes lines

Rayleigh scattering of light is the familiar phenomenon that is responsible for the blue colour of the sky. Light from the sun strikes air molecules and is scattered in all directions without losing energy or changing frequency. The blue colour arises because the strength of the scattering depends strongly on the fourth power of the frequency so that blue light is much more strongly scattered than yellow or red.

Questions: The frequency of violet light is even greater than that of blue. Why isn't the sky violet? Why is the sun yellow at noon, but red at sunset?

In 1928 C.V. Raman discovered a second, much weaker type of scattering of light, in which the frequency changes when the light is scattered. The frequency shift Δv occurs, when some of the energy of the scattered photon is taken up by a molecule, which excites the molecule's atoms into vibrational motion. Most of the molecules are initially in the ground state but because of thermal agitation some molecules will be in an excited state. The scattering process can be thought of as the incoming photon raising the molecule to a virtual (non-existent) excited state.

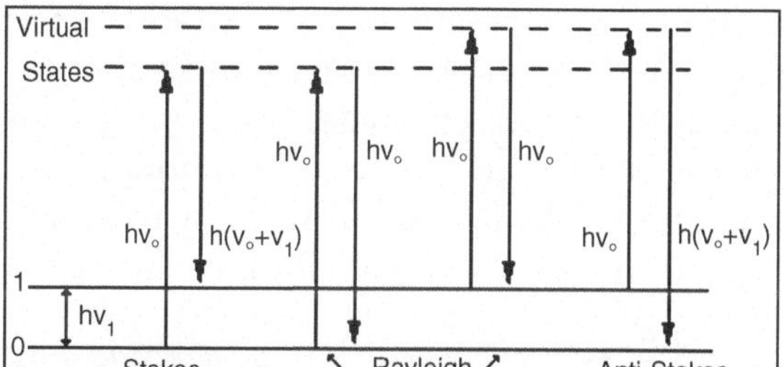

Fig: Raman and Rayleigh Scattering of Light

Since the molecule cannot remain in this virtual level, it must immediately fall back down to a lower level with the emission of a photon. If the molecule falls into the same level as it started from, there is no frequency shift in the emitted photon and we have Raleigh scattering. But there will be a direction change with photons being scattered in all directions.

If the molecule falls into a different level, the energy of the emitted photon must differ from that of the incoming photon in order to conserve total energy; the emitted photon has a different frequency from that of the exciting photon. This process is called Raman scattering. The frequency can decrease (giving rise to Stokes lines in the spectrum) or increase (anti-Stokes lines), depending on whether the molecule starts in the ground state or an excited state. Since the initial population of the excited states is usually very small, the anti-Stokes lines are much weaker than the Stokes lines and sometimes cannot be observed. (The larger the Raman shift, the higher the excited state, and the less likely it is to be thermally populated. Therefore, anti-Stokes lines with small Raman shifts are most likely to be observed.)

Wave numbers (reciprocal centimeters)—cm^{-1}: Spectroscopists, and especially chemists, frequently use wave numbers ν^*, expressed in units of reciprocal centimeters, to measure frequency. A wave number is defined as $\nu^* = \nu/c = 1/\lambda$, where c is the speed of light in cm/s and λ is the wavelength in cm. The wave number gives the number of wavelengths of light that will fit into one centimetre.

Notice from Fig. above that the Raman shift $\Delta\nu = \nu_o - (\nu_o \pm \nu_1) = \pm \nu_1$ does not depend on the frequency ν_o of the incident light; the shift only depends on the excitation energy of the excited state. Therefore, in reporting Raman spectra, only $\Delta\nu^*$ is given in cm^{-1}. The spectrometer you will use sweeps the wavelength linearly with time and is calibrated in nm. It is straightforward to calculate $\Delta\nu^*$ from the wavelength λ_0 of the incident photon and λ_1 of the Raman scattered photon measured in nm:

$$\Delta\nu^* = [1/\lambda_0 - 1/\lambda_1]10^7 = (\lambda_1 - \lambda_0)/ \lambda_0 \lambda_1 10^7 \ (cm^{-1})$$

Interpretation of Raman Spectra: The atoms of a molecule can vibrate in many ways called the normal modes of vibration. The normal modes have different excitation energies so the Raman spectrum will consist of more than one line. The number of normal modes is easily deduced; if the number of nuclei in the molecule is N, the total number of degrees of freedom (i.e., the number of coordinates required to specify the positions of all of the nuclei) is 3N. Of these, three account for translation of the molecule as a whole and three more for its rotation. This leaves 3N-6 coordinates to account for the relative positions of the nuclei relative to each other, i.e., for internal motions. This, then, is the number of normal modes. [However, this calculation only puts an upper limit on the number of lines in the Raman spectrum since some normal modes may be degenerate (have the same energy), while others, due to their symmetry, cannot Raman scatter a photon (are not "Raman active").]

For a simple molecule like carbon tetrachloride, CCl_4, N = 5 and there are 9 classical normal modes. *Only five Raman lines can be observed:* Δv^* = 218, 314, 459, 762 and 790 (may not be resolved) and 1539 (weak) cm^{-1}. The strongest line at 459 cm^{-1} corresponds to a symmetric stretching of the four Cl ions along their bonds to the C. If the resolution of the spectrometer were better it would show a splitting caused by a slight difference in excitation energy depending upon whether the molecule has 1, 2, 3, or 4 atoms of the heavier ^{37}Cl isotope rather than ^{35}Cl.

Description of the modes of a particular molecule, and application of selection rules to predict the Raman spectrum, require knowledge of group theory beyond the scope of this experiment. However, the basic idea is that when light strikes a molecule it sets the electron cloud in oscillation. This oscillating polarization then reradiates the energy as scattered light. In order for the vibration of the nuclei to interact with this oscillating (accelerated) charge polarization and produce a Raman shift, it is necessary that some component of the electron cloud polarization have the same symmetry as the normal mode transition. We shall not attempt to interpret individual lines but, rather, treat the Raman spectrum as a characteristic pattern which can be used to identify unknown substances, or whose relative intensity can give a quantitative measure of the composition of mixtures of liquids.

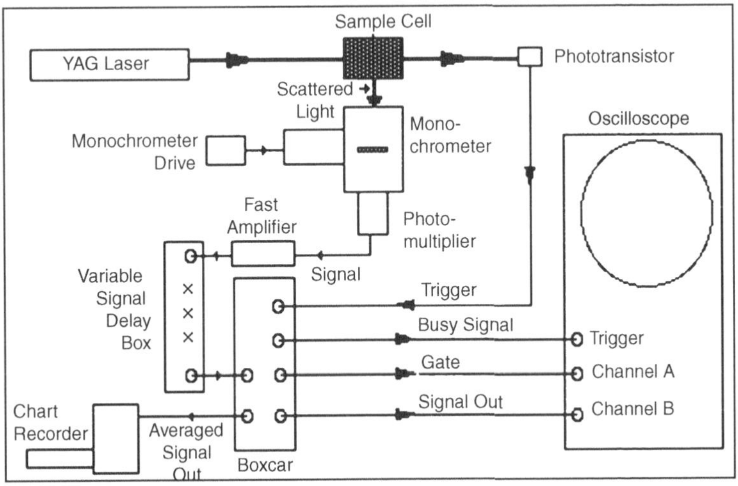

Fig: Block Diagram of the Raman Spectrometer

EXPERIMENTAL SETUP OF RAMAN SCATTERING

Raman scattering is an extremely weak process. Only about 10^{-7} of the incident photons are scattered as compared to 10^{-4} in Rayleigh scattering. [Despite this weakness, Raman discovered the scattering using sunlight as the source and his eyes as the detector!] To get quantitative results in this experiment we will have to use some rather sophisticated light detection apparatus.

YAG LASER OF LIGHT SOURCE

The light source is a pulsed laser, whose operation is discussed in Appendix A. The intensity of Raman scattering increases as the fourth power of the frequency. To get a large signal, we want to use as high a frequency light source as possible. The YAG laser puts out ~ 5 ns wide pulses with an ultraviolet wavelength of 355 nm at a pulse rate of 10 per second. The pulse energy is 4.5 mJ, which translates into a peak power of 0.9 MW. The laser pulse contains some residual 1064 nm infrared light as well. Both of these wavelengths are invisible to the human eye. Although this might seem to be a rather small amount of energy, it can damage the eyes and is especially dangerous since the beam is invisible. Be sure to wear goggles whenever the laser is operating.

SAMPLE CELL OF RAMAN SCATTERING

One of the strengths of Raman scattering as an analytical tool is that no special sample preparation is required. The liquid (or solid dissolved in a solvent) is placed in a 1 cm thick quartz sample cell. The only requirement for the sample is that is be transparent to the incident beam and not fluoresce. Because of the danger to your eyes from stray laser light, the path from the laser output to the sample cell is enclosed and the sample cell is covered with a light shield.

PHOTOGATE TRIGGER

Since the signal is weak and the laser is pulsed, we can use pulsed electronics to detect the signal. The laser has a 5 ns jitter (variation in the starting time of the pulses) after the flashlamp fires. In order to eliminate the effects of this jitter on the detection process, a phototransistor is placed in the beam path after it passes through the sample cell. When a pulse strikes the phototransistor, it generates a voltage pulse (trigger) that is used to synchronize the detection electronics with the laser.

MONOCHROMETER SCATTERING OF LIGHT

The scattered light from the sample cell is a mixture of all the Raman lines, plus the intense Rayleigh scattered light. In order to measure the spectrum, the light is resolved into its components with a grating monochrometer. The diffraction grating is mounted on a motor driven gear mechanism so that the wavelength reaching the exit slit varies linearly with time. The grating has a spectral range of 3—850 nm. It is calibrated to ± 1 nm and has a linear dispersion of 4 nm/mm (i.e. if the exit slit is 1 mm wide, it will pass a 4 nm wide band of light). The entrance and exit slits are ~ 0.1 mm wide, and thus the bandpass is 0.4 nm.

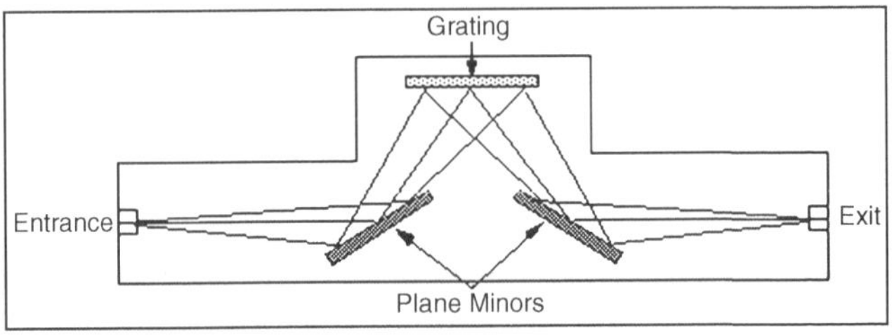

Fig: The Grating Monochrometer

The widths of the entrance and exit slits to the monochrometer are fixed (~ 0.1 mm) but the height (8 mm max) can be varied using the "fish-tail" slides located at the each end of the spectrometer. Pushing them all the way in gives maximum height and transmitted light, but reduces the resolution. There is a trade-off between resolution and signal-to-noise and the length of time it takes to perform the experiment.

PHOTOMULTIPLIER (PM)

The light from the monochrometer is detected with a Hamamatsu phototube, which has a quantum efficiency in excess of 5% over the range 150 to 700 nm (i.e. it detects more than 5% of the photons striking it). The PM is highly sensitive and must be protected from ambient light at all times when the accelerating voltage (800 to 1000 V) is applied to the tube. The tube is equipped with a shutter to be closed whenever the high voltage is on if there is a possibility of ambient light reaching the tube. Be sure that the high voltage is turned off or the shutter is closed whenever you remove the sample shield to change samples. To avoid damaging the boxcar with a voltage pulse from the PM, always turn the high voltage power supply down to zero before turning it off or on.

BOXCAR INTEGRATOR

The output of the PM consists of 5 ns wide, negative pulses, occurring at a rate of 10 pps (pulses per second) and partially obscured by considerable noise generated in the phototube. *To obtain a signal with adequate signal-to-noise ratio, we will use two techniques:*

The first is signal averaging (or integrating); the PM signal will be integrated over P pulses. Since the desired Raman signal from the PM will always be negative, the integrated signal after P pulses will be P times larger than that of a single pulse. The phototube noise on the other hand will fluctuate randomly with both positive and negative polarity. Thus the integrated noise will partially cancel out. Calculation shows that if P pulses are integrated the signal-to-noise will improve by $\sqrt{P}$. For this experiment you will integrate over 10 to 30 pulses for a S/N gain of 3 to 5.5.

A much more significant improvement in the S/N will be achieved by using a boxcar integrator, an integrating circuit that is gated (turned on) only during the time period when a gate pulse is present. The Raman signal is present for only a small fraction of the time (.000005% of the time for a 5 ns pulse repeated at a 10 pps rate). During the time between pulses there is no useful signal from the PM; if we integrate during this time, we only add noise. Thus by using a boxcar integrator gated to coincide with the PM signal we can integrate only during the short time when the desired signal is present and ignore all the intervening noise.

Timing: The measurement process is initiated by the photogate trigger pulse travelling from the phototransistor to the boxcar. There are a number of sources of delay in the system: the PM cannot respond instantly to the laser pulse, the phototransistor and other electronic circuits do not respond instantly, and there is a propagation delay of about 5 ns/m in the coax cable connecting the PM to the input amplifier. We also intentionally delay the amplified signal by about 30 ns so that when we observe the signal on the oscilloscope, it does not fall at the edge of the screen. We compensate for these delays using an adjustable delay in the boxcar between the time the boxcar receives the trigger pulse and when it generates the gate pulse that initiates the integration. Adjustment of the timing is simple; the gate signal and the delayed PM signal are observed on the oscilloscope and the boxcar delay is adjusted so that the gate pulse coincides with the PM pulse. The width of the gate can also be adjusted to improve the S/N. It should be set narrow enough that it only covers the time when the pulse from the photomultiplier is present but not so narrow that it excludes too much signal. The S/N is sufficiently large that neither the gate pulse delay setting nor the gate-width is critical.

Resolution: The resolution of a spectrometer measures how close in wavelength two spectral features can be before the spectrometer will no longer be able to resolve them as separate features. We saw in the discussion of the monochrometer that the bandpass is ~0.4 nm. Thus we cannot expect to resolve features much smaller than 0.4 nm. But there is another possible limit on the resolution: In order to measure the wavelength dependence of the Raman scattering, the monochrometer grating is rotated so that the wavelength reaching the PM increases linearly with time. The boxcar is the continual average of the signal received from the last P pulses. Thus if P = 100 and the laser pulse rate is 10 pps, the boxcar averaging time is 100/10 = 10 s. In order to avoid distorting the spectrum, the rate at which the wavelength is swept must be slow enough that the spectrum does not change appreciably in 10 s. Thus the resolution depends on the interplay of sweep speed and the number of samples averaged. If, for the example considered above, the monochrometer is swept at its slowest rate of 2.5 nm/mm, then the spectrometer will not be able to resolve features closer than about tow or three times 2.5(10)/60 = 0.42 nm. This exceeds the 0.4 nm bandpass and thus degrades the resolution of the spectrometer. In practice, the number of samples averaged should be kept at 30 or less.

THE CHART RECORDER

The boxcar output is recorded with a chart recorder. Since the paper moves past the pen at a constant rate, and the wavelength is also swept at a constant rate, the x-axis is proportional to the wavelength. In order to calibrate this axis you must make marks on the paper corresponding to the wavelength readings on the monochrometer. For this purpose the push button on the back of the recorder momentarily shorts the input and makes a vertical mark on the paper. After using the recorder be sure to turn off the chart paper drive and put the cap back on the pen to prevent it from drying out.

STRUCTURE AND NUCLEAR MAGNETIC RESONANCE

In order to identify the chemical structure of molecules, chemists often use spectroscopic techniques to analyse molecules. Spectroscopy is defined as an experimental process in which the energy differences between allowed states of a system are measured by determining the frequency of the light absorbed. In lab, you will use ^{13}C and ^{1}H nuclear magnetic resonance (NMR) spectroscopy to determine the structure of several compounds. ^{13}C and ^{1}H NMR spectroscopy allow you to determine the kind, location, and number of non-equivalent carbon and hydrogen atoms in a molecule. NMR spectrometers detect nuclei that generate a magnetic field when they spin.

The spinning nuclei behave like a bar magnet, and when placed in the presence of an external field, a super-conducting magnet, they will align with (parallel) or against (antiparallel) the external field. The parallel orientation is lower in energy than the antiparallel orientation by an amount that depends on the strength of the external magnetic field. A ^{13}C nucleus has the ability to generate a magnetic field when it spins; ^{12}C nuclei do not. ^{13}C isotopes occur at an abundance of about 1 in every 100 (1.1%) in an organic sample. All hydrogen nuclei have the ability to generate a magnetic field when they spin. The ^{13}C and ^{1}H nuclei will spin-flip when exposed to a radio wave frequency that is equal to the energy needed to flip the nucleus from the parallel to the antiparallel spin. When a nucleus spin-flips it is said to be in resonance, and this is what the instrument records.

The chemical environment of a nucleus plays a major role in determining when a nucleus will come into resonance. The denser the electron cloud around a nucleus, the less the nucleus feels the applied force of the magnet because the electrons shield the nucleus from the applied field. The chemical shift of a hydrogen or carbon resonance depends on how the atoms around it affect the density of its electron cloud. If the ^{13}C or ^{1}H is in the presence of electronegative atoms, such as O or F, its electron cloud is less dense, or its nucleus is deshielded. Deshielding of the nucleus occurs because the electronegative atoms pull the electron density away from the nucleus. The more deshielded a nucleus is the more downfield (to the left) its resonance will occur. The number of carbons attached to the ^{13}C nucleus also affects the density of the electron cloud. A carbon nucleus that is bound to three carbon atoms and one hydrogen atom is more deshielded than a carbon nucleus that is bound to three hydrogen atoms and one carbon atom because carbon atoms are more electro-negative than hydrogen atoms. The calibration peak is the signal for the solvent, d-chloroform ($CDCl_3$), and will occur at 77.16 ppm in ^{13}C NMR and 7.26 ppm in ^{1}H NMR.

So how do chemists put all of this information together and determine structures from NMR spectra? Let's start with an example. Let's take the ^{1}H and ^{13}C NMR spectra of the molecule methane (CH_4).

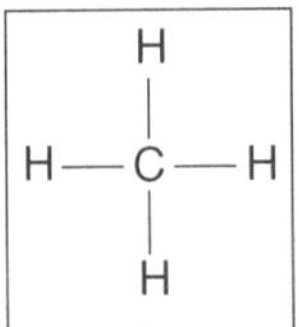

Methane

This molecule has four hydrogen atoms but all of them are chemically equivalent to each other. The ^{1}H NMR spectrum of this molecule would show a single peak to indicate the presence of hydrogen atoms chemically equivalent to each other and not interacting with anything else. The ^{13}C spectra would also show one peak to account for only one type of carbon.

Now try a more complex molecule such as the one below:

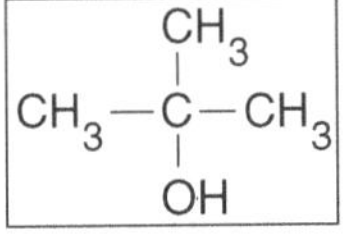

BASIC THEORY OF NUCLEAR MAGNETIC RESONANCE

Nuclear magnetic resonance (NMR) spectroscopy is the study of molecular structure through measurement of the interactions of an oscillating electromagnetic field with a collection of nuclei immersed in a strong external magnetic field. The nuclei are the central parts of the atom which are assembled into molecules by bonds formed by electron orbital overlaps. An NMR spectrum can provide detailed information about molecular structure, both static and dynamic. Without NMR such acquisition of data would be extremely difficult, if not impossible.

The phenomenal of the nuclei of certain atoms behaving strangely in the presence of strong external magnetic fields was first noticed by P. Zeeman. In 1902 he was awarded the Nobel Prize in physics for this discovery. However, it was not until 1952 that two physicists, Felix Bloch and Edward Purcell, were able to create a practical machine to observe the nuclear Zeeman Effect. Since the 1950's the NMR spectroscopy has revolutionized the way chemistry, biochemistry, and biology is studied. NMR has become arguably the single most widely used technique for elucidation of molecular structure. But to comprehend the NMR, a few fundamental principles of physics must be understood.

OVERVIEW OF ELECTROMAGNETIC RADIATION

"All spectroscopic techniques involve the interaction of matter with electromagnetic reaction" and measuring the response of the matter to a given electromagnetic condition. The light rays that allow eyes to see constitute only a narrow range called the visible region of the electromagnetic radiation spectrum. Each electromagnetic ray, can be visualized as a composition of two orthogonal waves that oscillate exactly in phase with each other. This means that each wave reaches the peaks and nodes at the same points. One of the waves is the electric field vector (E) oscillating in one plane, and the other wave is the magnetic field vector (B) oscillating in the plane perpendicular to the electric field.

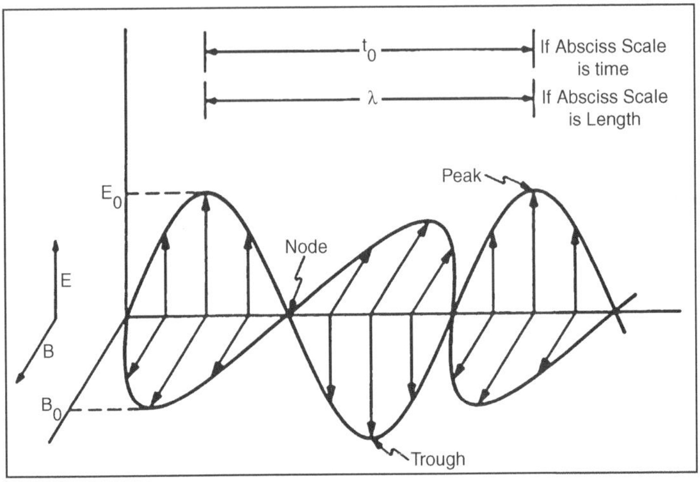

Fig: Electromagnetic wave with electric vector, E, and magnetic vector, B.

The electromagnetic waves consist of two independent parameters or properties, wavelength (λ) and the maximum amplitude (E_0 and B_0). However, the intensity of the wave is proportional to the square of its amplitude. Thus, given that the all electromagnetic radiation travels at a constant velocity c (3.00×10^{10} cm s^{-1} in vacuum), the wave can be described as having a frequency n, which is the inverse of the peak-to-peak time t_0:

$$v = \frac{1}{t_0}$$

where t_0 is measured in seconds and v has units of cycles per second or hertz (Hz).

Realizing that the electromagnetic waves travel a distance of λ in t_0 seconds, a second more important relationship can be deduced:

$$c = \frac{\lambda}{t_0} = \lambda v$$

The equation above shows that wavelength and frequency are not independent of each other, but are inversely proportional. A wave of high frequency has a short wavelength while a wave of low frequency must have a long wavelength. The electromagnetic spectrum ranges from the very small wavelength and high frequency of cosmic rays to the extremely large wavelengths and very low frequency of radio waves.

In addition to its wave-like behaviour, electromagnetic radiation also displays behaviour characteristic of particles. A particle, or quantum, of radiation is called a photon. In essence, a photon can be considered a discrete packet of energy that is directly proportional to its frequency and can be summarized by the following relationship:

$$E = hv$$

where h is Planck's constant with a value of 6.63×10^{-34} Js per photon (or 3.99×10^{-13} $kJsmol^{-1}$). Since the usual strength of a chemical bond is about 400 $kJmol^{-1}$, electromagnetic wave energies above the visible region more than enough energy to photodissociate (break) chemical bonds, while waves below the visible region cannot typically break molecular bonds. The frequency that NMR spectroscopy uses is in the radio frequency region which also is the same frequency range that communication signals between radios and televisions. Normally, the NMR uses frequencies from 200 to 759 MHz, which are at the low end of the energy scale, but happens to precisely correspond to the amount of energy that is needed for molecular resonance and measurement.

Classical Interaction of Radiation with Matter

Having briefly examined the properties of electromagnetic radiation, the parameters that control the interaction between waves and particles of matter can be examined. The three primary types of interaction of interest to spectroscopitists are absorption, emission, and scattering. During an absorption interaction, the photon disappears and its entire energy is transferred to the particle that absorbed it. The resulting particle with excess energy is said to be in an excited state. From its excited state, the particle can relax back to its ground state by emitting a photon (at a different wavelength than the incoming photon) which carries off the excess energy. Radiation is scattered when the direction of a travelling photon is shifted by some angle. The shift is due to the result of passing too close to a resonating molecule. If the frequency of the photon is unchanged the scattering is described as elastic. However, if the frequency has changed (inelastic scattering), this indicates that there must have been some exchange of energy between the photon and the particle.

In NMR spectroscopy, the main measurements are only absorption and emission of radio frequency radiation. Quantum mechanics, the field of physics that deals with energy at the atomic level and defines the rules that describe the probability for a photon to be absorbed or emitted under a given set of circumstances. But classical physics states a very important requirement shared by all forms of absorption and emission spectroscopy: for a particle to absorb (or emit) a photon, the particle itself must first be in some sort of uniform periodic motion with a characteristic fixed frequency. Most important, the frequency of the motion must exactly match the frequency of the absorbed (or emitted) photon:

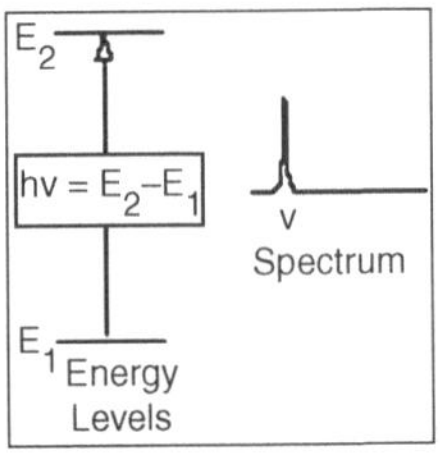

Fig: Energy Gap

This above fact, which at first glance might appear to be an incredible chance, is actually quite reasonable. If a photon is to be absorbed, it energy, which is originally in the form of the oscillating electric and magnetic fields, must be transformed into energy of the particles' motion. This transfer of energy can take place only if the oscillations of the electric and/or magnetic fields of the photon can constructively interfere with the oscillations of the particle's electric and/or magnetic fields. If the energy of the photon is equal to the oscillation energy gap for the particle, only then can there be a transfer of energy to particle from the photon. When such a condition exists, the system is said to be in resonance, and only then can the act of absorption take place.

At this point one might thing that the frequency-matching requirement places a heavy constraint on the types of absorption processes that can occur. After all, how many kinds of periodic motion can a particle have? The answer is that even a small molecule is constantly undergoing many types of periodic motion. Each of its bonds is constantly vibrating and the whole molecule and some if its individual parts are rotating in all three dimensions. The electrons are circulating through their orbital. And each of these processes has its own characteristic frequency and it own selection of rules governing absorption.

All of the above forms of microscopic motion are what is called intrinsic, which means the motion takes place all by itself, without intervention by any external agent. However, it is possible under certain circumstances to induce particles to engage in additional forms of periodic motion. Still to achieve resonance, one needs to match the frequency of the induced motion with that of the incident radiation.

For example an ion (or any charged particle) follows a curved path as it moves through a magnetic field and if one was to carefully adjust the strength of the magnetic filed, the ion will follow a perfectly circular path, with characteristic fixed frequency that depends on it mass, charge, velocity, and strength of the magnetic filed. Matching this characteristic cyclotron frequency with incident electromagnetic radiation of the same frequency ultimately can lead to absorption, and this is the basis of a technique known as ion cyclotron resonance (ICR) spectroscopy.

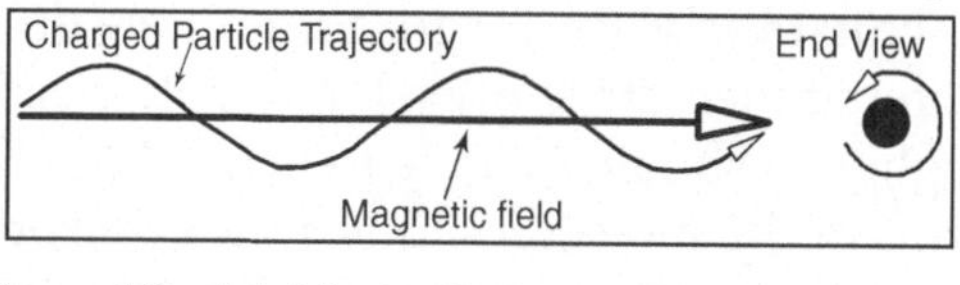

Fig: Charged Particle Moving in Perpendicular Magnetic Field.

Uncertainty and Time Scale

To take a photograph of moving object, one needs to know the shutter speed of the camera that must be set to avoid blurring the image. Therefore, the faster the object is moving, the shorter the exposure times to capture the motion of the object. Similar considerations in spectroscopy must be also taken.

Suppose one was looking at a particular dot which could turn white and black every 1 s. If one was to take a picture of this dot with a shutter speed of 10 s, the photograph of the dot would appear to be gray, because it would capture the average of the two colours of the dot. But if on decreased the exposure time to perhaps 0.01 s, the photograph would show a black one or white one dot. Thus to capture the individual colours, black or white in this case, the exposure time must be significantly shorter than the cycle time of the colour change. In a similar fashion, frequency, analogous to the shutter speed, must be high enough so that the motion of the particle can be captured. In addition, electrical hardware and computational power must be fast enough to capture the image of the particle.

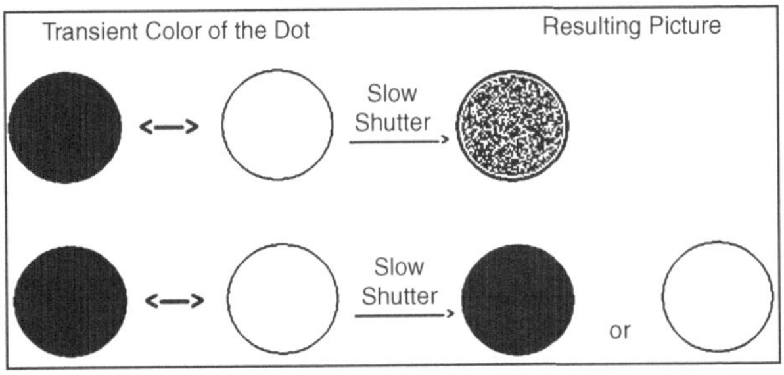

Fig: Freezing a Transient Condition Requires a "Fast" Shutter.

There are many types of molecular changes, that is, molecules constantly undergo some sort of reversible reorganization of their structures. If absorption of the photon is fast enough, one should be able to detect both "black" and "white" forms of the molecules. But if the absorption process is slower than the interconversion, the NMR will only detect some sort of the time-averaged structure, making the structure harder to decipher. The situation therefore boils down to the question: How long does it take for particle to absorb a photon? Unfortunately, such a question is impossible to answer with complete precision.

In 1927, W. Heisenberg, a pioneer of quantum mechanics stated his uncertainty principle: There will always be a limit to the precision with which we can simultaneously determine the energy and times scale of an event.

Stated mathematically, the product of the uncertainties of the energy and time can never be less than h.

$$\Delta E \Delta t \leq h$$

Thus, if we know the energy of a given photon to a high order of precision, we would be unable to measure precisely how long it takes for the photon to be absorbed. However, there is a useful generalization one can make by substitution of h, *giving*:

$$\Delta t \geq 1 / \Delta v \,,$$

where Δv is the uncertainty in frequency. As a result, the time required for a photon to be absorbed (Δt) must be approximately as long as it takes one cycle of the wave to pass the particle. The length of time t_0, is nothing more than 1/v. This result is not surprising if one considers that the particle would have to wait through at least one cycle before it could "sense" what the radiation frequency was. This allows an idea of the order-of-magnitude of how fast the "shutter" (frequency) speed of the NMR must be in order to "freeze" a given molecular transition.

MAGNETIC PROPERTIES OF NUCLEI

The Structure of an Atom

The compounds examined by NMR are composed of molecules, which are themselves aggregates of atoms. Each atom has some number of negatively charged electrons whizzing around a tiny dense bit of positively charged matter called the nucleus. The size of an atom is the volume of space that the electron cloud occupies. However, >99.9% of the mass of an atom is concentrated in its nucleus, though the nucleus occupies only one trillionth the atom's volume. Even the nucleus can be further dissected into other fundamental particles, including protons and neutrons, not to mention a host of other sub-nuclear particles that help hold the nucleus together and give nuclear physicists something to wonder about.

Composition of the Nucleus

The number of protons in an atoms nucleus (Z, the atomic number) determines both the atom's identity and the charge on its nucleus. In the periodic table of elements, the atomic number of each element is shown to the right of it chemical symbol. Every nucleus with just one proton is a hydrogen nucleus while every nucleus with six protons is a carbon nucleus, and so on. Yet, careful examination a large sample of hydrogen atoms, finds that not all their nuclei are identical. It is true that all have just one proton, but they differ in the number of neutrons. Most hydrogen atoms in nature (99.985%, to be exact) have no neutrons (N=0), but a small fraction, 0.015%, have one neutron (N=1) in addition to the proton. These two forms are the naturally occurring stable isotopes of hydrogen and they are given the symbols ^{1}H and ^{2}H, respectively.

The leading superscript is the mass number (A) of the isotope, which is the integer sum of Z and N:

$$A = Z + N$$

The isotope ^{2}H is usually referred to as deuterium (D), or heavy hydrogen, but most isotopes of other elements are identified simply by their mass number. The atomic mass listed for each element in the periodic table is a weighted means, the fractional abundance of each isotopes times its exact mass, summed over all naturally occurring isotopes.

Electron Spin

Before going further into the properties of the nucleus, a close examination of the electrons is needed to understand electron spin. Just like protons, electrons also exhibit wave and particle like properties. Each electron wave in an atom is characterized by four quantum numbers. The first three of these numbers (n, l, and m) can be taken as the electrons' address and describes the energy (n), shape (l), and orientation (m) of the volume the electron occupies in the atom. All three numbers define a specific volume of the electron which is called an orbital. The various electron orbitals as defined by the specific quantum numbers.

Nuclear Spin

The proton is a spinning charged (Z=1) particle as well and so it too exhibits a magnetic moment. And as with the electron, its magnetic moment has only two possible orientations that are degenerate in the absence of an external magnetic field. To differentiate nuclear spin states from the electronic spin states, the proton spin quantum number m is used. Thus for a proton, m can assume values of only +½ or –½ and can be described as having a nuclear spin I, (I= +½ or –½). Since nuclear charge is opposite in sign that of the electron, a nucleus whose magnetic moment is aligned with the magnetic field (m= +½) has the lower energy.

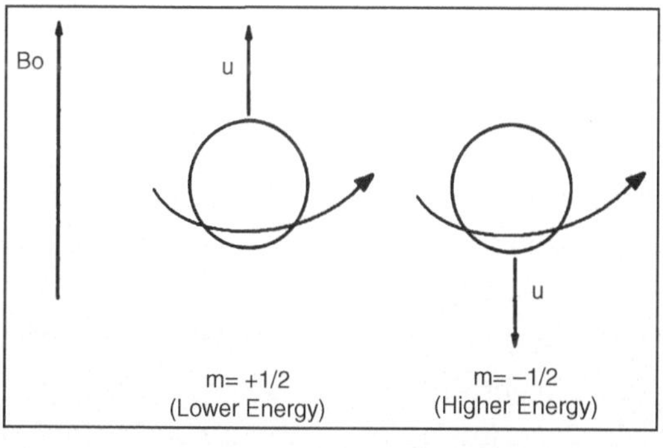

Fig: Two Possible Orientations of the Magnetic Moment μ of a Spinning Proton in an External Magnetic Field Bo.

Although neutrons are uncharged subatomic particles, neutrons also display magnetic moments and show a spin of I = ½.

As previously noted, Zeeman found only certain isotopes give rise to multiple nuclear spin state when immersed in an external magnetic field. This is because only isotopes with an odd number of protons (odd Z) and/or and odd number of neutrons (odd N) posses nonzero nuclear spin. Nuclei with zero nuclear spin (when Z and N are even) have zero nuclear magnetic moment and cannot be detected by NMR methods. Thus on of the limitations to NMR is that only certain isotopes can be detected.

ELECTRON SPIN RESONANCE (ESR)

An electron bound to an atom can absorb a photon (or packet of electromagnetic energy) of the right energy and make a transition to a higher energy state, provided that the photon energy precisely matches the energy difference between two allowed states. The energy of a photon depends on its frequency (which can also be considered in a semiclassical picture to be the frequency of oscillation of the electric and magnetic fields) by $E = h\nu$. Thus, an electron bound to an atom can absorb or emit only photons that have specific frequencies.

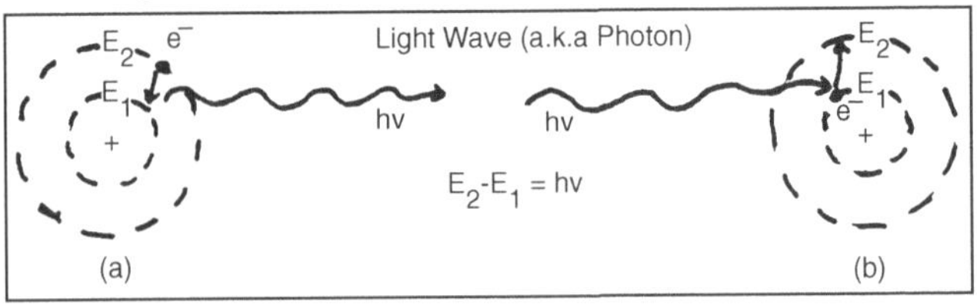

Fig: Electrons Bound to Atoms can Emit or Absorb Electromagnetic Energy (Photons) only in Discrete Quantities Corresponding to the different Allowed Energy States in the Atom. (a) Emission, (b) Absorption.

When free electrons (or nearly free electrons in a solid) are placed in a magnetic field, the z-component of the spin angular momentum (the component parallel to the magnetic field) can take on two values, and these two spin orientations correspond to different energies. These two energy states are due to the magnetic dipole moment of the electron and its orientation relative to the external magnetic field. A classical analogue of this phenomenon is the current loop in a magnetic field: To rotate the magnetic dipole moment of the loop opposite to the applied field, work must be done. For the spinning electron, there are only two allowed energy states associated with its interaction with the magnetic field, whereas the energy for a macroscopic current loop is continuous.

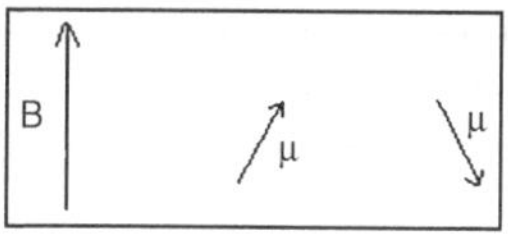

(a)

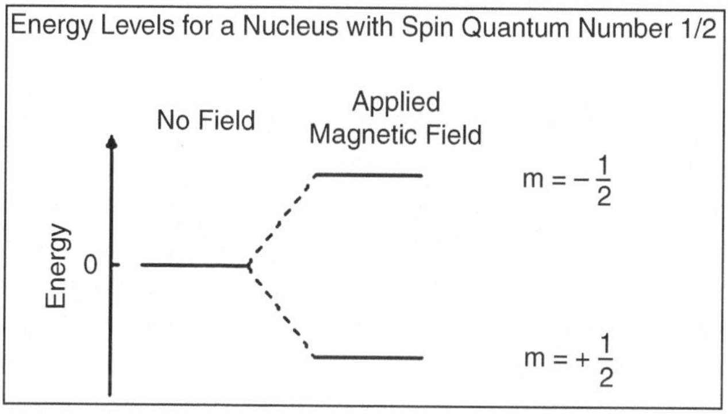

(b)

Fig: (a) Two Spin States of Electron in a Magnetic Field (b) This Image Shows the Energy Splitting due to a Magnetic Field for any Spin ½ Particle, such as Electrons, Protons, Neutrons or Certain Nuclei.

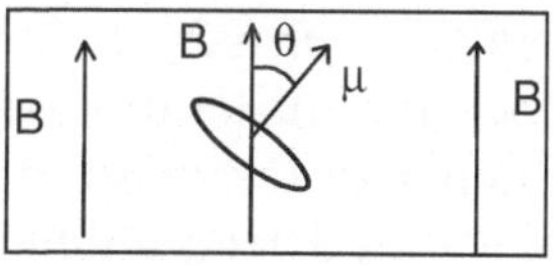

Fig: Energy of a Classical Current Loop in a Magnetic Field

The magnetic moment of the electron differs from the classical analogy of a current in a loop in one other aspect. The classical magnetic moment is easily calculated from the circulating current. The electron, on the other hand, is a point charge so its magnetic dipole moment cannot be viewed simply as a classical circulating charge. The magnetic moment of an electron is a fundamental, quantum mechanical property of the electron. As for the current loop, the magnetic moment and the spin angular momentum of the electron are proportional, but the constant of proportionality is different.

For electron spins, a correction factor, known as the *g*-factor, must be included in the above equation, and we refer to the component of the magnetic moment along the z axis by substituting $h/4\pi$ for the magnitude of the angular momentum along this axis, so that $\mu_e = g_e(q/2m)(h/4\pi)$. The *g*-factor for the electron is now known to high accuracy through both experiment and theory to be 2.002319134.

The energy associated with a classical magnetic dipole, of moment μ, in a magnetic field B (oriented along the z-axis) is given by $E = -\mu \bullet B = -\mu_z B$. The two allowed quantum spin energy states of the electron, then, are $\pm\mu_e B$, with the lower state corresponding to "parallel" alignment of the magnetic moment with the B-field, or when the spin of the *negative* charge is anti-aligned. (Note that the when there is no external magnetic field, *i.e.*, $B = 0$, the two states have the same energy and are therefore indistinguishable. In quantum mechanical terms, we say that these states are degenerate.) Since the magnetic dipole moment of an electron along the magnetic field axis is given by me, as defined above, the energy difference between the two allowed energy states, and therefore the energy that can be absorbed by the electrons is $2\mu_e B$. The requirement for electrons to absorb a photon and flip its spin, then, is that $hn = 2\mu_e B$. This is considered a resonance situation because the natural response frequency of the system (the frequency of radiation that the electrons will absorb) equals the applied frequency (of the oscillating EM field).

In this experiment, the oscillating electromagnetic field is in the radio frequency range, and is created by an oscillating current in a coil. A quantum of this oscillating electromagnetic field has energy hv, where v is the frequency of oscillation. The electrons will be located inside this coil and inside a larger-scale *external* magnetic field, created by a set of Helmholtz coils. When $hv = 2\mu_e B$ the electrons will absorb energy from the oscillating EM field.

The DPPH contains the electrons whose spins will produce the desired resonance. DPPH is the organic salt diphenyl-picryl-hydrazil, $(C_6H_5)_2N\text{-}NC_6H_2(N0_{2;}$ it contains an electron that is unpaired and has 0 orbital angular momentum (it is in an s orbital) and therefore behaves like an isolated electron. We use DPPH, in part because it has a very strong and narrow absorption line, with a g=2.0036 factor very close to the value for free electrons, and also because it's used in chemistry as a free radical, and ESR actually is used to study its properties.

EXPERIMENTAL PROCEDURE

To measure the magnetic moment, μ_e, of the electron, you are to find the resonance condition described in the introduction and given by $2\mu_e B = h\nu$. You will need to find resonance for a situation with known B and ν. You will create a known uniform B field with a set of Helmholtz coils and create an oscillating EM field of known frequency ν by using smaller coils carrying an AC current of known frequency. Then, by placing the electrons inside the small coils and the small coils inside the Helmholtz coils, you will provide the electrons with the necessary condition for spin flip transitions. You could either set a fixed B and vary ν until absorption from the EM field is seen or you can fix ν and vary B. You will use the latter approach in this experiment. This is easier because you can put the 60 Hz current from the wall through the Helmholtz coils, which will vary the magnetic field at a rate much faster than you could vary the frequency of the AC current through the small coils. Note that the electrons respond to a frequency of tens of MHz, so on the timescale of the electrons, the magnetic field from the Helmholtz coils is effectively constant. The 60 Hz frequency is also suitable for monitoring with an inexpensive oscilloscope. When resonance occurs, a drop in the voltage across the small coils will be seen because the electrons absorb the energy of the electromagnetic field created by the current, thereby altering the impedance of the coil.

4

Spectra of Polyatomic Molecules

THE VIBRATIONAL SPECTRA OF A POLYATOMIC MOLECULE

The vibrational motion of a molecule is quantised and the resulting energy level spacings giverise to transitions in the mid-IR portion of the electromagnetic spectrum (4000 to ca. 400 cm^{-1}).The diatomic harmonic oscillator, the energies (or wavenumber positions, cm^{-1}) of these transitions are related to the bond strength (force constant), bond length,and atomic masses (reduced mass). In polyatomic spectra, the positions and relative intensitiesof the vibrational modes depend on the symmetry (*i.e.,* shape or structure) of the molecule, aswell as the bond strengths and masses. For this reason, vibrational spectra (IR and Raman) canprovide detailed structural information. This structural information is the objective of this lab,and it is obtained by this analysis, or interpretation, of the infrared and Raman spectra.

In this experiment you will obtain infrared and Raman spectra of a polyatomic molecule, predictthe selection rules, assign vibrational modes, and then compare these with the vibrational modepositions and intensities predicted for that molecule using HyperChem®. Using group theory, weshall predict the spectral selection rules, *i.e.,* predict the spectra for a particular structural model. Assignment of vibrational modes in a spectrum involves relating the experimental spectrum andthe predicted spectrum so that each observed vibrational band is identified as to its theoreticalorigin. A series of empirical rules is provided below to aid in this assignment. Also, a chartdefining the well-known positions of group frequencies will be available. (These chartssummarise the vast knowledge obtained from the extensive, experimental spectral database thathas been collected, litreally, over the past 65 years.) Finally, the results of the HyperChem®calculation will be compared with the above. Because these calculated normal mode positions will be harmonic frequencies, they must be multiplied by a constant to relate them to the empirical, anharmonic band positions. This constant depends upon the orbital basis set that you use.

BACKGROUND

For a non-linear polyatomic molecule containing n atoms, there will be 3n-6 vibrational degrees of freedom (3n-5 for a linear molecule). This number represents the maximum number of vibrational modes for the molecule. However, often the observed number is smaller because of degeneracies and selection rules. Because of the symmetry (*i.e.,* structure), some transitions maybe degenerate, and some transitions may be forbidden and not observed; others will be allowedand observed. Allowed or forbidden transitions are also referred to as active or inactive vibrational modes, respectively.

Vibrational transitions may also be observed using IR or Raman spectroscopy. For an IRabsorption to be allowed between two vibrational levels, a change in dipole moment (μ) mustoccur as the atoms move, and Δv must equal + 1. To be Raman active (*i.e.,* allowed), there mustbe a change in polarizability (α_{ij}) during the vibration and Δv must equal $\pm$ 1. This polarizability can be better understood as an induced dipole. A fundamental vibrational mode will involve a transition from the $v = 0$ level to the $\upsilon = 1$ level. The selection rules for IR and for Raman spectra differ so that the two techniques provide complementary information, not redundant information. Therefore, the Raman spectrum provides significant new structural information, in addition to that provided by the IR spectrum. Group theory is used to predict the characteristic or normal modes of vibration for a molecule. (Normal refers to the fact that these modes of vibration are orthogonal to each other, *i.e.,* independent of each other.)

For molecules with many atoms, 3n-6 becomes very large, and this can result in a seemingly complex spectral pattern. However, the presence of symmetry in a molecule often simplifies the vibrational spectrum. Recognition of this symmetry simplifies and allows the interpretation of even complex vibrational spectra, both IR and Raman. The predicted symmetry species define the activity (allowed or forbidden) of each vibrational mode in the IR and in the Raman spectra, and these are referred to as selection rules. Also, the stretching mode scan be predicted to distinguish them from the bending and torsional vibrations.

The atom masses and force constants determine the precise region of the spectrum at which each normal mode vibrates, *i.e.,* the energy (or frequency or wavenumber) for each. The general region in which various molecular groups will occur can be obtained from group frequency charts, which summarise extensive collections of empirical data.

EMPIRICAL RULES USED TO INTERPRET SPECTRA

When we interpret a spectrum, we shall relate (or assign) each band in the spectrum to its origin as predicted by the group theoretical selection rules. The following empirical rules are used in this assignment process for molecular species. The band position (cm^{-1}) provides information about the type of vibration.

Vibrational modes can be of three basic types, stretching modes (u), bending modes (δ) or torsional modes (τ). Stretching modes of vibration occur at higher energy, *i.e.,* higher wavenumber, than bending modes. Torsional modes appear at even lower energy. Both the type of vibration and the symmetry species of each vibrational mode influence the relative band intensities. The intensities of asymmetric stretching modes will be greater than asymmetric bending (or torsional) modes in the IR. If one compares asymmetric species with symmetric species of each type (stretch or bend), the asymmetric species will, in general, best ronger in the IR spectrum.

For a Raman spectrum, the opposite is true; the symmetric species are stronger. The spectra, both the IR and Raman, will contain some weak bands that are fundamental vibrations and some weak bands that are overtone or combination bands. (Overtone and combination bands are not allowed in the harmonic approximation, and therefore exhibit reduced intensities.) To distinguish the two, compare the IR and Raman spectra. If a band is weak in both the IR and the Raman, it is more likely to be an overtone.

A fundamental is expected to be strong in one and weak in the other. However, it is possible, on occasion, to have a mode be weak in both. When comparing IR and Raman band positions, how do you decide if the bands may be ascribed to the 'same' vibrational mode, *i.e.,* that these are coincident in the IR and the Raman? This is defined by the experimental error in each spectrum. The maximum precision (for a sharp band) is defined by the spectral resolution used for the scan. For example, if you used 2 cm^{-1} resolution, then your precision (or uncertainty) is ±2 cm^{-1}. For broad bands, the precision will be less. The criterion for coincidence is then the sum of the two uncertainties.

GROUP THEORETICAL ANALYSIS

The first choice of point group used to predict the IR and Raman spectral selection rules should be the "ideal" structure, the highest symmetry point group possible. Sometimes, more than one structure (and point group) is possible. Do the group theoretical calculation for both and determine which applies to the real spectrum. For example, when calculating the minimum energy geometry, you may find that this geometry has lower symmetry than the "ideal" and belongs to a lower symmetry point group. You will then need to predict the IR and Raman selection rules for this point group, as well as the "ideal," high symmetry point group. When comparing the two sets of predictions with the experimental data, you may then decide which agrees better with the experimental results.

There are two 'background' pages that will be given to you as handouts in class.

These are:

1. 'How is Group Theory Used?' and
2. 'Applying Group Theory: Representations of Vibrational Motion'.

Copies of these follow this experiment for your convenient reference.

HYPERCHEM® OUTPUT, ANHARMONICITY CORRECTION, NEGATIVE FREQUENCIES, AND DEGENERACY

HyperChem® calculates all of the fundamental modes, both IR and Raman, as well as the IRintensities. Thus it outputs two spectra, one with all of the bands plotted, and the second with just the IR active modes. Since it does not calculate Raman intensities, it cannot plot a Raman spectrum. HyperChem® also identifies the symmetry species of each mode. Since you know the assignments from your group theoretical results, you can predict the approximate Raman intensity expected for each calculated mode. (The totally symmetric species will be stronger in the Raman.)

The frequencies calculated using HyperChem® (or any other ab initio calculation) are harmonic frequencies. To correct for anharmonicity the calculated, harmonic frequencies are multiplied by a constant. This constant depends upon the basis set used. Professor Brown recommends use of the HF/6-13G* basis set (select the 6-13G* basis in the setup) to minimize the energy and to calculate the geometry.

Multiply your calculated values by 0.8929, if you use the 6-13G* basis set. This correction will allow you to compare your experimental values with these corrected values. These should agree quite will, but will not give a perfect agreement. Any drasticd is agreement here may indicate an error in your group theoretical analysis and empirical assignments. Be sure to describe and discuss this comparison. This correction factor is an empirically determined value which can vary from 0.89 to 0.99.

The precise value needed for each molecule or even for each fundamental vibrational mode may differ slightly. This is especially true for the lower frequency vibrational modes such as bending and torsional modes. After you 'assign' each fundamental vibration and compare the experimental and calculated harmonic values, you can calculate the precise coefficient needed for each mode. The overall average coefficient for your molecule, as well as the average values for just the stretching modes and for just the bending plus torsional modes will be interesting to calculate and discuss in your report.

How much do these differ from the literature value reported above (0.8929)?A negative frequency means that you have not obtained a minimum. A negative frequency indicates an imaginary energy, which occurs if you are at a saddle point. You are not at the minimum energy structure. Go back and recalculate the minimum energy structure. If your molecule exhibits degenerate vibrational modes (E or T species), HyperChem® will calculate 2 or 3 essentially identical (*i.e.*, within experimental error) frequencies for doubly or triply degenerate vibrational modes, respectively.

SYMMETRIC TOP MOLECULE

These are the settings for a symmetric molecule as a whole, *i.e.*, those common to all states (but perhaps different for different isotopologues).

SETTINGS

nNuclei	Number of nuclei to calculate hyperfine structure for. Leave this at 0 unless you want the hyperfine structure resolved.
Jmin	Minimum J to use in calculation - set to -1 (default) to use value from species.
Jmax	Maximum J to use in calculation - set to -1 (default) to use value from species.
Colour	Colour - set to "None" to take value from elsewhere.
PointGroup	Point group of molecule. Possible values are: C_{3v}, C_{4v}, C_{5v}, C_{6v}, C_{7v}, C_{8v}, D_{3h}, D_{4h}, D_{5h}, D_{6h}, D_{7h}, D_{8h}, D_{2d}, D_{3d}, D_{4d}, D_{5d}, D_{6d}, D_{7d}, D_{8d}
Wt0	Statistical Weight for each possible rovibronic symmetry. The number of settings here depends on the point group set as above, with one setting per rovibronic symmetry.

INTENSITIES OF ROTATION AND VIBRATION-ROTATION RAMAN TRANSITIONS IN ASYMMETRIC TOP MOLECULES

The derivation of the intensities of rotation and rotation-vibration Raman transitions for asymmetric top molecules is given, based on irreducible spherical tensor formalism. A computer programme package written to calculate such intensities is described. Its use is demonstrated by reproducing the observed contours of the pure rotational band and the asymmetric stretching vibrational band in the Raman spectrum of the SO_2 molecule. The polarizability tensor component ratio required to simulate the pure rotational contour is combined with literature values for mean polarizability and depolarisation ratio to obtain the principal values of the SO_2 polarizability tensor. A correlation of the polarizability tensor component ratio with band types is discussed for totally symmetric bands which have been reproduced using our programme and those of others.

ROTATIONAL TRANSITION

A rotational transition is an abrupt change in angular momentum in quantum physics. Like all other properties of a quantum particle, angular momentum is quantised, meaning it can only equal certain discrete values, which correspond to different rotational energy states. When a particle loses angular momentum, it is said to have transitioned to a lower rotational energy state. Likewise, when a particle gains angular momentum, a positive rotational transition is said to have occurred.

Rotational transitions are important in physics due to the unique spectral lines that result. Because there is a net gain or loss of energy during a transition, electromagnetic radiation of a particular frequency must be absorbed or emitted. This forms spectral lines at that frequency which can be detected with a spectrometer, as in Rotational spectroscopy or Raman spectroscopy.

SYMMETRY PROPERTIES OF THE ROTATIONAL ENERGY LEVELS

The symmetry properties of the rotational energy levels of diatomic molecules. The rotational levels of all diatomic molecules can be classified as + or – according to their parity, *i.e.*, according to the behaviour of the complete molecular wave function (apart from translation) when the laboratory-fixed Cartesian coordinates of all particles are replaced by their negatives. The rotational energy levels of homonuclear diatomic molecules can be classified in addition as s (symmetric) or a (antisymmetric) with respect to permutation of identical nuclei. The symmetry designations +, -, s, a are very important, since perturbations and optical transitions between two rotational levels are limited by selection rules on these quantities.

It turns out that the two permutation-inversion symmetry operations mentioned in the preceding paragraph, *i.e.,* the laboratory-fixed inversion operation I, and the permutation P of identical nuclei in a homonuclear diatomic molecule, are related to the geometric symmetry operations found in the usual group theory tables, *i.e.,* rotation, reflection, inversion. and rotation-reflection operations. It is convenient at this time to consider these two kinds of symmetry operations in more detail.

GEOMETRIC SYMMETRY OPERATIONS

Heteronuclear diatomic molecules belong to the point group $C_{\infty v}$. This point group contains as symmetry elements the identity (E), one infinite-fold rotation axis (C_∞), and an infinite number of reflection planes (σ_v) containing the rotation axis.

Homonuclear diatomic molecules belong to the point group D8h. This point group contains, in addition to the symmetry elements found in $C_{\infty v}$, an inversion center (i), one infinite-fold rotation-reflection axis (S_∞), and an infinite number of twofold rotation axes (C_2) perpendicular to the C_∞ axis.

It is relatively easy to visualise the effect of these geometric symmetry operations on an electron belonging to the diatomic molecule, and to determine in this way the precise effect of these geometric symmetry operations on the coordinates of the electron. Let

$$x_e = \rho_e \sin\theta_e \cos\psi_e$$
$$y_e = \rho_e \sin\theta_e \sin\psi_e$$
$$z_e = \rho_e \cos\theta_e$$

be the Cartesian coordinates and spherical polar coordinates of an electron in an axis system fixed in the diatomic molecule such that the internuclear axis is the z axis. The new coordinates of this electron, after it has been subjected to representative symmetry operations of the point groups $C_{\infty v}$ and $D_{\infty h}$.

When one of these symmetry operations acts on a function containing the electron coordinates, its effect is to replace, everywhere in the function, each coordinate by the quantity at the intersection of the appropriate row and column. For example,

$$\begin{aligned} C_\infty^E(z).i.C_2(y).f(\ldots,\psi_e,\ldots) &= C_\infty^e(z).i.f(\ldots,\pi-\psi_e,\ldots) \\ &= C_\infty^e(z).f(\ldots,\pi-(\pi+\psi_e),\ldots) \\ &= f(\ldots,-\psi_e-\in,\ldots). \end{aligned}$$

Table 4.1 The Effect of Various Symmetry Operations on Electron Coordinates.

Symmetry operation	Coordinates acted upon					
	x_e	y_e	z_e	ρ_e	θ_e	φ_e
E	x_e	y_e	z_e	ϱ_e	θ_e	ϕ_e
$C_\infty^\varepsilon(z)$	$x_e \cos\varepsilon - y_e \sin\varepsilon$	$y_e \cos\varepsilon + x_e \sin\varepsilon$	$+z_e$	ϱ_e	$+\theta_e$	$\phi_e+\varepsilon$
$\sigma_v(xz)$	$+x_e$	$-y_e$	$+z_e$	ϱ_e	$+\theta_e$	$-\phi_e$
i	$-x_e$	$-y_e$	$-z_e$	ϱ_e	$\pi-\theta_e$	$\pi+\phi_e$
$S_\infty^\varepsilon(z)$	$x_e \cos\varepsilon - y_e \sin\varepsilon$	$y_e \cos\varepsilon + x_e \sin\varepsilon$	$-z_e$	ϱ_e	$\pi-\theta_e$	$\phi_e+\varepsilon$
$C_2(y)$	$-x_e$	$+y_e$	$-z_e$	ϱ_e	$\pi-\theta_e$	$\pi-\phi_e$

These geometric symmetry operations also act on the vibrational and rotational variables of a diatomic molecule. The transformations of the vibrational variable can be obtained by considering the effect of the various symmetry operations on the vibrational displacement vectors. Pictorially speaking, these displacement vectors are subjected to the various symmetry operations while the molecular framework, *i.e.*, the equilibrium position of each atom in the molecule, is left unchanged.

The effect of representative symmetry operations of $C_{\infty v}$ and $D_{\infty h}$ on arbitrary displacement vectors (d_1, d_2) for the two nuclei of a diatomic molecule. The vibrational variable for diatomic molecules is usually taken to be the internuclear distance r, given by $|(a_1+d_1)-(a_2+d_2)|$, where a_1 and a_2 represent equilibrium positions for the two atoms. Since the equilibrium positions a_i lie on the z axis, and since they are not changed in value by any of the symmetry operations, it is easy to show that the transformations leave the vibrational variable r unaltered.

Table 4.2 The Effect of Various Symmetry Operations on Nuclear Displacement Vectors

Symmetry operation	Displacement vector component acted upon					
	d_{1x}	d_{1y}	d_{1z}	d_{2x}	d_{2y}	d_{2z}
E	d_{1x}	d_{1y}	d_{1z}	d_{2x}	d_{2y}	d_{2z}
$C_\infty^{\varepsilon}(z)$	$d_{1x}\cos\varepsilon - d_{1y}\sin\varepsilon$	$d_{1y}\cos\varepsilon + d_{1x}\sin\varepsilon$	$+d_{1z}$	$d_{2x}\cos\varepsilon - d_{2y}\sin\varepsilon$	$d_{2y}\cos\varepsilon + d_{2x}\sin\varepsilon$	$+d_{2z}$
$\sigma_v(xz)$	$+d_{1x}$	$-d_{1y}$	$+d_{1z}$	$+d_{2x}$	$-d_{2y}$	$+d_{2z}$
i	$-d_{2x}$	$-d_{2y}$	$-d_{2z}$	$-d_{1x}$	$-d_{1y}$	$-d_{1z}$
$S_\infty^{\varepsilon}(z)$	$d_{2x}\cos\varepsilon - d_{2y}\sin\varepsilon$	$d_{2y}\cos\varepsilon + d_{2x}\sin\varepsilon$	$-d_{2z}$	$d_{1x}\cos\varepsilon - d_{1y}\sin\varepsilon$	$d_{1y}\cos\varepsilon + d_{1x}\sin\varepsilon$	$-d_{1z}$
$C_2(y)$	$-d_{2x}$	$+d_{2y}$	$-d_{2z}$	$-d_{1x}$	$+d_{1y}$	$-d_{1z}$

The effect of geometric symmetry operations on rotational variables is not as obvious as the effect on electronic and vibrational variables. The rotational variables of a molecule actually represent Eulerian angles, indicating how the (right handed) molecule-fixed axis system is rotated with respect to some (right handed) laboratory-fixed axis system. For every orientation of the molecule-fixed axis system there is a set of corresponding Eulerian angles. For every set of Eulerian angles there is a corresponding orientation of the molecule-fixed axis system.

It thus seems intuitively obvious that a geometric symmetry operation corresponding to a pure rotation should effect a change in the Eulerian angles corresponding to that pure rotation. It is not possible, however, to represent the change from a right handed to a left-handed axis system by a set of Eulerian angles. Consequently, it is not intuitively obvious how sense-reversing symmetry operations (reflections, inversion, rotation-reflections) should affect the Eulerian angles. It turns out that a consistent and useful scheme of geometric symmetry operations can be obtained if a sense-reversing operation is defined to have the same effect on the Eulerian angles as does the pure rotation obtained from the sense-reversing operation by multiplication by the inversion. According to this prescription, i and E have the same effect on the rotational variables; σ_p(xz) and C_2(y) have the same effect; and $S_{\&infinity;}$ $^{\varepsilon}$(z) and $C_\infty^{\pi+\varepsilon}$ (z) have the same effect.

The rotational variables of linear molecules present an additional complication since they consist of two Eulerian angles rather than three. Because the third Eulerian angle is missing, it is not possible to carry out the operation $C_\infty{}^{\varepsilon}$(z) on the rotational variables. Thus, this operation and $S_\infty{}^{\varepsilon}$(z), both of which were used in classifying electronic and vibrational levels, cannot be used in classifying rotational energy levels. The remaining symmetry operations are E, σ υi, and C_2. Of these, we need only investigate the effect of C_2 on the rotational variables. Note added in proof: A recently published article by Bunker and Papoušek presents a more sophisticated discussion of the complications associated with symmetry operations for linear molecules than does reference.

The rotational variables θ and ϕ represent for a diatomic molecule the polar and azimuthal angles of the internuclear axis in the laboratory-fixed axis system. Since C_2(y) corresponds to a twofold rotation about an axis perpendicular to the internuclear axis, this symmetry operation reverses the direction of the internuclear axis. Thus, $C_2(y)$ acting on a function of the rotational variables replaces θ by $\pi - \theta$ and ϕ by $\pi + \phi$ everywhere in the function. The functions of the rotational variables most often considered, of course, are the rotational basis set functions ΩJM themselves. Explicit expressions for these functions, corresponding precisely to the phase conventions used in this monograph, can be obtained by setting $\alpha = \pi/2$, $\beta = \theta$, $\gamma = \phi$, $j = J$, $\mu' = \Omega$ and $\mu = M$ in the quantity $\left[(2j+1)/4\pi\right]^{1/2}.D^{(j)}([\alpha\beta\gamma])\mu'\mu$, where $D^{(j)}(\alpha\beta\gamma)\mu'\mu$ is given in equation of Wigner's book on group theory In this same connection, the 3 × 3 rotation matrices used in eqs can be obtained by setting $x = \pi/2$, $\theta = \theta$, and $\phi = \phi$.

The effect of $C_2(y)$ on the polar and azimuthal angles of the internuclear axis, as defined above, is different from the effect of $C_2(y)$ on the polar and azimuthal angles of an electron. This difference arises because $C_2(y)$ represents a rotation about an axis which is always perpendicular to the internuclear axis, but which is not in general perpendicular to the position vector from the origin to a given electron.

FRANCK-CONDON PRINCIPLE

Franck-Condon principle was proposed by German physicist James Franck (1882–1964) and U.S., physicist Edward U. Condon (1902–1974) in 1926. This principle states that when an electronic transition takes place, the time scale of this transition is so fast compared to nucleus motion that we can consider the nucleus to be static, and the vibrational transition from one vibrational state to another state is more likely to happen if these states have a large overlap. It successfully explains the reason why certain peaks in a spectrum are strong while others are weak (or even not observed) in absorption spectroscopy.

$$M = \int \psi_e^{'}(r,R_e).\mu_e.\psi_e^{''}(r,R_e)dr \int \psi_\upsilon^{'}(R).\psi_\upsilon^{''}(R)dR$$

The second integral in the above equation is the vibrational overlap integral between one eigenstate and another eigenstate. In addition, the square of this integral is called the Franck-Condon factor:

$$\text{Franck}-\text{Condon Factor}=\left|\int \psi_{\upsilon}^{'}\psi_{\upsilon}^{''}dR\right|^{2}$$

It governs the vibrational transition contribution to the transition probability and shows that in order to have a large vibrational contribution, the vibrational ground state and excited state must have a strong overlap.

The above figure shows the Franck-Condon principle energy diagram, since electronic transition time scale is small compared to nuclear motion, the vibrational transitions are favoured when the vibrational transition have the smallest change of nuclear coordinate, which is a vertical transition in the figure above. The electronic eigenstates favours the vibrational transition v'=0 in the ground electronic state to v'=2 in the excited electronic state, while peak intensity of v'=0 to v'=0 transition is expected to be low because the overlap between the v'=0 wavefunction and v"=0 wavefunction is very low.

The figure above is the photoelectron spectrum of the ionisation of hydrogen molecule (H_2), it is also a beautiful example to formulate the Franck-Condon principle. It shows the appropriate energy curves and the vibrational energy levels, and with the help of the Franck-Condon principle, the transition between ground vibrational state v_0' and excited vibrational state v_2' is expected to be the most intense peak in the spectrum.

Vibronic Coupling

Why can some electronic-forbidden transitions be observed as weak bands in spectrum? It can be explained by the interaction between the electronic and vibrational transitions. The word 'vibronic' is the combination of the words 'vibrational' and 'electronic.' Because the energy required for one electronic state to another electronic state (electronic transition, usually in the UV-Vis region) is larger than one vibrational state to another vibrational state (vibrational transition, usually in the IR region), sometimes energy (a photon) can excite a molecule to an excited electronic and vibrational state. The bottom figure shows the pure electronic transition (no vibronic coupling) and the electronic transition couples with the vibrational transition (vibronic coupling).

We now can go back to the original question: Why can some electronic-forbidden transitions be observed as weak bands in spectrum? For example, the d–d transitions in the octahedral transition metal complexes are Laporte forbidden (same symmetry, parity forbidden), but they can be observed in the spectrum and this phenomenon can be explained by vibronic coupling.

Now we consider the $Fe(OH_2)_6^{2+}$ complex which has low spin d^6 as ground state. Let's examine the one-electron excitation from t_{2g} molecular orbital to e_g molecular orbital. The octahedral complex has Oh symmetry and therefore the ground state has A_{1g} symmetry from the character table. The symmetry of the excited state, which is the direct product of all singly occupied molecular orbitals (e_g and t_{2g} in this case):

$$\Gamma_{t2g} \otimes \Gamma_{cg} = T_{1g} + T_{2g}$$

The transition moment integral for the electronic transition can be written as,

$$\vec{M} = \int_{\psi}'^{*} \hat{\mu} \psi \, dr$$

where ψ is the electronic ground state and ψ' is the electronic excited state. The condition for the electronic transition to be allowed is to make the transition moment integral non-zero. The $\hat{\mu}$ is the transition moment operator, which is the symmetry of the $\hat{x}, \hat{y}, \hat{z}$, operators from the character table. For octahedral symmetry, these operators are degenerate and have T_{1u} symmetry. Therefore, we can see that both ${}^1T_{1g} \leftarrow {}^1A_{1g}$ and ${}^1T_{2g} \leftarrow 1A_{1g}$ are electronically forbidden by the direct product (do not contain the totally symmetric A_{1g}):

$$T_{1g} \times T_{1u} \times A_{1g} = A_{1u} + E_u + T_{1u} + T_{2u}$$

$$T_{2g} \times T_{1u} \times A_{1g} = A_{2u} + E_u + T_{1u} + T_{2u}$$

For octahedral complex, there are 15 vibrational normal modes. From the Oh character table we can get these irreducible representations:

$$\Gamma_{vib} = \alpha_{1g} + e_g + e_g + 2t_{1u} + t_{2g} + t_{2u}$$

When we let the vibrational transition to couple with the electronic transition, the transition moment integral has the form:

$$\vec{M} = \int \psi^{*'}_{e} y^{*'}_{\upsilon} \vec{\mu} \psi_e \psi_e dr$$

For the vibronic coupling to be allowed, the transition moment integral has to be non-zero. Use these vibrational symmetries of the octahedral complex to couple with the electronic transition:

$$A_{1g} \times \{T_{1g} \times T_{1u} \times A_{1g}\} = A_{1u} + E_u + T_{1u} + T_{2u}$$

$$E_g \times \{T_{1g} \times A_{1g}\} = E_g \times \{A_{1u} + E_u + T_{1u} + T_{2u}\} = A_{1u} + A_{2u} + 2_{Eu} + 2T_{1u} + 2T_{2u}$$

$$T_{1u} \times \{T_{1g} \times T_{1u} \times A_{1g}\} = T_{1u} \times \{A_{1u} + E_u + T_{1u} + T_{2u}\} = A_{1g} + \ldots$$

$$T_{2g} \times \{T_{1g} \times T_{1u} \times A_{1g}\} = T_{2g} \times \{A_{1u} + E_u + T_{1u} + T_{2u}\} = A_{1u} + A_{2u} + 2E_u + 3T_{1u}\{3_{T1g} + 4T_{2u}\}$$

$$T_{2u} \times \{T_{1g} \times T_{1u} \times A_{1g}\} = T_{2u} \times \{A_{1u} + E_u + T_{1u} + T_{2u}\} = A_{1g} + ..$$

Since the t_{1u} and t_{2u} representation can generate the totally symmetric representation in the integrand. Therefore, we can see that t_{1u} and t_{2u} can couple with the electronic transition to form the allowed vibronic transition. Therefore, the d-d transition band for $Fe(OH_2)_6{}^{2+}$ complex can be observed through vibronic coupling.

Rotational Selection Rules

- Transitions with $\Delta J = \pm 1$ are allowed;

Photons do not have any mass, but they have angular momentum. The conservation of angular momentum is the fundamental criteria for spectroscopic transitions. As a result, the total angular momentum has to be conserved after a molecule absorbs or emits a photon. The rotational selection rule relies on the fact that photon has one unit of quantised angular momentum. During the photon emission and absorption process, the angular moment J cannot change by more than one unit.

Let's consider a single photon transition process for a diatomic molecule. The rotational selection rule requires that transitions with $\Delta J = \pm 1$ are allowed. Transitions with $\Delta J=1$ are defined as R branch transitions, while those with $\Delta J= -1$ are defined as P branch transitions. Rotational transitions are conventional labeled as P or R with the rotational quantum number J of the lower electronic state in the parentheses. For example, R(2) specifies the rotational transition from J=2 in the lower electronic state to J=3 in the upper electronic state.

- DJ=0 transitions are allowed when two different electronic or vibrational states are involved: $(X'', J''=m) \rightarrow (X', J'=m)$.

The Q branch transitions will only take place when there is a net orbital angular momentum in one of the electronic states. Therefore, Q branch does not exist for $^1\Sigma \leftrightarrow ^1\Sigma$ electronic transitions because Σ electronic state does not possess any net orbital angular momentum. On the other hand, the Q branch will exist if one of the electronic states has angular momentum. In this situation, the angular momentum of the photon will cancel out with the angular momentum of the electronic state, so the transition will take place without any change in the rotational state.

The schematic of P, Q, and R branch transitions are shown below:

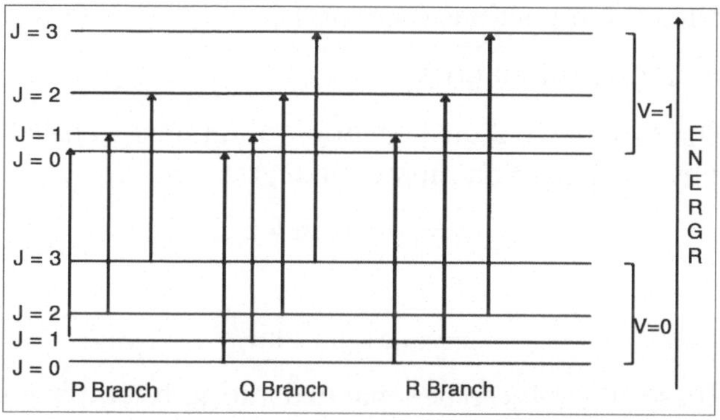

Schematic Diagram of P,Q, and R Branch Transitions

With regard to closed-shell non-linear polyatomic molecules, the selection rules are more complicated than diatomic case. The rotational quantum number J remains a good quantum number as the total angular momentum if we don't consider the nuclear spin. Under the effect of single photon transition, the change of J is still limited to a maximum of ± 1 based on the conservation of angular momentum. However, the possibility of Q branch is greatly enhanced irrelevant to the symmetry of the lower and upper electronic states. The rotational quantum number K is introduced along the inertial axis. For polyatomic molecules with symmetric top geometry, the transition moment is polarised along inertial axis. The selection rule becomes $\Delta K = 0$.

COMBINATION BANDS, OVERTONES AND FERMI RESONANCES

Fundamental vibrational frequencies of a molecule corresponds to transition from $v = 0$ to $v = 1$. For a non-linear molecule there will by 3N–6 (where N is the number of atoms) number vibrations. The same holds true for linear molecules, however the equations 3N–5 is used, because a linear molecule has one less rotational degrees of freedom.

The levels denoted by vibrational quantum numbers v represent the potenital energy for the harmonic (quadratic) oscillator. The transition 0--> 1 is fundamental, transitions 0--> n (n>1) are called overtones, and transitions 1--> n (n<1) are called hot transitions (hot bands).

Symmetry Requirements

The symmetry requirement of vibrational transisition is given by the transition moment integral,

$$u = \int \psi^* \mu \psi dr \neq 0$$

where,

$$\mu = i\mu_x + j\mu_y + k\mu_z$$

These integrals can be separated into each component: x,y, and z. Because the ground state contains the totally symmetric representation, the coordinate x, y, or z and ψ^* must belong to the same representation so that the direct product will contain the totally symmetric representation.

HARMONIC OSCILLATOR BREAKDOWN

The harmonic oscillator approximation is convenient to use for diatomic molecules with quantised vibrational energy levels given by the following equation:

$$E_\upsilon\left(cm^{-1}\right)=\left(\upsilon+\frac{1}{2}\right)\omega_e.$$

A more accurate description of the vibrational energies is given by the anharmonic oscillator (also called Morse potential) with energy of,

$$E_\upsilon\left(cm^{-1}\right)=\omega_e\left(\upsilon+\frac{1}{2}\right)-w_e x_e\left(\upsilon+\frac{1}{2}\right)^2+w_e y_e\left(\upsilon+\frac{1}{2}\right)^2+\ldots$$

where ω_e is the vibrational frequency for the re internuclear separation and $\omega_e >> \omega_e x_e >> \omega_e y_e$. This accounts for the fact that as the higher vibrational states deviate from the perfectly parabolic shape, the level converge with increasing quantum numbers. It is because of this anharmoniticity that overtones can occur. While it may seem that the harmonic oscillator and the anharomic oscillator are closely related, this is in fact not the case. The differences in the wavefunctions lead to a breakdown of selection rules, specifically, $\Delta v = \pm 1$ selection rule can not be applied, and higher order terms must be accounted in the energy calculations.

There is only a small correction from the ground state to the first excited state for the anharmonic correction, but it becomes much larger for more highly excited states which are populated as the temperature increases. The deviation from the harmonic oscillator to the anharmonic oscillator results in expanding the energy function with additional terms and treating these terms with perturbation theory. The results in the correct vibrational energies and also relaxes the selection rules. A $\Delta v = \pm 1$ is still most predominant, however, weaker overtones with $\Delta v = \pm 2, \pm 3, \ldots$ can occur. It should be noted that a $\Delta v = 2$ transition does not occur at twice the frequency of the fundamental transition, but at a lower frequency.

Overtones

Overtones occur when a vibrational mode is excited from v=0 to v=2, which is called the first overtone, or v=0 to v=3, the second overtone. The fundamental transitions, $v = \pm 1$, are the most commonly occurring, and the probability of overtones rapid decreases as $v = \pm n$ increases. Based on the harmonic oscillator approximation, the energy of the overtone transition will be about n times the fundamental associated with that particular transition. The anharmonic oscillator calculations show that the overtones are usually less than a multiple of the fundamental frequency. Overtones are generally not detected in larger molecules. This is demonstrated with the vibrations of the diatomic HCl in the gas phase:

Table 4.8 HCl Vibrational Spectrum

Transition	$\tilde{\nu}_{obs}$ [cm^{-1}]	$\tilde{\nu}_{obs}$ Harmonic [cm^{-1}]	$\tilde{\nu}_{obs}$ Anharmonic [cm^{-1}]
0 --> 1 (fundamental)	2885.9	2885.9	2885.3
0 --> 2 (first overtone)	5668.0	5771.8	5665.0
0 --> 3 (second overtone)	8347.0	8657.7	8339.0
0 --> 4 (thirdovertone)	10 923.1	11 543.6	10 907.4
0 --> 5 (fourth overtone)	13 396.5	14 429.5	13 370.

We can see from the table above that the anharmonic frequencies correspond much better with the observed frequencies, especially as the vibrational levels increase.

Special Case

If one of the symmetries is doubly degenerate in the excited state a recursion formula is required to determine the symmetry of the vth wave function, given by,

$$x_{\upsilon}(R) = \frac{1}{2}\left[x(R)x_{\upsilon} - 1(R) + x\left(R^{\upsilon}\right)\right]$$

where Xv(R) is the character under the operation R for the vth energy level; X(R) is the character under R for the degenerate irreducible representation; $X_{v-1}(R)$ is the character of the (v–1)th energy level; and $X(R^{v})$ is the character of the operation R^{v}.

COMBINATION BANDS

Combination bands are observed when more than two or more fundamental vibrations are excited simultaneously. One reason a combination band might occur is if a fundamental vibration does not occur because of symmetry.

This is comparable to vibronic coupling in electronic transitions in which a fundamental mode can be excited and allowed as a "doubly excited state." Combination implies addition of two frequencies, but it also possible to have a difference band where the frequencies are subtracted.

To determine if two states can be excited simultaneous the transition moment integral must be evaluated with the appropriate excited state wavefunction. For example, in the transition,

$$\psi^1(0)\psi^2(0)\psi^3(0) \to \psi^1(2)\psi^2(0)\psi^3(1)$$

the symmetry of the excited state will be the direct product of the irreducible representation for ψ_1 (2) and ψ_3 (1).

For example, in the point group $C_{4v,}$ v_1 has symmetry e and v_3 has symmetry a_2. By performing the calcualtions listed above, it is determined that $\psi_1(2)$ has $(a_1 + b_1 + b_2)$ symmetry:

$$\Gamma[\psi_{cs}] = \Gamma[\psi_1(2)] \otimes \Gamma[\psi_3(1)] = (a_1 + b_1 + b_2) \times a_2 = a_2 + b_2 + b_1$$

A pratical use for understanding overtones and combination bands is applied to organic solvents used in specroscopy.

Most organic liquids have strong overtone and combination bands in the mid-infrared region, therefore, acetone, DMSO, or acetonitrile should only be used in very narrow spectral regions. Solvents such at CCl_4, CS_2 and $CDCl_3$ can be used above 1200 cm^{-1}.

HOT BANDS

Hot bands are observed when an already excited vibration is further excited. For example an v1 to v1' transition corresponds to a hot band in its IR spectrum. These transitions are temperature dependent, with lower signal intensity at lower temperature, and higher signal intensity at higher temperature.

This is because at room temperature only the ground state is highly populated (kT ~ 200 cm^{-1}), based on the Boltzmann distribution.

The Maxwell-Boltzmann distribution law states that if molecules in thermal equilibrium occupy two states of energy ε_j and ε_i, the relative populations of molecules occupying these states will be, $\frac{n_j}{n_i} = \frac{e^{-c}j/RT}{e^{-c}i/RT} = e^{-\Delta}e/RT$ where, k is the Boltzmann constant and T is the temperature in Kelvin.

In the harmonic oscillator model, hot bands are not easily distinguished from fundamental transitions because the energy levels are equally spaced. Because the spacing between energy levels in the anharmonic oscillator decrease with increasing vibrational levels, the hot bands occur at lower frequencies than the fundamentals.

Also, the transition moment integrals are slightly different since the ground state will not necessarily be totally symmetric since it is not in v=0.

Example: $\psi^1(0)\psi^2(0)\psi^3(1) \rightarrow \psi^1(0)\psi^2(0)\psi^3(2)$

FERMI RESONANCES

Fermi resonance results in the splitting of two vibrational bands that have nearly the same energy and symmetry in both IR and Raman spectroscopies. The two bands are usually a fundamental vibration and either an overtone or combination band.

The wavefunctions for the two resonant vibrations mix according to the harmonic oscillator approximation, and the result is a shift in frequency and a change in intensity in the spectrum. As a result, two strong bands are observed in the spectrum, instead of the expected strong and weak bands. It is not possible to determine the contribution from each vibration because of the resulting mixed wave function.

If the symmetry requirements are fulfilled and the energies of the two states are similar, mixing occurs, and the resulting modes can be described by a linear combination of the two interacting modes. The effect of this interaction is to increase the splitting between the engery levels. The splitting will be larger if the original energy difference is small and the coupling energy is large. The mixing of the two states also equalised the intensities of the vibrations which allows a weak overtone or combination band to show significant intensity from the fundamental with which it has Fermi resonance with.

Because the vibrations have nearly the same frequency, the interaction will be affected if one mode undergoes a frequency shift from deuteration or a solvent effect while the other does not.

The molecule most studied for this type of resonance (even what Fermi himself used to explain this phenomena), is carbon dioxide, CO_2. The three fundamental vibrations are v_1= 1337 cm^{-1}, v_2 = 667 cm^{-1}, v_3 = 2349 cm^{-1}. The first overtone of v_2 is $v_1 + 2v_2$ with symmetries σ_g+ and $(\sigma_g+ + \delta_g^+)$, respectively, and frequencies of 1337 cm^{-1} (v_1) and 2(667) = 1334 cm^{-1} (v_2). According to group theory calculations, CO_2 belongs to the point group D_{8h} and should only have one Raman (symmetric stretching vibrations) and two IR active modes (asymmetric stretching and bending vibrations). CS_2 is an analog to this system.

Another typical example of Fermi resonance is found in the vibrational spectra of aldehydes, where the C-H bond in the CHO group interacts with the second harmonic level, 2δ(CHO), derived from the fundamental frequency of the deformation vibration of the CHO group (2*1400 cm^{-1}). The result is a Fermi doublet with branches around 2830 and 2730 cm^{-1}. It is important for Fermi resonance that the vibrations connected with the two interacting levels be localised in the same part of the molecule.

When bands have non-negligible widths, Fermi resonance perturbation of localised levels cannot be applied. This broadening can be the result of a number of things, such as, intermolecular interaction, shortened excited state lifetimes, or interaction of vibrational modes with phonons. In place of perturbation theory, the distribution of interacting vibrational states can be approximated as a collection of discrete level. The influence from each level can be calculated.

It is useful to understand Fermi resonance because it helps assign and identify peaks within vibrational spectra (ie. IR and Raman) that may not otherwise be accounted for, however it should not be used lightly when assigning spectra.It is easy to jump to the conclusion that an unidentifiable band is the result of Fermi resonance, however this explanation may not fully account for the inconsistency and further characterisation may be required for the system being investigated. It is important to assign spectra before doing the normal mode (coordinate) calculations because doing these calculations beforehand often leads to incorrect assignments of the peaks in the spectra.

5

Electronic States of Molecular

MOLECULAR ELECTRONICS

The use of molecules for electronic devices was suggested by Mark Ratner of Northwestern University and Avi Aviram of IBM as early as the 1970s, but proper nanotechnology tools did not become available until the turn of the 21st century. Wiring up molecules some half a nanometre wide and a few nanometres long remains a major challenge, and an understanding of electrical transport through single molecules is only beginning to emerge. A number of groups have been able to demonstrate molecular switches, for example, that could conceivably be used in computer memory or logic arrays.

Current areas of research include mechanisms to guide the selection of molecules, architectures for assembling molecules into nanoscale gates, and three-terminal molecules for transistor-like behaviour. More-radical approaches include DNA computing, where single-stranded DNA on a silicon chip would encode all possible variable values and complementary strand interactions would be used for a parallel processing approach to finding solutions. An area related to molecular electronics is that of organic thin-film transistors and light emitters, which promise new applications such as video displays that can be rolled out like wallpaper and flexible electronic newspapers.

MOLECULAR ELECTRONIC PROCESS

Essentially all electronic processes in nature, from photosynthesis to signal transduction, occur in molecular structures.

For electronics applications, molecular structures have four major advantages:

- *Size:* The size scale of molecules is between 1 and 100 nm, a scale that permits functional nano-structures with accompanying advantages in cost, efficiency, and power dissipation.
- *Assembly and recognition:* One can exploit specific intermolecular interactions to form structures by nanoscale self-assembly. Molecular recognition can be used to modify electronic behaviour, providing both switching and sensing capabilities on the single-molecule scale.
- *Dynamical stereochemistry:* Many molecules have multiple distinct stable geometric structures or isomers (an example is the rotaxane molecule, in which a rectangular slider has two stable binding sites along a linear track). Such geometric isomers can have distinct optical and electronic properties. For example, the retinal molecule switches between two stable structures, a process that transduces light into a chemoelectrical pulse and allows vision.
- *Synthetic tailorability:* By choice of composition and geometry, one can extensively vary a molecule's transport, binding, optical, and structural properties. The tools of molecular synthesis are highly developed. Molecules have disadvantages, though, such as instability at high temperatures. But overall, the four advantages render molecules ideal for electronics applications, as Richard Feynman noted in his famous 1959 speech, 'There is Plenty of Room at the Bottom.'

MECHANISMS OF MOLECULAR CHARGE TRANSPORT

The synthesis and characterisation of molecules are endeavours typically conducted in solution. Decades of research have given chemists intuitive models that serve as a guide for using synthetic control to design physical properties into a molecule. A key challenge in molecular electronics is to translate that solution-phase intuition into a solid-state device setting. Certain molecular structures have emerged as models for relating intramolecular electron transfer rates in solution to solid-state molecular junction conductance.

A picture of electron transport through molecular devices is emerging, and it couldn't be more different from what is observed for more traditional conductors. Disregard, for the moment, the details of the electrical contact. In a semiconductor or metal wire, charge transport is ohmic: For a given wire diameter, longer wires have proportionately higher resistance. Such a picture is usually wrong for molecules because of the localised nature of most molecular electronic states.

Four types of molecular-electronic junctions are represented, with examples of molecular structures. One electrode functions as an electron donor and the other as an electron acceptor. The electrodes are bridged by a linear chain (an alkane). In 1961, Harden McConnell wrote down the rate constant for electron transfer across a molecular bridge: k_{ET} = $Ae-_{bt'}$ where l is the bridge length and b is an energy-dependent parameter characterising the molecule. For alkanes up to a certain length and for small applied voltages, this approximation works well: Current through a junction decreases exponentially with increasing chain length, and the alkane effectively serves as a simple energy barrier separating the two electrodes.

The possible mechanisms for electron transport are much richer for the electron donor-bridge-electron acceptor (DBA) molecular junction. DBA complexes serve as models for understanding how charge transport mechanisms in solution translate into the conductivity of solid-state molecular junctions. In DBA complexes, the donor and acceptor sites are part of the molecule, and the lowest unoccupied sites on the donor and acceptor components are separated from one another by a bridging component that has molecular orbitals of differing energy. In a process called electron-type superexchange, electrons that tunnel from the right electrode into the acceptor state when a bias is applied may coherently transfer to the donor state before tunnelling to the left electrode.

Alternatively, in hole-type superexchange, the tunnelling from the molecule into the left electrode might occur first, followed by refilling of the molecular level from the right. In fact, both processes will occur, and it is their relative rates that determine the nature of coherent conductance through a DBA junction. A third possibility is that an electron from the donor can jump to the acceptor due to either thermal or electrical excitation. That incoherent, diffusive process is quite closely related to ohmic charge flow.

Electrode Effects

The molecule–electrode interface is a critically important component of a molecular junction: It may limit current flow or completely modify the measured electrical response of the junction. Most experimental platforms for constructing molecular-electronic devices are based on practical considerations. This pragmatic approach is, in many ways, the boon and the bane of the field. For example, the sulfur–gold bond is a terrific chemical handle for forming self-assembled, robust organic monolayers on metal surfaces.

Other methods, such as using a scanning probe tip to contact the molecule, are frequently employed, in part because they avoid processing steps that can damage or unpredictably modify the molecular component. Ideally, the choice of electrode materials would be based not on the ease of fabrication or measurement, but rather on firstprinciples considerations of molecule–electrode interactions. However, the current state of the art for the theory of molecule-electrode interfaces is primitive.

Poor covalent bonding usually exists between the molecule and electrode. Consequently, at zero applied bias some charge must flow between molecule and electrodes to equilibrate the chemical potential across the junction. That flow can cause partial charging of the molecule, and local charge buildup gives Schottky-like barriers to charge flow across the interface.

Such barriers, which can partially or fully mask the molecule's electronic signature, increase for larger electronegativity differences. For this reason— and others, including stability, reproducibility, and generality—chemical bonds such as carbon–carbon or carbon– silicon will likely be preferred over gold–sulfur linkages at the interfaces.

Very little theory exists that can adequately predict how the molecular orbitals' energy levels will align with the Fermi energy of the electrode. Small changes in the energy levels can dramatically affect junction conductance, so understanding how the interface energy levels correlate is critical and demands both theoretical and experimental study. A related consideration involves how the chemical nature of the molecule–electrode interface affects the rest of the molecule.

The zero-bias coherent conductance of a molecular junction may be described as a product of functions that describe the molecule's electronic structure and the molecule–electrode interfaces. However, the chemical interaction between the molecule and the electrode will likely modify the molecule's electron density in the vicinity of the contacting atoms and, in turn, modify the molecular energy levels or the barriers within the junction.

The clear implication (and formal result) is that the molecular and interface functions are inseparable and thus must be considered as a single system.

MOLECULAR SCALE ELECTRONICS

Molecular scale electronics, also called single molecule electronics, is a branch of nanotechnology that uses single molecules, or nanoscale collections of single molecules, as electronic components. Because single molecules constitute the smallest stable structures imaginable, this miniaturisation is the ultimate goal for shrinking electrical circuits.

Conventional electronic devices are traditionally made from bulk materials. The bulk approach has inherent limitations in addition to becoming increasingly demanding and expensive. Thus, the idea was born that the components could instead be built up atom for atom in a chemistry lab (bottom up) as opposed to carving them out of bulk material (top down).

In single molecule electronics, the bulk material is replaced by single molecules. That is, instead of creating structures by removing or applying material after a pattern scaffold, the atoms are put together in a chemistry lab. The molecules utilised have properties that resemble traditional electronic components such as a wire, transistor or rectifier.

Single molecule electronics is an emerging field, and entire electronic circuits consisting exclusively of molecular sized compounds are still very far from being realised. However, the continuous demand for more computing power together with the inherent limitations of the present day lithographic methods make the transition seem unavoidable. Currently, the focus is on discovering molecules with interesting properties and on finding ways to obtaining reliable and reproducible contacts between the molecular components and the bulk material of the electrodes.

Molecular electronics operates in the quantum realm of distances less than 100 nanometers. Miniaturisation down to single molecules brings the scale down to a regime where quantum effects are important. As opposed to the case in conventional electronic components, where electrons can be filled in or drawn out more or less like a continuous flow of charge, the transfer of a single electron alters the system significantly.

The significant amount of energy due to charging has to be taken into account when making calculations about the electronic properties of the setup and is highly sensitive to distances to conducting surfaces nearby.

One of the biggest problems with measuring on single molecules is to establish reproducible electrical contact with only one molecule and doing so without shortcutting the electrodes. Because the current photolithographic technology is unable to produce electrode gaps small enough to contact both ends of the molecules tested (in the order of nanometers) alternative strategies are put into use.

These include molecular-sized gaps called break junctions, in which a thin electrode is stretched until it breaks. Another method is to use the tip of a scanning tunnelling microscope (STM) to contact molecules adhered at the other end to a metal substrate.

Another popular way to anchor molecules to the electrodes is to make use of sulfur's high affinity to gold; though useful, the anchoring is non-specific and thus anchors the molecules randomly to all gold surfaces, and the contact resistance is highly dependent on the precise atomic geometry around the site of anchoring and thereby inherently compromises the reproducibility of the connection. To circumvent the latter issue, experiments has shown that fullerenes could be a good candidate for use instead of sulfur because of the large conjugated π-system that can electrically contact many more atoms at once than a single atom of sulfur.

One of the biggest hindrances for single molecule electronics to be commercially exploited is the lack of techniques to connect a molecular sized circuit to bulk electrodes in a way that gives reproducible results. Also problematic is the fact that some measurements on single molecules are carried out in cryogenic temperatures (close to absolute zero) which is very energy consuming.

MOLECULAR MATERIALS FOR ELECTRONICS

Chemical structures of some conductive polymers. From top left clockwise: polyacetylene; polyphenylene vinylene; polypyrrole (X = NH) and polythiophene (X = S); and polyaniline (X = NH/N) and polyphenylene sulfide (X = S).

Molecular materials for electronics is a term used to refer to bulk applications of conductive polymers. Conductive polymers or, more precisely, intrinsically conducting polymers (ICPs) are organic polymers that conduct electricity in their bulk state. Such compounds may have metallic conductivity or can be semiconductors. The biggest advantage of conductive polymers is their processability, mainly by dispersion. Conductive polymers are not plastics, *i.e.,* they are not thermoformable, but they are organic polymers, like (insulating) polymers. They can offer high electrical conductivity but do not show mechanical properties as other commercially used polymers do. The electrical properties can be fine-tuned using the methods of organic synthesis and by advanced dispersion techniques.

The linear-backbone 'polymer blacks' (polyacetylene, polypyrrole, and polyaniline) and their copolymers are the main class of conductive polymers. Historically, these are known as melanins. PPV and its soluble derivatives have similarly emerged as the prototypical electroluminescent semiconducting polymers. Today, poly(3-alkylthiophenes) are the archetypical materials for solar cells and transistors.

Conducting polymers have backbones of contiguous sp^2 hybridised carbon centers. One valence electron on each center resides in a p_z orbital, which is orthogonal to the other three sigma-bonds. The electrons in these delocalised orbitals have high mobility when the material is 'doped' by oxidation, which removes some of these delocalised electrons. Thus the conjugated p-orbitals form a one-dimensional electronic band, and the electrons within this band become mobile when it is partially emptied. Despite intensive research, the relationship between morphology, chain structure and conductivity is poorly understood yet.

Due to their poor processability, conductive polymers enjoy few large-scale applications. They have some promise in antistatic materials and they have been incorporated into commercial displays and batteries, but there have had limitations due to the manufacturing costs, material inconsistencies, toxicity, poor solubility in solvents, and inability to directly melt process. Nevertheless, conducting polymers are rapidly gaining attraction in new applications with increasingly processable materials with better electrical and physical properties and lower costs.

With the availability of stable and reproducible dispersions, PEDOT and polyaniline have gained some large scale applications. While PEDOT (poly(3,4-ethylene-dioxythiophene)) is mainly used in antistatic applications and as a transparent conductive layer in form of PEDOT:PSS dispersions (PSS=polystyrene sulfonic acid), polyaniline is widely used for printed circuit board manufacturing – in the final finish, for protecting copper from corrosion and preventing its solderability.The new nanostructured forms of conducting polymers particularly, provide fresh air to this field with their higher surface area and better dispersability.

BORN-OPPENHEIMER OR ADIABATIC APPROXIMATION

The Born-Oppenheimer or adiabatic approximation is based on the observation, that the electrons are much lighter particles than the nuclei. The electron-nucleus mass ration MI/me amounts to 1836 for a proton and to order of 104 for typical elements such as carbon or silicon. Due to their smaller mass electrons bound in the potential of the nuclei move more rapidly than the heavy nuclei themselves and on the average follow their motion. This can be expressed by making an ansatz for the wave function $\psi(\{rj\},\{RJ\})$ in terms of a wave function of the nuclei X and of the electron ϕ that adiabatically follow them,

$$\psi(\{rj\},\{RJ\}) = x(\{RJ\}\phi(\{rj\};\{RJ\}))$$

For simplicity, the set of all electron coordinates {rj} will be denoted q in the following and correspondingly the set of all nuclear coordinate $\{_{RJ}\}$ by Q . insertion of this ansatz and neglecting the Q -dependence of Φ (q,Q) with respect to the kinetic energy operator Q allows the separation into an entirely electronic problem for each momentary set of nuclear coordinates and a Schrödinger equation for the nuclei that move on an effective potential surface that accounts for their interaction with the electrons,

$$(Te \wedge + Vee \wedge + Vek \wedge (Q))\phi n(q;Q)(TK \wedge VKK \wedge + En(Q))$$

$$\phi n(q;Q) = En_{\upsilon} X(Q)$$

NON-ADIABATIC INTERACTION

The parametric dependence $Vek_{\wedge}$ on Q requires that the electronic eigenvalues are also functions of Q . n and υ are the quantum numbers of electron and nuclei.

The En(Q) as function of the coordinates act as an effective potential of the adiabatic electron-nuclei interaction, which depends on the quantum state the electronic subsystem occupies. Together with the repulsive Coulomb interaction between the nuclei it provides an effective potential in which the electrons move,

$$Vn(Q)=Vkk(Q)+En(Q)$$

The effective potential $V_0(Q)$ associated with the electronic ground state is called the Born-Oppenheimer surface. The electronic terms are often well separated near the equilibrium positions and the vibrational motion in solids or the vibration and rotational motion in molecules leads to a finely spaced energy spectrum associated with each electronic quantum states.

HOMONUCLEAR DIATOMIC MOLECULES

Other homonuclear diatomic molecules (*e.g.*, $Li_2, O_2, He_2, F_2, N_2, ... H_2^+$ ..) can be described according to the LCAO approach introduced with the study of the molecule. A general feature of the LCAO method is that a combination of two atomic orbitals on different centers gives two molecular orbitals (MO). One of these molecular orbitals is called bonding and the other one is called antibonding. The bonding state is more stable than the system of infinitely separated atomic orbitals. On the other hand, the antibonding state is less stable than the isolated atomic orbitals. The description of the H_2^+ molecule can be summarised by the following diagram:

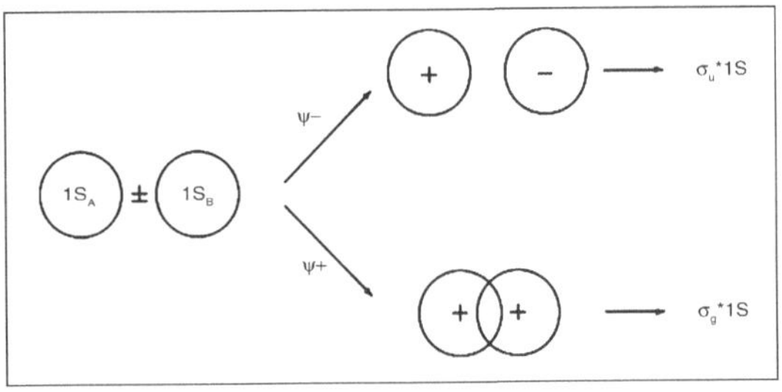

The Nomenclature of States of Homonuclear Diatomic Molecules

This diagram introduces the nomenclature of states of homonuclear diatomic molecules, which is determined by the following aspects:

- Nature of the atomic orbitals in the linear combination (*e.g.*, 1S orbitals in the study of the H_2^+ molecules).
- Eigenvalue of $\hat{L}_z$, with z the internuclear axis (*e.g.*, such eigenvalue is zero for the H_2^+ molecule and, therefore, the orbital is called s).
- Eigenvalue of the inversion operator through the

center of the molecule (*e.g.,* g when the eigenvalue is 1, and u when the eigenvalue is –1).

- Stability with respect to the isolated atoms (*e.g.,* an asterisk indicates that the state is unstable relative to the isolated atoms).

Other homonuclear diatomic molecules involve linear combinations of ρ orbitals. Such linear combinations give rise to σ type orbitals when there is no component of the angular momentum in the bond axis (*e.g.,* we choose the bond axis to be the z axis). An example of such linear combination is represented by the following diagram:

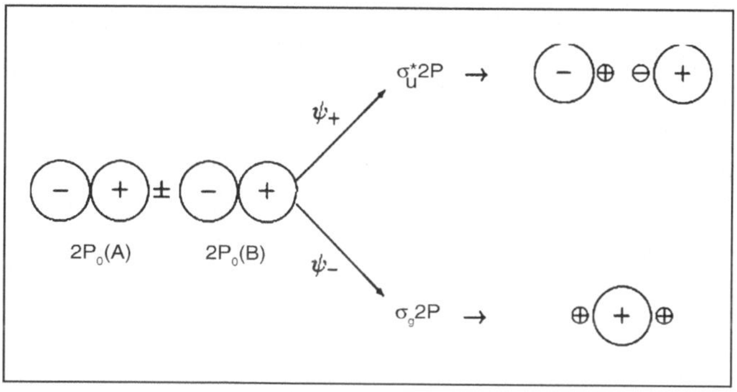

Linear Combination

In order to classify molecular states according to eigenvalues of $\hat{L}_z$, we make linear combinations of eigen-functions of $\hat{L}_z$ with common eigenvalues. There are four possible states:

$$\text{m}=1: \quad 2P_{+1}(A) \pm 2P_{+1}(B), \quad \overbrace{\pi_u 2P_{+1}}^{\oplus}, \overbrace{\pi_g^* 2P_{+1}}^{\ominus},$$

$$\text{m}=-1: \quad 2P_{-1}(A) \pm 2P_{-1}(B), \quad \pi_u 2P^{-1}, \pi_g^* 2P_{-1}.$$

All of these linear combinations are π states, because $\lambda = |m| = 1$ for all of them. In order to justify their symmetry properties with respect to inversion we analyse the following particular case,

$$\pi_u 2P_{+1} = 2P_{+1}(A) + 2P_{+1}(B) = \frac{1}{8\sqrt{\pi}}\left(\frac{z}{a}\right)^{5/2}\left(e^{i\phi A}e - \frac{zrA}{2n} rA\right)$$

$$\sin\theta_A + e^{i\phi B} e - \frac{zrB}{2a} rB \quad \sin\theta_B),$$

which is represented by the following diagram:

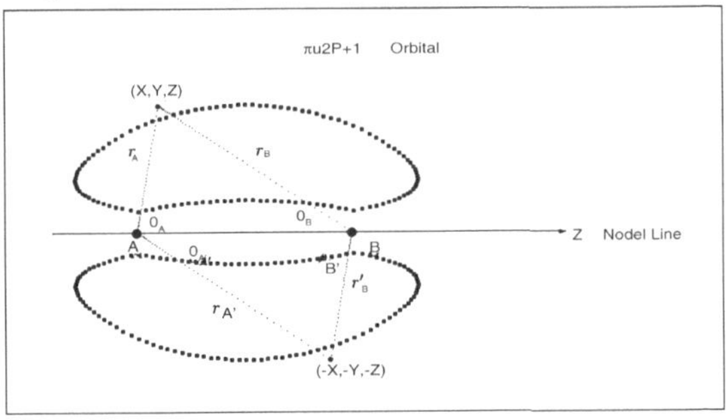

Under Inversion Through the Origin

This diagram shows that under inversion through the origin, coordinates are transformed as follows,

$$r_A \to r_B, \qquad \theta_A \to \theta_B,$$
$$r_B \to r_A, \qquad \theta_B \to \theta_A,$$
$$\phi_A = \phi_B = \phi,$$
$$\phi \to \phi + \pi,$$

$$e^i(\phi+\pi) = e^{i\phi} e^{i\pi} = -e^{i\phi}, \text{ because } e^{i\pi} = \underbrace{\text{Cos}\pi}_{-1} + i\underbrace{\text{Sin}\pi}_{0}.$$

The states constructed with orbitals P_{-1} differ, relative to those constructed with orbitals p+1, only in the sign of phase ϕ introduced by the following expression,

$$\pi_g^* 2P_{+1} = \frac{1}{8\sqrt{\pi}}\left(\frac{z}{a}\right)^{5/2} e - \frac{-zrA}{2a} rA \sin\theta_A + e - \frac{zrB}{2a} rB \quad \sin 0_B).$$

This function has a nodal xy plane and is described by the following diagram:

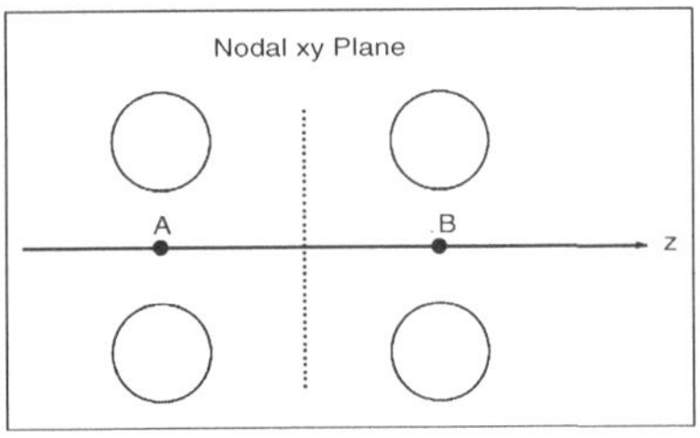

Since atomic orbitals $2p_x$, and $2p_y$ are linear combinations of atomic orbitals $2P_{+1}$and $2P^{-1}$ molecular orbitals $\pi_u 2p_{+1}$ and $\pi_u 2p_{-1}$ can be combined to construct molecular orbitals $\pi_u 2p_x$ and $\pi_u 2p_y$ as follows,

$$\pi_u 2p_x = 2p_x(A) + 2P_x(B),$$
$$\pi_u 2p_y = 2p_y(A) + 2p_y(B).$$

Note, however, that molecular orbitals $\pi_u 2p_x$, and $\pi_u 2p_y$ are not eigenfunctions of $\hat{L}_z$.

The order of increasing energy for homonuclear diatomic orbitals is described by the following diagram:

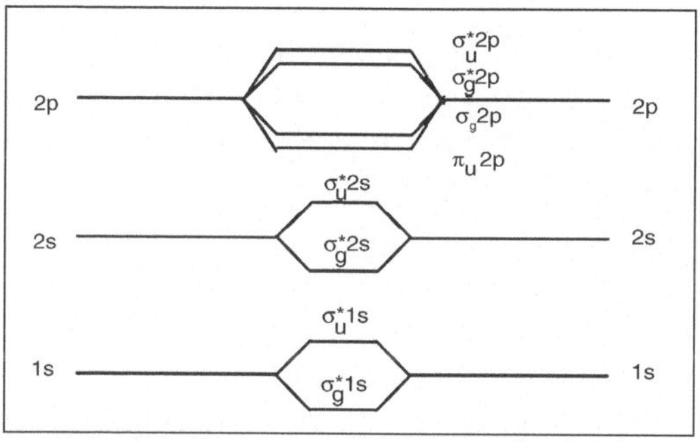

The electronic structure of homonuclear diatomic molecules can be approximated to zeroth order by filling up the unperturbed states according to the Pauli exclusion principle. However, we should always keep in mind that we are using the H_2^+ molecular orbitals (*i.e.*, the unperturbed states) and, therefore, we are neglecting the repulsive interaction between electrons.

This is the same kind of approximation implemented in the construction of zeroth order wave functions of atoms according to hydrogenlike atomic orbitals, where the repulsion energy between electrons was disregarded and the electronic configuration was constructed by filling up hydrogenlike atomic orbitals according to the Pauli exclusion principle.

6

The Electronic Structure of Diatomic Molecules

A knowledge of the electronic structure of molecules is of the greatest importance, both to the physicist and the chemist; to the physicist because the facts of molecular spectra can only be interpreted in terms of electronic structure, to the chemist because a detailed knowledge of electronic structure is necessary to indicate the exact conditions (of excitation, etc.), under which atoms will combine to form molecules. A number of methods, both experimental and theoretical, have recently been converging to a solution of this problem. On the experimental side there is the important work of Franck and his collaborators, who have shown how a molecule splits up by light absorption into its component atoms (or ions). This work shows that in most cases a normal molecule splits up (adiabatically) into two unexcited atoms or ions.

This work must now be supplemented by the important results of Herzberg, who has shown that in some cases a molecule in its normal state splits up into one normal and one excited component. In these cases it is an excited molecule which leads on dissociation to two normal components. The converse must be true, so that, for example, an excited C atom and a normal N atom are necessary to produce a normal CN molecule.

The recent advances on the theoretical side are the direct outcome of the new quantum mechanics, as the older theory was incapable of dealing with the simplest molecules. The first new and important concept was Heisenberg's idea of resonance in atoms. This led, as is well known, to a satisfying explanation of the ortho- and para-system of helium, and to a general explanation of multiplet spectra. Of the possible spectral terms, which can arise from a given outer group of electrons, the one of greatest multiplicity has the lowest energy and of the terms with the same multiplicity the one with the greatest 'l' value is lowest. The same result is doubtless true also of molecular terms.

The natural extension of the resonance principle of Heisenberg to an 'Austausch' principle was made by Heitler and London. Although the underlying ideas are somewhat different, the mathematical analysis is practically identical. It was shown that the exchange between the electrons of two hydrogen atoms led to an energy lower than that of the separated atoms; in other words, it led to the formation of a molecule.

This important result has since been extended by Heitler and London. The latter has shown that the new theory gives a quantum mechanical explanation of the empirical ideas of Lewis and others concerning chemical valency and correlates the idea of valency with that of electron spin. Although the general conditions under which binding can occur in a quantum mechanical sense, have now been well developed, only one case has been worked out quantitatively, *viz.*, that of the hydrogen molecule.

Certain difficulties have appeared in more complicated cases, as, for instance, in O_2 and F_2, where the theory is unable to account for molecular binding, and at the same time to account for the $^3\Sigma$ ground level of O_2. We shall refer to this point later and shall suggest a possible explanation. Of the possible molecular states which can arise from atoms in given atomic states, the theory as developed at present indicates that the one of lowest multiplicity has the lowest energy, though this is not always true (as in O_2, for example). The theory is not yet able to say what is the relative energy of terms of like multiplicity.

An exhaustive treatment of the relation between atomic spectral terms and the molecular terms which are possible on bringing two atoms together has been made by Wigner and Witmer. This theory gives all the molecular terms which are theoretically possible to satisfy the requirements of group theory, but it gives no indication which of the possible terms correspond to stable molecular states and which to unstable. Thus, two F atoms in ^2P states could give rise to one Δ molecular state, two Π states and three Σ states, and each could be a singlet or a triplet. The theory gives no idea which of them actually occur or what is the relative depth of the energy levels.

The most important work on the problem of the detailed electronic structure of molecules has been done by Hund and Mulliken, who have ascribed to each electron in a molecule a definite and unique quantum notation. In the first place, each electron is regarded as having a definite quantised angular momentum about the molecular axis. When this is zero, the electron is described as a σ electron; similarly, when it has the values, 1, 2 . . ., it is said to be a π, δ . . . . electron, in analogy with the s, p, d.... notation in atoms. In the second place, the electron is given those atomic quantum numbers which it would have, if the atoms of the molecule were pushed together to form one united atom.

This defines each electron uniquely. Thus, we may have $2s\sigma$, $2p\sigma$, $2p\pi$ . . . . electrons. The Pauli Principle is assumed to hold in molecules as in atoms, so that it is assumed that there are not more than two electrons in the same σ-state, but as a π-electron may have an angular momentum of +1 or – 1, there can be four, and not more than four, electrons in the same π-state. The electronic structure of a molecule may then be given unambiguously, as, for example, $1s\sigma^2$, $2p\sigma^2$, $2s\sigma^2$, $2p\pi^3$, $3p\sigma$, the upper index indicating in each case the number of 'equivalent' electrons.

The next problem considered by Hund is the relative energies of these various electron levels. This is known, of course, in the limiting case when the internuclear distance is zero and molecular states become atomic states. Thus, we have the series $1s^2$, $2s^2$, $2p^2$, $3s^2$ . . . When the nuclei are pulled slightly apart, Hund gives reasons for supposing that the series of corresponding molecular states is $1s\sigma^2$, $2s\sigma^2$, $2p\sigma^2$, $2p\pi^4$,

$3s\sigma^2$. . . . Again, the energy levels of another limiting case is known, *viz.*, that in which the component atoms are infinitely distant. By considering the splitting of the degenerate states which the work of researchers indicates, another series of energy levels can be written down. For the intermediate stages which actual molecules occupy, a series of energy levels is assumed by interpolation, and is adjusted so as to fit in with many known facts and to give a smooth transition from the one extreme limiting case to the other.

The character of a molecular term is determined in the first place by the resultant angular momentum of all the electrons about the nuclear axis. When this is zero, the term is described as a Σ term; similarly, when it is one, two, the terms are denotedby Π, Δ..., in analogy with the S, P, D, notation of atoms. The multiplicity is denoted as usual by an index on the left-hand side, as in $^2\Pi$, $^3\Sigma$, and so on. A closed molecular group, whether σ or π, must give a $^1\Sigma$ term, as the resultant angular momentum and the resultant electron must both be zero.

Researchers have found it necessary to supplement the table of energy levels by certain empirical rules. The former uses a working hypothesis to limit the intersections of the possible transitions from a given state of the separated atoms to the corresponding states of the united atom. The latter uses the hypothesis that the number of σ, π.... electrons remains constant during possible transitions. Both methods have met with considerable success, and have led to a better understanding of the structure of the more complicated diatomic molecules, like N_2. Further, they have obtained analogous electronic structures for certain series of diatomic molecules with a like number of electrons and are thus able to explain why these molecules should have similar physical properties, a well-known but otherwise unexplained fact.

There are, however, certain difficulties in the theories of Hund and Mulliken, as has been pointed out by Herzberg. In particular, they are not capable of explaining the experimental results obtained by Herzberg, and interpreted by Heitler and Herzberg, *viz.*, that N_2^+ in the normal state, splits up into a normal N atom and an excited N ion. Similar results hold also in the cases of CN, CO^+, BO and SiN. Herzberg has proposed a modification of the Hund-Mulliken scheme to bring it more in line with the Heitler and London ideas, and has used as a working hypothesis that each electron in the transition from atom to molecule retains its own characteristic quantum numbers (in the Hund-Mulliken notation).

It seems to the writer that there is a great disadvantage in relating the notation of electrons in molecules to a condition which cannot be realised. It is more important to know what happens to a molecule on dissociation than to know what happens when it is compressed to form a single atom. Further, the Hund-Mulliken notation would become somewhat complicated if extended to heavy atoms for there is a progressive increase in the quantum numbers required. Even for atoms with principal quantum number 2, it is necessary to use the symbols $3d\pi$ and $4p\sigma$ for the molecular states, and such states are not readily interpreted.

Further, the notation gives no indication as to whether the various electronic states in a molecule correspond to binding or repulsion. These difficulties are due to the attempt to preserve the Pauli Principle in molecules so as to have not more than two electrons with given quantum numbers. There are thus only two electrons in each molecule with principal quantum 1.

There must, however, be a limit for practical purposes to such an application of the Pauli Principle, otherwise it would be necessary to give a different notation for every pair of K electrons in a solid (say, a lump of lead). It seems more reasonable and practicable in heavy molecules to allot two K electrons to each nucleus. We shall regard the Pauli Principle as fulfilled when we say that two K electrons ' belong' to a nucleus A and two to a nucleus B. Similarly, there must be a stage when it is more convenient to assign a complete group of L electrons to each nucleus. A distinction is therefore drawn in this paper between atomic levels and molecular levels, even in a molecule.

The latter are those which arise from an 'Austausch' phenomenon in the Heitler and London sense, and give binding. There is also a set of levels, which give rise to repulsion, the corresponding eigenfunctions having a certain asymmetry not possessed by the ' binding' or 'molecular' levels. The main purpose of this paper is to show that these levels should not be considered in the process of building molecules in their normal states.

An 'Aufbau' Principle is adopted which assigns the electrons one by one to a molecule, and places them in the lowest available molecular and atomic levels subject to certain rules which have to be observed in order not to conflict with the Heitler-London requirements.

The assigning of electrons to molecular levels leads to the idea of resonance between molecular states when two electrons are in different molecular levels. In such a case, that state is held to be lowest which has the greatest multiplicity, as is the case in atoms. Examples occur in Bo_2, [sic] and O_2, which should both be $^3\Sigma$ states in the normal level, and therefore paramagnetic, while the lowest state of N_2 is a $^1\Sigma$ state, and is therefore diamagnetic.

In the older quantum theory, one was guided in the assignment of quantum numbers to electrons in atoms by the quantum numbers necessary to specify the different orbits in the simple hydrogen atom.

Owing to the effect of the core, the energy levels of electrons in the outer shells were different from those of hydrogen, but nevertheless 'effective' quantum numbers were deduced for the various levels, and it was in general easy to infer the correct 'true' quantum numbers. Except in the more complicated atoms, it was possible to use an Aufbau Principle, whereby the electrons were added one at a time to the nucleus, and were placed in the orbits corresponding to the progressive changes in the hydrogen quantum numbers. The Bohr (or, later, the Stoner) subgroups were successively filled by electrons. It was found permissible to assume as a first approximation that the energy of electrons in outer incomplete groups was not seriously modified by the other outer electrons, that is, electrons with the same n, but different l.

As a second approximation, it was possible to combine the 'l' (or angular momentum) values of incompleted groups vectorially to give different effective or resultant L values. This resultant L determined the spectral type, which was denoted by S, P, D... according as it had the values 0, 1, 2....

Next, the coupling between spin momenta of the electrons gave a 'resultant' spin vector S, which determined the multiplicity. The multiplicity was given by $R = 2S + 1$, if S was measured in units of $h/2\pi$. Finally, the components of a multiplet were regarded as determined by the coupling between the resultant L vector and the resultant S vector.

These vectors methods have proved not to be of general applicability, but the results obtained thereby are in most cases confirmed by the more well-founded 'resonance' methods of Heisenberg. In particular, both lead to the same relative energy values of the various multiplet terms, which can arise from a given number of outer electrons with prescribed n and l values.

We seek a similar and analogous method for molecule-building. First we consider the possible energy levels of one electron in the presence of a two-nuclear system. An accurate analytical solution of the two centre-problem is not yet possible, but certain approximate methods can now be used to indicate the relative position of the various energy levels -- in each case as a function of internuclear distance.

We use this system of energy levels for the many-electron problem just as was done in atoms. We then suppose a molecule built up in the following way. We add one charge at a time to each nucleus and then, supposing the nuclei held fixed, add to the system two electrons successively. The system is then allowed to take up its equilibrium value adiabatically.

Next, we add the components of the angular momenta about the nuclear axis. This determines the spectral type, Σ, Π, or Δ, etc. Then as in atoms, we add the electron spins to determine the multiplicity.

In most molecules, the electronic energy is much greater than that due to vibration and so, when the nuclei are no longer held fixed, a series of energy levels arise due to the same electron configuration but different quantised vibrations. We assume that the vibration does not seriously modify the electron configuration.

Again, when rotation takes place, it may in general be assumed that neither the electronic configuration nor the vibration energy are greatly perturbed. This is not true of the light molecule He2, where an uncoupling of the 'l' values from the nuclear axis takes place when the rotation is large. We shall not enter this problem, but shall mostly confine ourselves to ground levels or to excited states of the heavier molecules.

THE ELECTRONICALLY EXCITED STATES

EXCITED STATES OF MOLECULES

Most molecules have bound higher energy excited electronic states in addition to the ground electronic state E_0. These states may be thought of as arising from the promotion of one of the electrons from the occupied orbital in the ground state to a vacant higher energy orbital.

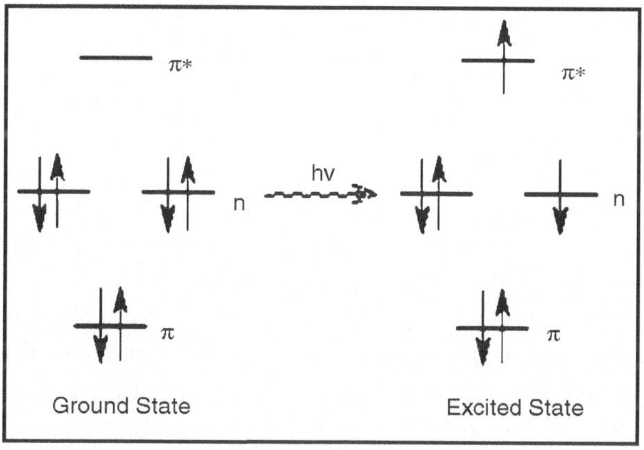

Fig. 6.1

The excitation of an electron from the occupied orbital to a higher-energy orbital occurs when a photon with the energy that matches the difference between the two states interacts with the molecule.

The classical Franck-Condon principle states that because the rearrangement of electrons is much faster than the motion of nuclei, the nuclear configuration does not change significantly during the energy absorption process. Thus, the absorption spectrum of molecules is characterised by the vertical excitation energies.

VIBRATIONAL FINE STRUCTURE OF ABSORPTION LINES

The ground state (E_0) supports a large number of vibrational energy levels. At room temperature, only the lowest vibrational level is populated, and electronic transitions originate from the n=0 vibrational level. The bound excited states (E_1) also support several vibrational levels. However, because the excited state potential energy curve is typically shifted, the vertical excitations from the lowest vibrational level of the ground electronic state take the system into one of several vibrational levels of the excited electronic state.

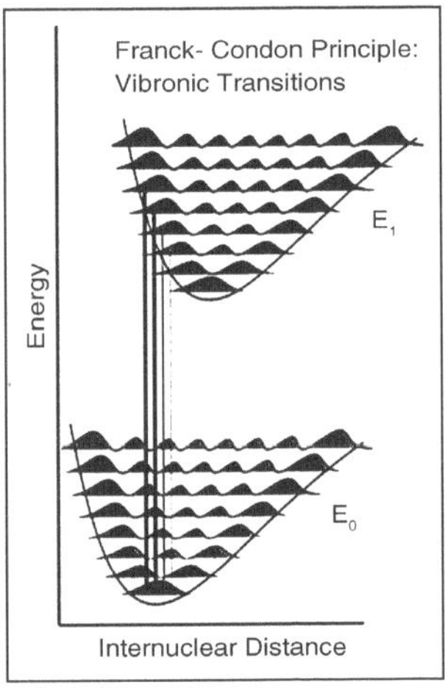

Fig. 6.2

Thus, valence transitions, such as n →π* in carbonyl compounds show vibrational fine structure which may be useful for the characterisation of the excited state. The quantum mechanical Franck-Condon principle states that the probability of each transition is determined by the extent of overlap between the ground state and excited state vibrational wave functions. These individual vibronic bands can be sometimes observed in the gas phase absorption spectra of molecules but the assignment of vibronic bands to specific states can be challenging.

For example, if the two potential energy curves are significantly shifted, the 0 ← 0 transition may have so low intensity that it can escape detection. The spectra of molecules in solvents that interact strongly with the chromophore are broad and often featureless.

CLASSIFICATION OF ABSORPTION BANDS

The absorption bands are typically classified as valence bands (for example, the local π → π* transition in many unsaturated organic molecules), Rydberg bands (transitions to very diffuse orbitals around the molecule), and charge transfer bands (involving electron transfer from one part of the molecule to another part). The lower energy bands typically arise from transitions from occupied valence orbitals to unoccupied valence orbitals. Many far-ultraviolet bands (below 200 nm) arise from Rydberg transitions. These bands can be recognised by the lack of vibrational fine structure and by the convergence of their energies towards the ionisation potential of the molecule. The lowest energy transition in molecules that contain both lone pairs and π bonds is typically the $n \rightarrow \pi^*$ transition. However, in some symmetric molecules, the intensity of the $n \rightarrow \pi^*$ transition is very low because the transition is symmetry forbidden.

FATES OF EXCITED STATES

Excited states have limited life times (typically in the order of a nanosecond) and they can decay via several modes. Sometimes the excited state is so weakly bound that it will dissociate. For example, ozone undergoes a photodissociation to O_2 and atomic oxygen after absorbing a photon of ultraviolet light.

A second possibility is that the excited state returns to the ground state without emitting a photon. Such radiationless decay occurs readily when the excited state and the ground state potential energy curves meet via a conical intersection. For example, the excited states of DNA bases in Watson-Crick base paired geometry are very short-lived thanks to efficient radiationless decay; this protects DNA from photochemical damage. The third possibility of return to the ground state is via the emission of photon. Such radiative decay is commonly called fluorescence.

It is usually observed that the fluorescent light from molecules or nanoparticles has a longer wavelength than the exciting light. This immediately suggests that the emission of a photon from the electronically excited state is not a perfect mirror process of the absorption. Instead, the excited vibronic state rapidly relaxes on the excited state potential energy surface: the nuclei adopt a new optimum geometry that is at equilibrium with the excited state electronic wavefunction. In simple words, fluorescence usually takes place from the ground vibrational level of the electronically excited state E1. Again, because the rearrangement of electrons is very fast, the emission is vertical and reaches one of the vibrational levels of the ground electronic state E_0. The energy difference between the relaxed excited state energy and the ground state energy is called the adiabatic excitation energy. Adiabatic excitation energies can be measured from the emission spectra of molecules.

Fluorescence occurs very quickly after excitation. There is another radative decay mode, called phosphoresence, which takes the system back to ground state over much longer timescales.

In the case of phosphoresence, the excited state undergoes a change in the spin state. In a typical scenario, the potential energy surface of a singlet excited state crosses with the potential energy surface of a lower-laying triplet energy state, and the system becomes trapped in the triplet excited state. Spontaneous emission from triplet excited state to singlet ground state is spin forbidden, and thus occurs with a low probability. The phenomena of fluorescence and phosphoresence are two manifestations of luminescent emission.

COMPUTATIONAL METHODS FOR EXCITED STATES

Computational methods could, in principle give accurate information about the excited electronic states. For example, the vertical excitation energy can be obtained in the first approximation as the energy difference between the excited state potential energy curve and the ground state potential energy curve at the ground state minimum energy geometry. Optimisation of geometry of the excited electronic state allows to calculate adiabatic excitation energies.

Thus, computations could be used to predict absorption and fluorescence emission spectra of molecules. With a little more effort, the absorption of chiral light can be characterised, allowing one to predict the circular dichroism spectra. Such calculations are often valuable for chemists interested in the identification of molecules solely on the basis of their spectra.

A large number of computational methods have been developed for the description of excited states. On one hand, we have easy-to-apply methods, such as Configuration Interaction Singles (CIS) or Time Dependent Density Functional Theory (TDDFT) but these have a generally limited accuracy, and can fail spectacularly for certain situations. On the other hand, multireference configuration interaction methods typically offer an accuracy of about 0.1 eV (2.3 kcal/mol) but require expertise in setting up the calculation. In general, meaningful excited state calculations can be difficult to carry out. There are special cases where a simple method like (CIS) will give useful answers.

In general, however, one must be aware of pitfalls such as:

- The basis functions that are used to construct molecular orbitals are typically optimised to describe ground states. Calculation with such basis functions are biased to stabilise the ground state over the excited state. Excited states are often more diffuse and basis sets lacking adequate diffuse functions will not describe such states correctly. Typically, small basis sets lead to an overestimation of the transition energy because of poor description of the excited state. Oftentimes, special basis sets are used at the expense of higher computational cost.
- Accounting for electron correlation in excited states is not as straightforward as in the ground state. Finding a method that offers a well-balanced treatment of both states is often problematic. The methods needed are computationally demanding and require judgement in their application. For example, one may have to specify beforehand a limited set of occupied and virtual orbitals that are 'active' in the transition. Making a good selection is not trivial in many systems.

MULTIPARTICLE WAVEFUNCTIONS AND SYMMETRY

TWO ELECTRONS IN A ONE DIMENSIONAL WELL

So far, we have used Schrödinger's equation to see how a single particle, usually an electron, behaves in a variety of potentials. If we are going to think about atoms other than hydrogen, it is necessary to extend the Schrödinger equation so that it describes more than one particle. As a simple example of a two particle system, let us consider two electrons confined to the same one-dimensional infinite square well,

$$V(x) = 0, \quad -L/2 < x < L/2$$

$$V(x) = \infty \quad \text{otherwise.}$$

To make things even simpler, let us assume that the electrons do not interact with each other—we switch off their electrostatic repulsion. Then by analogy with our construction of the Schrödinger equation for a single electron, we write,

$$-\frac{\hbar^2}{2m}\frac{\partial^2\Psi(x_1,x_2,t)}{\partial x_1^2}-\frac{\hbar^2}{2m}\frac{\partial^2\psi(x_1,x_2,t)}{\partial x_2^2}=E\psi(x_1,x_{2,}t)$$

inside the well, with the wave function going to zero for x1 or x2 equal to L/2 or -L/2.

On looking at this equation, we see it is the same as the Schrödinger equation for a single electron in a two dimensional square well, and so can be solved in the same way, by separation of variables. For example, the wave function we plotted for the two dimensional rectangular well is in the square case:

$$\psi_{(2,3)}(x_1,x_2,t) = A\sin(2\pi x_1/L)\cos(3\pi x_2/L)e^{-IEt/\hbar}$$

has the same energy,

$$E = \frac{\hbar^2}{2m}\frac{\pi^2}{L^2}\left(2^2+3^2\right)$$

as the physically distinct wavefunction:

$$\psi_{(3,2)}(x_1,x_2,t) = A\sin(2\pi x_2/L)\cos(3\pi x_1/L)e^{-iEt/R}$$

INTERPRETING THE WAVEFUNCTION

We have already discussed how the above wavefunctions are to be interpreted if they are regarded as two-dimensional wavefunctions for a single electron: $|\psi(x_1,x_2)|^2 dx_1dx_2$ is the probability of finding the electron in a small area dx_1dx_2 at (x_1, x_2).

The natural extension of this interpretation to two electrons is to assume now $|\psi(x_1,x_2)|^2 dx_1dx_2$ is the joint probability of finding electron 1 in a small line length dx1 at position x_1, and at the same time finding electron 2 in a small length dx_2 at x_2.

This, however, leads to a real problem. Consider the wavefunction,

$$\psi_{(2,3)}(x_1,x_2,t)=A\sin(2\pi x_1/L)\cos(3\pi x_2/L)e^{-iEt/\hbar}$$

again. Let us now take specific points, $x_1 = 0$, $x_2 = L/4$. Then the probability of finding electron 1 in an infinitesimal interval at x_1 and electron 2 similarly at x_2 is zero, because y is zero at $x_1 = 0$. On the other hand, the probability of finding electron 2 at x_1 (= 0) and electron 1 at x_2 (= L/4) is not zero.

The problem is this: the electrons are identical (we assume their spins point the same way). We can't tell which is which, and nobody else can either. The indistinguishability of elementary particles is not like that of apparently identical macroscopic objects, where one could always place some tiny mark. There is no way to mark an electron. This means, though, that the best we can do is to talk about the probability of finding one electron at x_1 and another at x_2, we cannot specify which electron we find where. Therefore, any alleged wave function that gives different probabilities for finding electron 1 at x_1, 2 at x_2 and finding 2 at x_1, 1 at x_2 is not physically meaningful.

That is to say, a wave function describing two identical particles must have a symmetric probability distribution,

$$|\psi(x_1,x_2)|^2=|\psi(x_2,x_1)|^2.$$

This is definitely not the case with our function $\psi_{(2,3)}(x_1,x_2)$, so although it is a solution to the two particle Schrödinger equation, it is not a physically meaningful wave function for two particles in a box.

In fact, this is not difficult to fix—recall that the function $\psi_{(2,3)}(x_1,x_2)$ has the same energy, and in fact just corresponds to the two particles being switched around, that is to say, $\psi_{(2,3)}(x_1,x_2) = \psi_{(2,3)}(x_2,x_1)$.

It follows that the symmetric function,

$$\psi^{s}_{(2,3)}(x_1,x_2) = \frac{1}{\sqrt{2}}\left(\psi_{(2,3)}(x_1,x_2) + \psi_{(2,3)}(x_2,x_1)\right)$$

and the antisymmetric function,

$$\psi^{s}_{(2,3)}(x_1,x_2) = \frac{1}{\sqrt{2}}\left(\psi_{(2,3)}(x_1,x_2) + \psi_{(2,3)}(x_2,x_1)\right)$$

are both solutions to Schrödinger's equation for the energy E, and both satisfy the requirement $|\psi(x_1,x_2)|^2 = |\psi(x_2,x_1)|^2$. necessary for identical particles, so these are the appropriate candidate wave functions for the two particles in the one-dimensional box.

BOSONS, FERMIONS AND THE PAULI EXCLUSION PRINCIPLE

It turns out that both symmetric and antisymmetric wavefunctions arise in nature in describing identical particles. In fact, all elementary particles are either fermions, which have antisymmetric multiparticle wavefunctions, or bosons, which have symmetric wave functions. Electrons, protons and neutrons are fermions; photons, a-particles and helium atoms are bosons.

It is important to realise that this requirement of symmetry of the probability distribution, arising from the true indistinguishability of the particles, has a large effect on the probability distribution, and, furthermore, the effect is very different for fermions and bosons. The simplest way to see this is just to plot $|\psi(x_1,x_2)|^2$ for the symmetric and for the antisymmetric wave functions, and compare them.

For the symmetric case, the probability distribution (unnormalised) looks like:

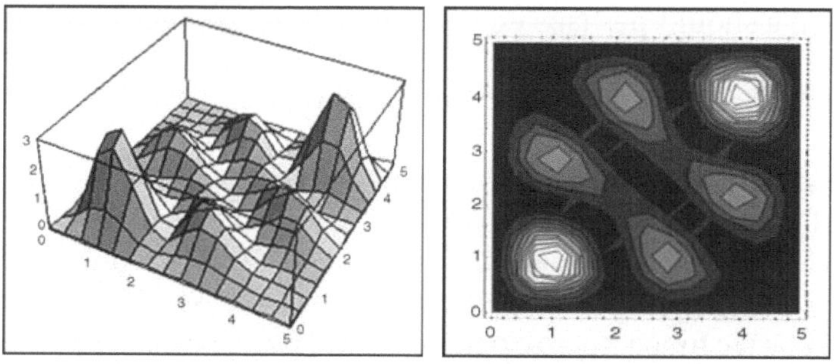

Fig. 6.3 The Graytone Figure is a Contour Map

The main point to note here is that the highest joint probability is that of finding the two particles close together, near (1,1) and (4,4). (These actual points depend on the wave function we chose initially, of course).

Now look at the antisymmetric case:

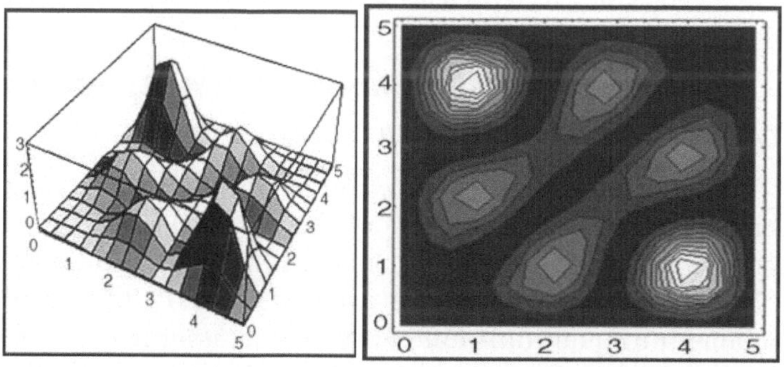

Fig. 6.4

The difference is dramatic. For the antisymmetric wave function, the particles are most likely to be found far away from each other. In fact, there is zero probability that they will be found at the same spot, because if $|\psi(x_1,x_2)|=|\psi(x_2,x_1)|$, obviously $\psi(x,x)=0$ A more general statement is that two fermions cannot be in the same quantum state, because if they were, the wave function would be of the symmetric form $f(x_1)\ f(x_2)$, and could not be antisymmetrised.

This is the Pauli Exclusion Principle—it is the basis of the periodic table, and consequently of almost everything else.

We should perhaps emphasise that these wave functions were calculated with the electrostatic repulsion between the electrons switched off. That is not what is keeping the electrons apart, although it will increase the separation if it is included. We should also warn against a simple classical picture of the Pauli principle, the thought that two things can't be in the same place, after all, so perhaps it's no surprise two electrons can't be in the same state. Two electrons can be in the same identical space wave function provided that their spins point in opposite ways. Furthermore, two bosons can be in the same state, and although that is perhaps reasonable sounding for photons, it is equally true for heavy atoms. In Bose-Einstein Condensation, a large number of atoms occupy the same quantum state. This happens in liquid Helium below about two kelvin, it becomes a superfluid and flows without friction. BE condensation has also been achieved with laser cooled collections of large atoms in a trap.

ANGULAR MOMENTUM QUANTUM NUMBERS

ORBITAL NAME ABBREVIATIONS S P D F

The orbital names s, p, d, and f stand for names given to groups of lines in the spectra of the alkali metals. These line groups are called sharp, principal, diffuse, and fundamental.

The orbital letters are associated with the angular momentum quantum number, which is assigned an integer valuc from 0 to 3. s correlates to 0, p – 1, d – 2, and f – 3. The angular momentum quantum number can be used to give the shapes of the electronic orbitals. s orbitals are spherical; p orbitals are polar. It may be simpler to think of these two letters in terms of orbital shapes (d and f aren't described as readily).

The electron configuration of an atom denotes the distribution of electrons among available shells. The standard notation lists the subshell symbols, one after another. The number of electrons contained in each subshell is stated explicitly. For example, the electron configuration of beryllium, with an atomic (and electron) number of 4, is $1s^2 2s^2$ or $[He]2s^2$.

TOTAL ANGULAR MOMENTUMQUANTUM NUMBER

In quantum mechanics, the total angular quantum momentum number parameterises the total angular momentum of a given particle, by combining its orbital angular momentum and its intrinsic angular momentum (*i.e.*, its spin).

If s is the particle's spin angular momentum and ℓ its orbital angular momentum vector, the total angular momentum j is,

$$j = s + \ell$$

The associated quantum number is the main total angular momentum quantum number j. It can take the following range of values, jumping only in integer steps:

$$|\ell - s| \leq j \leq \ell + s$$

where ℓ is the azimuthal quantum number (parameterising the orbital angular momentum) and s is the spin quantum number (parameterising the spin).

The relation between the total angular momentum vector j and the total angular momentum quantum number j is given by the usual relation,

$$\|j\| = \sqrt{j(j+1)}\hbar$$

the vector's z-projection is given by,

$$j \approx = m_j \hbar$$

where m_j is the secondary total angular momentum quantum number. It ranges from –j to +j in steps of one. This generates 2j + 1 different values of mj.

The total angular momentum corresponds to the Casimir invariant of the Lie algebra so(3) of the three-dimensional rotation group.

QUANTISATION OF ELECTRONIC ANGULAR MOMENTUM

Rutherford proposed that electrons orbit about the nucleus of an atom. One problem with this model is that, classically, orbiting electrons experience a centripetal acceleration, and accelerating charges lose energy by radiating; a stable electronic orbit is classically forbidden. Bohr nevertheless assumed stable electronic orbits with the electronic angular momentum quantised as,

$$l = m\upsilon r = n\hbar \quad (2)$$

Quantisation of angular momentum means that the radius of the orbit and the energy will be quantised as well. Bohr assumed that the discrete lines seen in the spectrum of the hydrogen atom were due to transitions of an electron from one allowed orbit/energy to another. He further assumed that the energy for a transition is acquired or released in the form of a photon as proposed by Einstein, so that,

$$\Delta E = h\nu \quad (3)$$

This is known as the Bohr frequency condition. This condition, along with Bohr's expression for the allowed energy levels, gives a good match to the observed hydrogen atom spectrum. However, it works only for atoms with one electron.

ELECTRONIC STRUCTURE OF ATOMS

Each electron in an atom is described by four different quantum numbers. Three of these quantum numbers (n, l, and m) represent the three dimensions to space in which an electron could be found. A wave function for an electron gives the probability of finding the electron at various points in space. A wave function for an electron in an atom is called an atomic orbital. The fourth quantum number (m_s) refers to a certain magnetic quality called spin.

N-THE PRINCIPAL QUANTAM NUMBER

Fig. 6.5

The n quantam number relates to the size of the atomic orbital. n can have any positive integer value from 1 to 7. The smaller the n, the lower the energy, the higher the value of n, the higher the energy. In the case of any single-electron atom, or hydrogen atom, n is the only quantum number which determines the energy. The size of an orbital depends on n. The larger the orbital, the larger the value of n.

Orbitals of the same quantum state belong the the same shell. To use an analogy for n, why not relate it to the size of a computer, where larger values would represent larger houses.

M-MAGNETIC QUANTUM NUMBER

The third quantum number has to do with the orientation of an orbital in a magnetic field. Because of this, we can relate its values to different directions the computer might be facing.

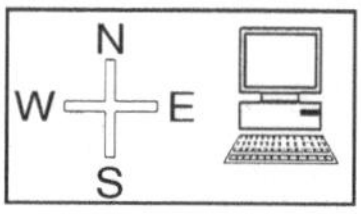

Fig. 6.6

Often times you will be asked to find the electron configuration for something that looks like this: $_{53}I$

The 53 denotes the number of electrons in an atom of iodine. You would now proceed to do the electron configuration by looking at the filling order chart.

$$1s^2 2s^2 2p^6 3s^2 3p^6 4s^2 3d^{10} 4p^6 5s^2 4d^{10} 5p^5$$

PERIODICITY

With increasing atomic number, the electron configuration of the atoms display a periodic variation. Because of this the elements show periodic variations of both physical and chemical behaviour. The periodic law is a law stating that when the elements are arranged by atomic number, their physical and chemical properties vary periodically. We are going to be looking at three physical properties of an atom: atomic radius, ionisation energy, and electron affinity.

Atomic Radius

The size of the electron cloud increases as the principal quantum number increases. Therefore, as you look down the periodic table, the size of atoms in each group is going to increase. When you look across the periodic table, you see that all the atoms in each group have the same principal quantum number. However, for each element, the positive charge on the nucleus increases by one proton. This means that the outer electron cloud is pulled in a little tighter. One periodic property of atoms is that they tend to decrease in size from left to right across a period of the table. So finally we have a good definition for how the atomic radii increases: the atomic radii increases top to bottom and right to left in the periodic table.

Ionisation Energy

The energy needed to remove the most loosely held electron from an atom is known as ionisation energy. Ionisation energies are periodic. The ionisation energy tends to increase as atomic number increases in any horizontal row or period. In any column or group, there is a gradual decrease in ionisation energy as the atomic number increases. Metals typically have a low ionisation energy. Non-metals typically have a high ionisation energy.

Electron Affinity

The attraction of an atom for an electron is called electron affinity. Metals have low electron affinities while non-metals have high electron affinities. The general trend as you go down a column is a decreasing tendancy to gain electrons. As you go across a row there is also a trend for a greater attraction for electrons.

ELECTRON CONFIGURATION

In atomic physics and quantum chemistry, the electron configuration is the distribution of electrons of an atom or molecule (or other physical structure) in atomic or molecular orbitals. For example, the electron configuration of the neon atom is $1s^2\ 2s^2\ 2p^6$.

According to the laws of quantum mechanics, an energy is associated with each electron configuration and, upon certain conditions, electrons are able to move from one orbital to another by emission or absorption of a quantum of energy, in the form of a photon.

Knowledge of the electron configuration of different atoms is useful in understanding the structure of the periodic table of elements. The concept is also useful for describing the chemical bonds that hold atoms together. In bulk materials this same idea helps explain the peculiar properties of lasers and semiconductors.

SHELLS AND SUBSHELLS

Electron configuration was first conceived of under the Bohr model of the atom, and it is still common to speak of shells and subshells despite the advances in understanding of the quantum-mechanical nature of electrons.

An electron shell is the set of allowed states electrons may occupy which share the same principal quantum number, n (the number before the letter in the orbital label). An atom's nth electron shell can accommodate $2n^2$ electrons, *e.g.*, the first shell can accommodate 2 electrons, the second shell 8 electrons, and the third shell 18 electrons. The factor of two arises because the allowed states are doubled due to electron spin—each atomic orbital admits up to two otherwise identical electrons with opposite spin, one with a spin +1/2 (usually noted by an up-arrow) and one with a spin –1/2 (with a down-arrow). A subshell is the set of states defined by a common azimuthal quantum number, l, within a shell. The values l = 0, 1, 2, 3 correspond to the s, p, d, and f labels, respectively. The maximum number of electrons which can be placed in a subshell is given by 2(2l + 1). This gives two electrons in an s subshell, six electrons in a p subshell, ten electrons in a d subshell and fourteen electrons in an f subshell.

The numbers of electrons that can occupy each shell and each subshell arise from the equations of quantum mechanics, in particular the Pauli exclusion principle, which states that no two electrons in the same atom can have the same values of the four quantum numbers.

Notation

Physicists and chemists use a standard notation to indicate the electron configurations of atoms and molecules. For atoms, the notation consists of a sequence of atomic orbital labels (*e.g.*, for phosphorus the sequence 1s, 2s, 2p, 3s, 3p) with the number of electrons assigned to each orbital (or set of orbitals sharing the same label) placed as a superscript. For example, hydrogen has one electron in the s-orbital of the first shell, so its configuration is written $1s^1$. Lithium has two electrons in the

1s-subshell and one in the (higher-energy) 2s-subshell, so its configuration is written $1s^2$ $2s^1$ (pronounced "one-s-two, two-s-one'). Phosphorus (atomic number 15), is as follows: $1s^2$ $2s^2$ $2p^6$ $3s^2$ $3p^3$.

For atoms with many electrons, this notation can become lengthy and so an abbreviated notation is used, since all but the last few subshells are identical to those of one or another of the noble gases. Phosphorus, for instance, differs from neon ($1s^2$ $2s^2$ $2p^6$) only by the presence of a third shell. Thus, the electron configuration of neon is pulled out, and phosphorus is written as follows: [Ne] $3s^2$ $3p^3$. This convention is useful as it is the electrons in the outermost shell which most determine the chemistry of the element. The order of writing the orbitals is not completely fixed: some sources group all orbitals with the same value of n together, while other sources (as here) follow the order given by Madelung's rule. Hence the electron configuration of iron can be written as [Ar] $3d^6$ $4s^2$ (keeping the 3d-electrons with the 3s- and 3p-electrons which are implied by the configuration of argon) or as [Ar] $4s^2$ $3d^6$.

The superscript 1 for a singly occupied orbital is not compulsory. It is quite common to see the letters of the orbital labels (s, p, d, f) written in an italic or slanting typeface, although the International Union of Pure and Applied Chemistry (IUPAC) recommends a normal typeface (as used here). The choice of letters originates from a now-obsolete system of categorising spectral lines as 'sharp', 'principal', 'diffuse' and 'fundamental' (or 'fine'), based on their observed fine structure: their modern usage indicates orbitals with an azimuthal quantum number, l, of 0, 1, 2 or 3 respectively. After 'f', the sequence continues alphabetically 'g', 'h', 'i'... (l = 4, 5, 6...), skipping 'j', although orbitals of these types are rarely required.

The electron configurations of molecules are written in a similar way, except that molecular orbital labels are used instead of atomic orbital labels.

ENERGY — GROUND STATE AND EXCITED STATES

The energy associated to an electron is that of its orbital. The energy of a configuration is often approximated as the sum of the energy of each electron, neglecting the electron-electron interactions. The configuration that corresponds to the lowest electronic energy is called the ground state. Any other configuration is an excited state.

As an example, the ground state configuration of the sodium atom is $1s^22s^22p^63s$, as deduced from the Aufbau principle. The first excited state is obtained by promoting a 3s electron to the 3p orbital, to obtain the $1s^22s^22p^63p$ configuration, abbreviated as the 3p level. Atoms can move from one configuration to another by absorbing or emitting energy. In a sodium-vapour lamp for example, sodium atoms are excited to the 3p level by an electrical discharge, and return to the ground state by emitting yellow light of wavelength 589 nm.

Usually the excitation of valence electrons (such as 3s for sodium) involves energies corresponding to photons of visible or ultraviolet light. The excitation of core electrons is possible, but requires much higher energies generally corresponding to x-ray photons. This would be the case for example to excite a 2p electron to the 3s level and form the excited $1s^22s^22p^53s^2$ configuration.

The remainder of this article deals only with the ground-state configuration, often referred to as 'the' configuration of an atom or molecule.

AUFBAU PRINCIPLE AND MADELUNG RULE

The Aufbau principle (from the German Aufbau, 'building up, construction') was an important part of Bohr's original concept of electron configuration. It may be stated as:

- A maximum of two electrons are put into orbitals in the order of increasing orbital energy: the lowest-energy orbitals are filled before electrons are placed in higher-energy orbitals.

The principle works very well (for the ground states of the atoms) for the first 18 elements, then decreasingly well for the following 100 elements. The modern form of the Aufbau principle describes an order of orbital energies given by Madelung's rule (or Klechkowski's rule). This rule was first stated by Charles Janet in 1929, rediscovered by Erwin Madelung in 1936, and later given a theoretical justification by V.M. Klechkowski.

- Orbitals are filled in the order of increasing n+l;
- Where two orbitals have the same value of n+l, they are filled in order of increasing n.

This gives the following order for filling the orbitals:

1s, 2s, 2p, 3s, 3p, 4s, 3d, 4p, 5s, 4d, 5p, 6s, 4f, 5d, 6p, 7s, 5f, 6d, 7p, (8s, 5g, 6f, 7d, 8p, and 9s)

In this list the orbitals in parentheses are not occupied in the ground state of the heaviest atom now known (Uuo, Z = 118). The Aufbau principle can be applied, in a modified form, to the protons and neutrons in the atomic nucleus, as in the shell model of nuclear physics and nuclear chemistry.

Periodic table

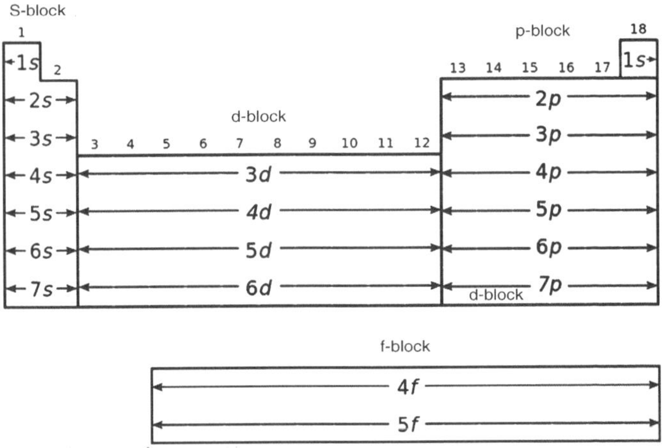

Fig. 6.7 Electron Configuration Table

The form of the periodic table is closely related to the electron configuration of the atoms of the elements. For example, all the elements of group 2 have an electron configuration of ns2 (where is an inert gas configuration), and have notable similarities in their chemical properties. In general, the periodicity of the periodic table in terms of periodic table blocks is clearly due to the number of electrons (2, 6, 10, 14...) needed to fill s, p, d, and f subshells.

The outermost electron shell is often referred to as the 'valence shell' and (to a first approximation) determines the chemical properties. It should be remembered that the similarities in the chemical properties were remarked more than a century before the idea of electron configuration, It is not clear how far Madelung's rule explains (rather than simply describes) the periodic table, although some properties (such as the common +2 oxidation state in the first row of the transition metals) would obviously be different with a different order of orbital filling.

Shortcomings of the Aufbau Principle

The Aufbau principle rests on a fundamental postulate that the order of orbital energies is fixed, both for a given element and between different elements: neither of these is true (although they are approximately true enough for the principle to be useful). It considers atomic orbitals as 'boxes' of fixed energy into which can be placed two electrons and no more. However the energy of an electron 'in' an atomic orbital depends on the energies of all the other electrons of the atom (or ion, or molecule, etc.). There are no 'one-electron solutions' for systems of more than one electron, only a set of many-electron solutions which cannot be calculated exactly (although there are mathematical approximations available, such as the Hartree–Fock method).

The fact that the Aufbau principle is based on an approximation can be seen from the fact that there is an almost-fixed filling order at all, that, within a given shell, the s-orbital is always filled before the p-orbitals. In a hydrogen-like atom, which only has one electron, the s-orbital and the p-orbitals of the same shell have exactly the same energy, to a very good approximation in the absence of external electromagnetic fields. (However, in a real hydrogen atom, the energy levels are slightly split by the magnetic field of the nucleus, and by the quantum electrodynamic effects of the Lamb shift).

Ionisation of the Transition Metals

The naive application of the Aufbau principle leads to a well-known paradox (or apparent paradox) in the basic chemistry of the transition metals. Potassium and calcium appear in the periodic table before the transition metals, and have electron configurations [Ar] $4s^1$ and [Ar] $4s^2$ respectively, *i.e.*, the 4s-orbital is filled before the 3d-orbital. This is in line with Madelung's rule, as the 4s-orbital has n+l = 4 (n = 4, l = 0) while the 3d-orbital has n+l = 5 (n = 3, l = 2). However, chromium and copper have electron configurations [Ar] $3d^5$ $4s^1$ and [Ar] $3d^{10}$ 4s1 respectively, *i.e.*,one electron has passed from the 4s-orbital to a 3d-orbital to generate a half-filled or filled subshell. In this case, the usual explanation is that 'half-filled or completely filled subshells are particularly stable arrangements of electrons'.

The apparent paradox arises when electrons are removed from the transition metal atoms to form ions. The first electrons to be ionised come not from the 3d-orbital, as one would expect if it were 'higher in energy', but from the 4s-orbital. The same is true when chemical compounds are formed. Chromium hexacarbonyl can be described as a chromium atom (not ion, it is in the oxidation state 0) surrounded by six carbon monoxide ligands: it is diamagnetic, and the electron configuration of the central chromium atom is described as 3d6, *i.e.*, the electron which was in the 4s-orbital in the free atom has passed into a 3d-orbital on forming the compound. This interchange of electrons between 4s and 3d is universal among the first series of the transition metals.

The phenomenon is only paradoxical if it is assumed that the energies of atomic orbitals are fixed and unaffected by the presence of electrons in other orbitals. If that were the case, the 3d-orbital would have the same energy as the 3p-orbital, as it does in hydrogen, yet it clearly doesn't. There is no special reason why the Fe^{2+} ion should have the same electron configuration as the chromium atom, given that iron has two more protons in its nucleus than chromium and that the chemistry of the two species is very different. When care is taken to compare 'like with like', the paradox disappears.

Other Exceptions to Madelung's Rule

There are several more exceptions to Madelung's rule among the heavier elements, and it is more and more difficult to resort to simple explanations such as the stability of half-filled subshells. It is possible to predict most of the exceptions by Hartree–Fock calculations, which are an approximate method for taking account of the effect of the other electrons on orbital energies. For the heavier elements, it is also necessary to take account of the effects of Special Relativity on the energies of the atomic orbitals, as the inner-shell electrons are moving at speeds approaching the speed of light. In general, these relativistic effects tend to decrease the energy of the s-orbitals in relation to the other atomic orbitals.

HELIUM ATOM GROUND STATE

The helium atom consists of two electrons with mass m and electric charge –e, around a essentially fixed nucleus of mass M » m and charge +2e. The Hamiltonian for it, neglecting the fine structure, is:

$$H = -\frac{\hbar^2}{2m}\left(\nabla_1^2 + \nabla_2^2\right) - \frac{e^2}{4\pi \epsilon_0}\left(\frac{2}{r_1} + \frac{2}{r_2} - \frac{1}{|r_1 - r_2|}\right)$$

where $\hbar$ is the reduced Planck constant, ε_0 is the vacuum permittivity, r_i (for i = 1, 2) is the distance of the i-th electron from the nucleus, and $|r_1 - r_2|$ is the distance between the two electrons.

If the term $V_{ee} = e^2/(4\pi\varepsilon_0 |r_1 - r_2|)$, representing the repulsion between the two electrons, were excluded, the Hamiltonian would become the sum of two hydrogen-like atom Hamiltonians with nuclear charge +2e. The ground state energy would then be $8E_1 = -109$ eV, where E_1 is the Rydberg constant, and its ground state wavefunction would be the product of two wavefunctions for the ground state of hydrogen-like atoms:

$$\psi(r_1, r_2) = \frac{Z^3}{\pi \alpha_0^3} e^{-Z}(r_1 + r_2)/\alpha_0.$$

where α_0 is the Bohr radius and Z = 2, helium's nuclear charge. The expectation value of the total Hamiltonian H (including the term V_{ee}) in the state described by ψ_0 will be a upper bound for its ground state energy. $\langle V_{ee}\rangle$ is $-5E_1/2 = 34$ eV, so $\langle H\rangle$ is $8E_1 - 5E_1/2 = -75$ eV.

A tighter upper bound can be found by using a better trial wavefunction with 'tunable' parameters. Each electron can be thought to see the nuclear charge partially 'shielded' by the other electron, so we can use a trial wavefunction equal with an 'effective' nuclear charge $Z < 2$: The expectation value of H in this state is:

$$\langle H \rangle = \left[-2Z^2 + \frac{27}{4} Z \right] E_1$$

This is minimal for Z = 27/16; Shielding reduces the effective charge to ~1.69. Substituting this value of Z into the expression for H yields $729E_1/128 = -77.5$ eV, within 2 per cent of the experimental value, –78.975 eV.

THE LCAO APPROXIMATION

To get the orbitals that give a Slater determinant with the lowest energy we have to solve the Fock equation. That is a partial differential equation, and these are generally extremely hard to solve.

Fortunately, we can turn the Fock equation into a (generalised) matrix eigenvalue equation. Such equations are relatively easy to solve with standard techniques from numerical mathematics.

The way to turn the Fock equation into a matrix eigenvalue equation is to write the orbitals as a linear combination of know functions. So if the ϕ_n's are the orbitals that we are trying to determine, and the X_m's are known functions, then we write,

$$\phi_n = \sum_m x_m C_{mn}.$$

Because we know the X's, the unknown quantities on the right-hand-side are the coefficients c_{mn}. If we substitute the linear combination in the Fock equation,

$$F\phi_n = \varepsilon_n \phi_n$$

we get,

$$F \sum_m X_m C_{mn} = \varepsilon_n \sum_m Xm^C{}_{mn}.$$

We convert this into a matrix eigenvalue equation for the coefficients by multiplying from the left by Xk.

$$\sum X_k F x_m C_{mn} = \sum X k X_m C_{mn} \varepsilon_n$$

and integrating over the electron coordinates,

$$\sum_m \langle X_k | F | X_m \rangle C_{mn} = \sum_m \langle X k | X m \rangle C_{mn} \varepsilon_n .$$

This is the desired from, although it might be a bit difficult to see that it is a matrix eigenvalue equation. We define the Fock matrix F,

$$F_{km} = \langle X_k | F | X_m \rangle ,$$

the overlap matrix S,

$$S_{km} = \langle X_k / X_m \rangle ,$$

and the vector $c^{(n)}$,

$$(c^{(n)})m = c_{mn}.$$

The equation above now becomes,

$$\sum_m F_{km} \left(C^{(n)} \right) m = \sum_m S_{km} \left(c^{(n)} \right) m^{\varepsilon} n,$$

or in matrix-vector notation,

$$Fc(n) = Sc(n)en.$$

(Strictly speaking this is a generalised matrix eigenvalue equation, because of the presence of the matrix S, but this does not really change the nature of the equation.) This eigenvalue equation is often called the Roothaan equation, and it's in this form that the Fock equation is generally solved.

When one is trying to determine the MO's of a molecule one usually takes as known functions χ atomic orbitals of the atoms forming the molecule. For example, in HF there is a molecular orbital that is formed from the 1s orbital of H and the $2p_z$ orbital of F. (It is a convention to take the molecular axis of a linear molecule as the z axis.)

Because the atomic orbitals are put in the linear combination the procedure is called the Linear Combination of Atomic Orbitals (LCAO) approximation. It is an approximation because it is not know in advance which and how many atomic orbitals to use. By taking more atomic orbitals in the linear combination the approximation can be made better. Nowadays it can be made very good.

Improvements on the Approximation

The LCAO approximation employed above leads to only a qualitatively correct description of chemical bonding in the H_2^+ molecule ion. The bond length and binding energy are quantitatively off from the exact values. In order to see how to improve the approximation, let us look at some of the limits of the LCAO approximation.

First in the limit $R \rightarrow 0$, the two protons are in approximately the same spatial location (exactly, strictly speaking, but this is unphysical), so that the wave function should have the same spatial dependence as that of a He wave function (the neutrons in an actual He nucleus have no significant effect on the electronic wave function). The ground state energy of He^+ should be $E_0 = Z^2 e^2 / 2\alpha_0 = -2e^2 / \alpha_0$. However, in the LCAO approximation employed above, the energy $E_- - e^2 / R$ (the nuclear repulsion term must be subtracted off because it becomes both infinite and unphysical if we fuse the two protons together into a single ``nucleus") becomes,

$$E_- - \frac{e^2}{R} \rightarrow -\frac{3e^2}{2\alpha_0}$$

Thus, this limit is not properly represented in the current LCAO scheme. In addition, the form of the wave function $\psi_-(r)$ does not reduce to a He^+ wave function when $R \rightarrow 0$ but rather reduces to,

$$\psi_-(r) \rightarrow \left(\frac{1}{\pi \alpha_0^3} \right)^{1/2} e^{-r/\alpha_0}$$

i.e., just a 1s orbital of hydrogen. In order to remedy this situation, one might imagine introducing Z, the atomic number, as a variational parameter into the LCAO approximation. That is, one could introduce atomic orbitals of the form,

$$\langle r|\psi_1(Z)\rangle = \psi_1(r;Z) = \left(\frac{Z^3}{\pi\alpha_0^3}\right)^{1/2} e^{-Z\left|x+\frac{E}{2}Z\right|/\alpha_0}$$

$$\langle r|\psi_2(Z)\rangle = \psi_2(r;Z) = \left(\frac{Z^3}{\pi\alpha_0^3}\right)^{1/2} e^{-Z\left|r-\frac{E}{2}Z\right|/\alpha_0}$$

and then construct a modified LCAO scheme with a trial wave function of the form,

$$|\psi\rangle = C_1|\psi_1(Z)\rangle| + C_2|\psi_2(Z)\rangle$$

The bond length and binding energy obtained in this case are 2.00 α_0 and 2.35 eV, respectively. While the bond length is now correct, the energy is still off from the exact value, which illustrates that the geometry tends to converge faster than the energy.

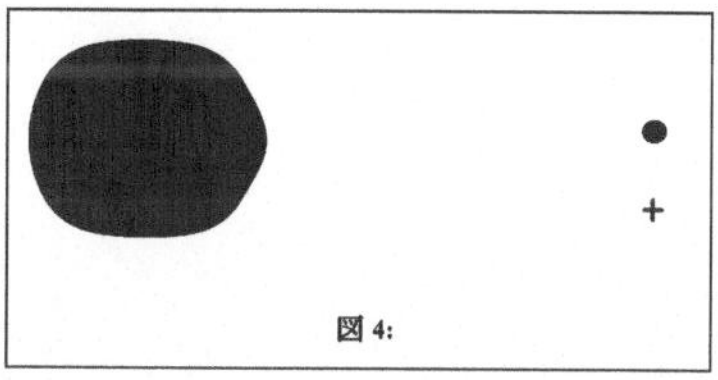

Fig

In the limit of R large but not infinite, the approximation of spherical atomic orbitals is also not entirely correct. The reason for this can be seen by the fact that a positive charge in the vicinity of a hydrogen atom will produce an electric field that causes a distortion of the electronic charge distribution about the hydrogen nucleus. (See figure)

This polarisation effect can be included in the trial wavefunction by mixing in a little bit of a ρ-orbital. For example, if we constructed a trial wavefunction of the form,

$$|\psi\rangle = C_1|\chi 1\rangle + C_2\ |\chi_2\rangle$$

where,

$$\langle r|\chi_1\rangle = \chi_1(r) = \psi_{1s}^2(r_1) + \sigma\psi_{2p}^2(r_1)$$

where σ is a mixing coefficient that is treated as a variational paraleter, then, with a similar definition for $|\chi_2\rangle$, a a variational scheme that includes the polarisation effect is obtained.

In order to include both limits, one would then introduce the Z dependence into the χ orbitals above and use as a trial wavefunction,

$$|\psi\rangle = C_1|\chi_1(Z)\rangle + C_2|\chi_2(Z')\rangle$$

which allows for an asymmetry due to the presence of Z and Z'. Thus, treating C_1, C_2, Z, Z', and σ as variational parameters, a bond length of 2.00 α_0 and binding energy of 2. 73eV are obtained, which are in very good agreement with the exact results.

7

Molecular Orbital Theory

ATOMIC AND MOLECULAR ORBITALS

By sharing electron, molecules can form bonds, and it is possible to regard the sharing of two electrons by two atoms as constituting a chemical bond. Atoms can share one, two or three electrons (forming single, double and triple bonds).

A hydrogen atom consists of a nucleus (a proton) and an electron. It is not possible to accurately determine the position of the electron, but it is possible to calculate the probability of finding the electron at any point around the nucleus. With a hydrogen atom the probability distribution is spherical around the nucleus and it is possible to draw a spherical boundary surface, inside which there is a 95 per cent possibility of finding the electron. The electron has a fixed energy and a fixed spatial distribution called an orbital. In the helium atom there are two electrons associated with the helium nucleus. The electrons have the same spatial distribution and energy (*i.e.*, they occupy the same orbital), but they differ in their spin (Pauli exlusion principle). In general: electrons in atomic nuclei occupy orbitals of fixed energy and spatial distribution, and each orbital only contains a maximum of two electrons with anti-parallel spins.

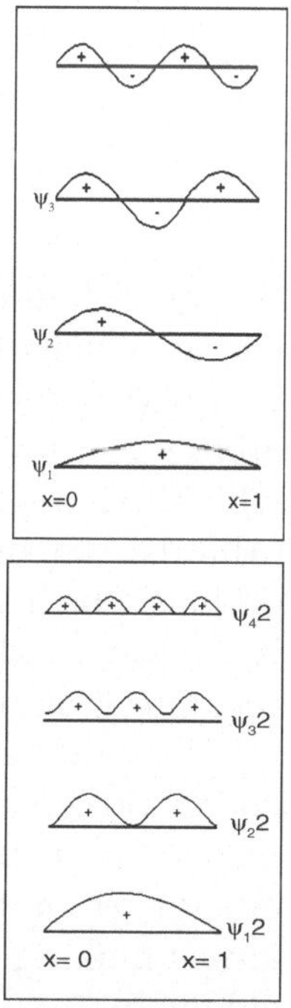

Fig. 7.1

In physics, periodic phenomena are associated with a 'wave equation', and in atomic theory the relevant equation is called the 'Schrödinger Equation'. The wave equation predicts discrete solutions in one dimension for a particle confined to a box with infinite walls, The solutions can be shown as in fig. 7.1.

$\psi_1 - \psi_4$ represent solutions of increasing energy. In three dimensions, the equation determines the energy and defines the spatial distribution of each electron. Solutions of the wave equations in three-dimensions allows calculation of the 'shape' of each orbital. The first five solutions of the wave equation for an electron associated with a proton can be shown in fig. 7.2.

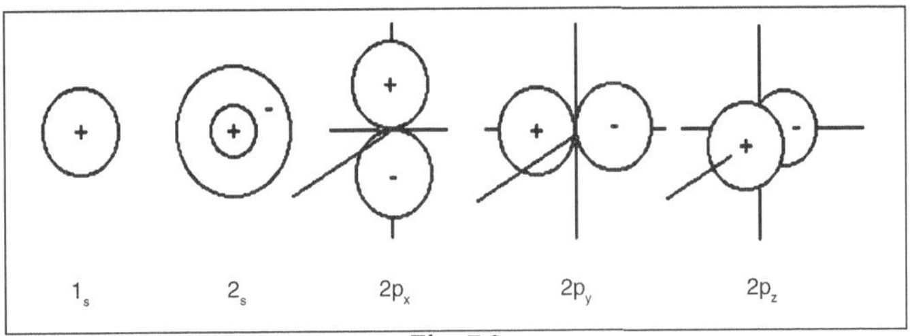

Fig. 7.2

In the hydrogen atom, the 1s atomic orbital has the lowest energy, while the remainder (2s, $2p_x$, $2p_y$ and $2p_z$) are of equal energy (*i.e.*, degenerate), but for all other atoms, the 2s atomic orbital is of lower energy than the $2p_x$, $2p_y$ and $2p_z$ orbitals, which are degenerate. In atoms, electrons occupy atomic orbitals, but in molecules they occupy similar molecular orbitals which surround the molecule. The simplest molecule is hydrogen, which can be considered to be made up of two separate protons and electrons.

There are two molecular orbitals for hydrogen, the lower energy orbital has its greater electron density between the two nuclei. This is the bonding molecular orbital - and is of lower energy than the two 1s atomic orbitals of hydrogen atoms making this orbital more stable than two separated atomic hydrogen orbitals. The upper molecular orbital has a node in the electronic wave function and the electron density is low between the two positively charged nuclei. The energy of the upper orbital is greater than that of the 1s atomic orbital, and such an orbital is called an antibonding molecular orbital.

Normally, the two electrons in hydrogen occupy the bonding molecular orbital, with anti-parallel spins. If molecular hydrogen is irradiated by ultraviolet (UV) light, the molecule may absorb the energy, and promote one electron into its antibonding orbital (σ*), and the atoms will separate. The energy levels in a hydrogen molecule can be represented in fig. 7.3 - showing how the two 1s atomic orbitals combine to form two molecular orbitals, one bonding (σ) and one antibonding (σ*).

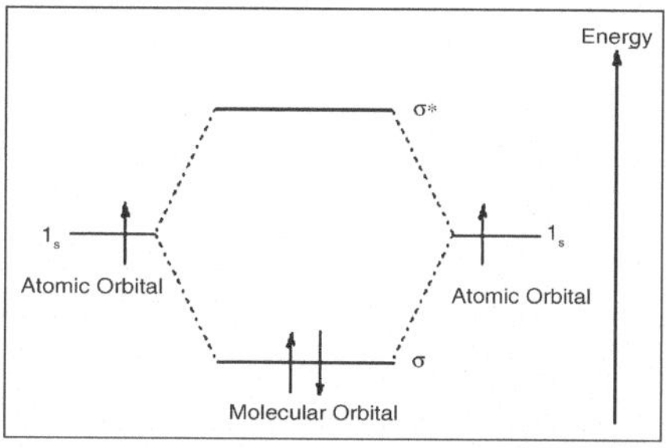

Fig. 7.3

VALENCE BOND MODEL VS. MOLECULAR ORBITAL THEORY

Because arguments based on atomic orbitals focus on the bonds formed between valence electrons on an atom, they are often said to involve a valence-bond theory.

The valence-bond model can't adequately explain the fact that some molecules contains two equivalent bonds with a bond order between that of a single bond and a double bond. The best it can do is suggest that these molecules are mixtures, or hybrids, of the two Lewis structures that can be written for these molecules.

This problem, and many others, can be overcome by using a more sophisticated model of bonding based on molecular orbitals. Molecular orbital theory is more powerful than valence-bond theory because the orbitals reflect the geometry of the molecule to which they are applied. But this power carries a significant cost in terms of the ease with which the model can be visualised.

Forming Molecular Orbitals

Molecular orbitals are obtained by combining the atomic orbitals on the atoms in the molecule. Consider the H_2 molecule, for example. One of the molecular orbitals in this molecule is constructed by adding the mathematical functions for the two 1s atomic orbitals that come together to form this molecule.

One of these orbitals is called a bonding molecular orbital because electrons in this orbital spend most of their time in the region directly between the two nuclei. It is called a sigma (σ) molecular orbital because it looks like an s orbital when viewed along the H-H bond. Electrons placed in the other orbital spend most of their time away from the region between the two nuclei. This orbital is therefore an antibonding, or sigma star (σ^*), molecular orbital. The σ bonding molecular orbital concentrates electrons in the region directly between the two nuclei. Placing an electron in this orbital therefore stabilises the H_2 molecule. Since the σ^* antibonding molecular orbital forces the electron to spend most of its time away from the area between the nuclei, placing an electron in this orbital makes the molecule less stable.

Electrons are added to molecular orbitals, one at a time, starting with the lowest energy molecular orbital. The two electrons associated with a pair of hydrogen atoms are placed in the lowest energy, or σ bonding, molecular orbital. This diagram suggests that the energy of an H_2 molecule is lower than that of a pair of isolated atoms. As a result, the H_2 molecule is more stable than a pair of isolated atoms.

Molecular Orbital Model to Explain

This molecular orbital model can be used to explain why He_2 molecules don't exist. Combining a pair of helium atoms with $1s^2$ electron configurations would produce a molecule with a pair of electrons in both the σ bonding and the σ^* antibonding molecular orbitals. The total energy of an He_2 molecule would be essentially the same as the energy of a pair of isolated helium atoms, and there would be nothing to hold the helium atoms together to form a molecule.

The fact that an He_2 molecule is neither more nor less stable than a pair of isolated helium atoms illustrates an important principle: The core orbitals on an atom make no contribution to the stability of the molecules that contain this atom. The only orbitals that are important in our discussion of molecular orbitals are those formed when valence-shell orbitals are combined. The molecular orbital diagram for an O_2 molecule would therefore ignore the 1s electrons on both oxygen atoms and concentrate on the interactions between the 2s and 2p valence orbitals.

Molecular Orbitals of the Second Energy Level

The 2s orbitals on one atom combine with the 2s orbitals on another to form a σ_{2s} bonding and a σ_{2s}^* antibonding molecular orbital, just like the σ_{1s} and σ_{1s}^* orbitals formed from the 1s atomic orbitals. If we arbitrarily define the Z axis of the coordinate system for the O_2 molecule as the axis along which the bond forms, the $2p_z$ orbitals on the adjacent atoms will meet head-on to form a σ_{2p} bonding and a σ_{2p}^* antibonding molecular orbital. These are called sigma orbitals because they look like s orbitals when viewed along the oxygen-oxygen bond.

The 2_{px} orbitals on one atom interact with the 2_{px} orbitals on the other to form molecular orbitals that have a different shape. These molecular orbitals are called pi (π) orbitals because they look like ρ orbitals when viewed along the bond. Whereas σ and σ^* orbitals concentrate the electrons along the axis on which the nuclei of the atoms lie, π and π^* orbitals concentrate the electrons. The 2px atomic orbitals combine to form a π_x bonding molecular orbital and a π_x^* antibonding molecular orbital. The same thing happens when the 2py orbitals interact, only in this case we get a π_y and a π_y^* antibonding molecular orbital. Because there is no difference between the energies of the 2px and 2py atomic orbitals, there is no difference between the energies of the π_x and π_y or the π_x^* and π_y^* molecular orbitals.

The interaction of four valence atomic orbitals on one atom (2s, $2p_x$, $2p_y$ and $2p_z$) with a set of four atomic orbitals on another atom leads to the formation of a total of eight molecular orbitals: σ_{2s}, σ_{2s}^*, σ_{2p}^*, π_x, π_x^*, and π_y^*. There is a significant difference between the energies of the 2s and 2p orbitals on an atom. As a result, the σ_{2s} and σ_{2s} orbitals both lie at lower energies than the σ_{2p}, σ_{2p}^*, π_x, σ_y, π_x^*, and π_y^* orbitals. To sort out the relative energies of the six molecular orbitals formed when the 2p atomic orbitals on a pair of atoms are combined, we need to understand the relationship between the strength of the interaction between a pair of orbitals and the relative energies of the molecular orbitals they form.

Because they meet head-on, the interaction between the $2p_z$ orbitals is stronger than the interaction between the $2p_x$ or $2p_y$ orbitals, which meet edge-on. As a result, the σ_{2p} orbital lies at a lower energy than the π_x and π_y orbitals, and the σ_{2p}^* orbital lies at higher energy than the π_x^* and π_y^* orbitals.

Unfortunately an interaction is missing from this model. It is possible for the 2s orbital on one atom to interact with the $2p_z$ orbital on the other. This interaction introduces an element of s-p mixing, or hybridisation, into the molecular orbital theory. The result is a slight change in the relative energies of the molecular orbitals. Experiments have shown that O_2 and F_2 are best described by the model in the figure above, but B_2, C_2, and N_2 are best.

Bond Order

The number of bonds between a pair of atoms is called the bond order. Bond orders can be calculated from Lewis structures, which are the heart of the valence-bond model. Oxygen, for example, has a bond order of two.

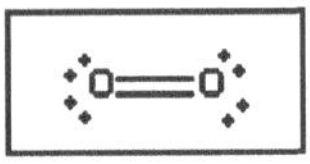

Fig. 7.4

When there is more than one Lewis structure for a molecule, the bond order is an average of these structures. The bond order in sulfur dioxide, for example, is 1.5 –the average of an S-O single bond in one Lewis structure and an S=O double bond in the other.

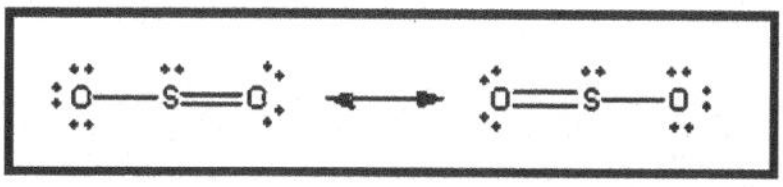

Fig. 7.5

In molecular orbital theory, we calculate bond orders by assuming that two electrons in a bonding molecular orbital contribute one net bond and that two electrons in an antibonding molecular orbital cancel the effect of one bond. We can calculate the bond order in the O_2 molecule by noting that there are eight valence electrons in bonding molecular orbitals and four valence electrons in antibonding molecular orbitals in the electron configuration of this molecule. Thus, the bond order is two.

Although the Lewis structure and molecular orbital models of oxygen yield the same bond order, there is an important difference between these models. The electrons in the Lewis structure are all paired, but there are two unpaired electrons in the molecular orbital description of the molecule. As a result, we can test the predictions of these theories by studying the effect of a magnetic field on oxygen. Atoms or molecules in which the electrons are paired are diamagnetic – repelled by both poles of a magnetic. Those that have one or more unpaired electrons are paramagnetic – attracted to a magnetic field. Liquid oxygen is attracted to a magnetic field and can actually bridge the gap between the poles of a horseshoe magnet. The molecular orbital model of O2 is therefore superior to the valence-bond model, which cannot explain this property of oxygen.

ATOMIC ORBITALS AND MOLECULAR ORBITAL THEORY

Molecular orbital theory rests on the notion that atomic orbitals are combined to form molecular orbitals. Because electron density from each atom is spread out over the span of the entire molecule, the electrons are lowered in energy. This accounts for the stabilisation that occurs during bonding. The amount of the stabilisation depends on the amount of overlap between atomic orbitals and the difference in energy between them. Atomic orbitals that overlap effectively produce stable molecular orbitals. One condition for overlap is that the overlapping atomic orbitals must be of similar energies.

The bonding in homonuclear and heteronuclear diatomic molecules will be discussed to show how molecular orbital theory works. Due to the complexities of describing the molecular orbitals in polynuclear molecules, we will introduce the notion of bonding through hybridised atomic orbitals to account for the bonding in such systems.

Molecular orbital theory can give us information about both ionic and covalent molecules and naturally predicts which molecules will be ionic and which will be covalent. It is a powerful and complex tool available to chemists for predicting the properties of molecules.

HOMONUCLEAR DIATOMIC MOLECULES

In atoms, as you know, electrons reside in orbitals of differing energy levels such as 1s, 2s, 3d, etc. These orbitals represent the probability distribution for finding an electron anywhere around the atom. Molecular orbital theory posits the notion that electrons in molecules likewise exist in different orbitals that give the probability of finding the electron at particular points around the molecule. To produce the set of orbitals for a molecule, we add together the valence atomic wavefunctions for the bonded atoms in the molecule. This is not as complicated as it may sound. Let's consider the bonding in homonuclear diatomic molecules--molecules of the formula A_2.

Perhaps the simplest molecule we can imagine is hydrogen, H_2. To produce the molecular orbitals for hydrogen, we add together the valence atomic wavefunctions to produce the molecular orbitals for hydrogen. Each hydrogen atom in H_2 has only the 1s orbital, so we add the two 1s wavefunctions.

As you have learned in your study of atomic structure, atomic wavefunctions can have either plus or minus phases - this means the value of the wavefunction y is either positive or negative. There are two ways to add the wavefunctions, either both in-phase (either both plus or both minus) or out-of-phase (one plus and the other minus). Figure 7.6 shows how atomic wavefunctions can be added together to produce molecular orbitals.

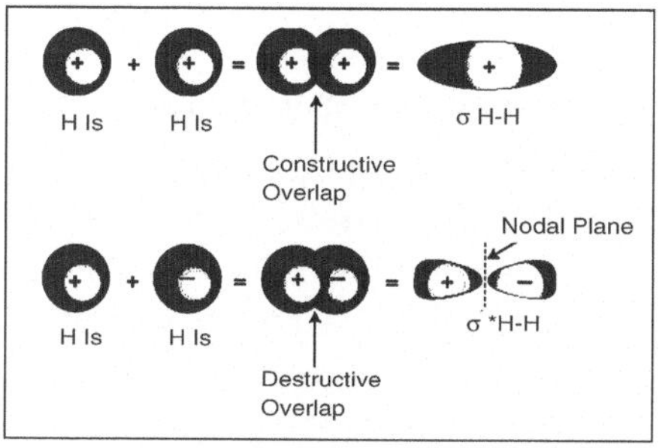

Fig. 7.6 Two 1s Orbitals Combine to form a Bonding and an Antibonding M.O

The in-phase overlap combination (top set of orbitals in) produces a build-up of electron density between the two nuclei which results in a lower energy for that orbital. The electrons occupying the s $_{H-H}$ orbital represent the bonding pair of electrons from the Lewis structure of H_2 and is aptly named a bonding molecular orbital. The other molecular orbital produced, s^*_{H-H} shows a decrease in electron density between the nuclei reaching a value of zero at the midpoint between the nuclei where there is a nodal plane. Since the s^*_{H-H} orbital shows a decrease in bonding between the two nuclei, it is called an antibonding molecular orbital. Due to the decrease in electron density between the nuclei, the antibonding orbital is higher in energy than both the bonding orbital and the hydrogen 1s orbitals. In the molecule H_2, no electrons occupy the antibonding orbital.

To summarise these findings about the relative energies of the bonding, antibonding, and atomic orbitals, we can construct an orbital correlation diagram, shown in fig. 7.7:

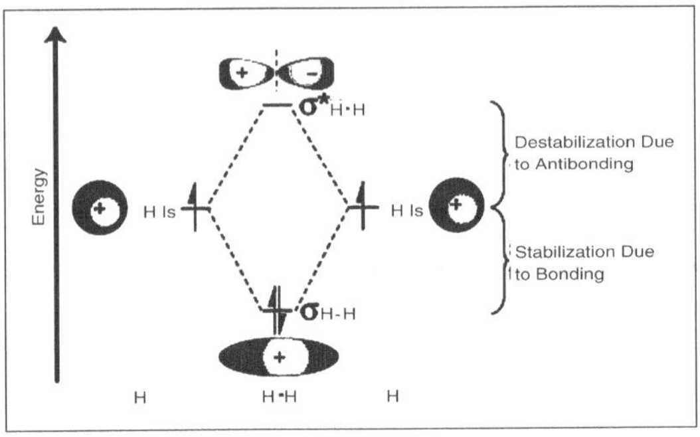

Fig. 7.7 An Orbital Correlation Diagram for Hydrogen

Notice that the orbitals of the separated atoms are written on either side of the diagram as horizontal lines at heights denoting their relative energies. The electrons in each atomic orbital are represented by arrows. In the middle of the diagram, the molecular orbitals of the molecule of interest are written. Dashed lines connect the parent atomic orbitals with the daughter molecular orbitals. In general, bonding molecular orbitals are lower in energy than either of their parent atomic orbitals. Similarly, antibonding orbitals are higher in energy than either of its parent atomic orbitals. Because we must obey the law of conservation of energy, the amount of stabilisation of the bonding orbital must equal the amount of destabilisation of the antibonding orbital.

The Lewis structure and the molecular orbital treatment of the hydrogen molecule agree with one another. In fact, they do. The Lewis structure for H_2 is H-H, predicting a single bond between each hydrogen atom with two electrons in the bond. The orbital correlation diagram in predicts the same thing--two electrons fill a single bonding molecular orbital. To further demonstrate the consistency of the Lewis structures with M.O. theory, we will formalise a definition of bond order--the number of bonds between atoms in a molecule. The bond order is the difference in the number of electron pairs occupying an antibonding and a bonding molecular orbital. Because hydrogen has one electron pair in its bonding orbital and none in its antibonding orbital, molecular orbital theory predicts that H_2 has a bond order of one-the same result that is derived from Lewis structures.

To demonstrate why it is important to take the number of antibonding electrons into account in our bond order calculation, let us consider the possibility of making a molecule of He_2. An orbital correlation diagram for He_2 is provided in fig. 7.8:

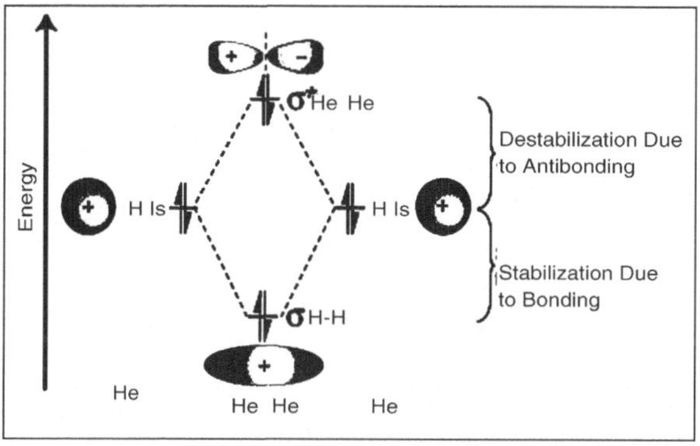

Fig. 7.8 An Orbital Correlation Diagram for a Hypothetical He-He Molecule

From the orbital correlation diagram above you should notice that the amount of stabilisation due to bonding is equal to the amount of destabilisation due to antibonding, because there are two electrons in the bonding orbital and two electrons in the antibonding orbital. Therefore, there is no net stabilisation due to bonding so the He_2 molecule will not exist. The bond order calculation shows that there will be a bond order of zero for the He_2 molecule--exactly what we should predict given that helium is a noble gas and does not form covalent compounds.

Both hydrogen and helium only have 1s atomic orbitals so they produce very simple correlation diagrams. However, we have already developed the techniques necessary to draw a correlation diagram (fig. 7.9) for a more complex homonuclear diatomic like diboron, B_2. Before we can draw a correlation diagram for B2, we must first find the in-phase and out-of-phase overlap combinations for boron's atomic orbitals. Then, we rank them in order of increasing energy. Each boron atom has one 2s and three 2p valence orbitals.

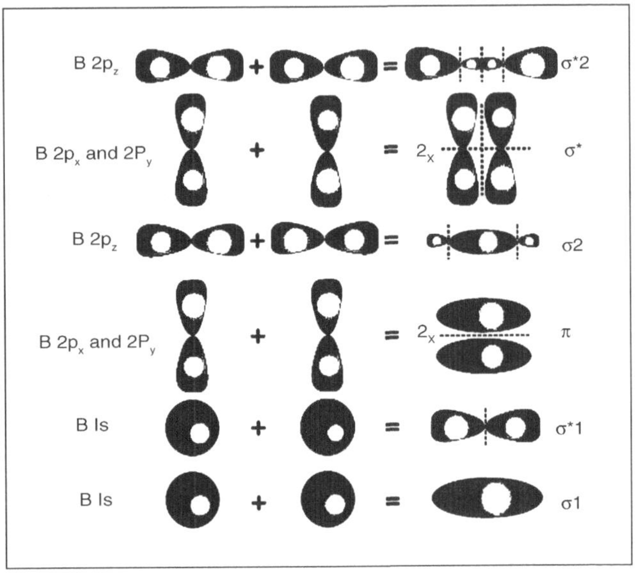

Fig. 7.9 The Molecular Orbitals of Diboron

Due to the great difference in energy between the 2s and 2p orbitals, we can ignore the overlap of these orbitals with each other. All orbitals composed primarily of the 2s orbitals will be lower in energy than those comprised of the 2p orbitals. shows the process of creating the molecular orbitals for diboron by combining orbitals of atomic boron. Note that the orbitals of lowest energy have the most constructive overlap (fewest nodes) and the orbitals with the highest energy have the most destructive overlap (most nodes).

Notice that there are two different kinds of overlap for p-orbitals--end-on and side-on types of overlap. For the p-orbitals, there is one end-on overlap possible which occurs between the two p_z.

Two side-on overlaps are possible--one between the two p_x and one between the two p y. P-orbitals overlapping end-on create s bonds. When p-orbitals bond in a side-on fashion, they create p bonds. The difference between a p bond and a s bond is the symmetry of the molecular orbital produced. s bonds are cylindrically symmetric about the bonding axis, the z-direction. That means one can rotate the s bond about the z-axis and the bond remains the same. In contrast, p bonds lack that cylindrical symmetry and have a node passing through the bonding axis.

The orbital correlation diagram for diboron, however, is not generally applicable for all homonuclear diatomic molecules. It turns out that only when the bond lengths are relatively short (as in B_2, C_2, and N_2) can the two p-orbitals on the bonded atoms efficiently overlap to form a strong p bond. Some textbooks explain this observation in terms of a concept called s-p mixing. For any atom with an atomic number greater than seven, the p bond is less stable and higher in energy than is the s bond formed by the two end-on overlapping p orbitals.

HETERONUCLEAR DIATOMIC MOLECULES

To draw the correlation diagrams for heteronuclear diatomic molecules, we face a new problem: where do we place the atomic orbitals on an atom relative to atomic orbitals on other atoms? For example, how can we predict whether a fluorine 2s or a lithium 2s orbital is lower in energy? The answer comes from our understanding of electronegativity. Fluorine is more electronegative than lithium.

Since lithium only has one occupied valence orbital, only one bonding and one antibonding orbital are possible. Furthermore, the electrons in orbitals on F that cannot bond with Li are left on F as lone pairs. As you can see, the electrons in the Li-F s bond are quite close in energy to fluorine's 2p orbitals. Then the bonding orbital is primarily composed of a fluorine 2p orbital, so the M.O. diagram predicts that the bond should be polarised towards fluorine--exactly what is found by measuring the bond dipole. Such an extreme polarisation of electron density towards fluorine represents a transfer of an electron from lithium to fluorine and the creation of an ionic compound.

The construction of other heteronuclear diatomic orbital correlation diagrams follows exactly the same principles as those we employed for LiF. To see more examples of such diagrams, consult your favourite chemistry textbook.

Bonding in Polyatomic Molecules

As you can imagine, to describe the bonding in polyatomic molecules, we would need a molecular orbital diagram with more than two dimensions so we could describe the bonds both between the central atom and each terminal atom and between the terminal atoms themselves. Such diagrams are impractically difficult to draw or require complex methods to collapse such multidimensional figures into two dimensions. Instead we will describe a simple yet powerful method to describe the bonding in polyatomic molecules called hybridisation. By adding together certain atomic orbitals, we can produce a set of hybridised atomic orbitals that have the correct shape and directionality to account for the known bond angles in polyatomic molecules. Hybrid orbitals describe the bonding in polyatomic molecules one bond at a time.

From the geometry of the molecules, as predicted by VSEPR, we can deduce the hybridisation of the central atom. Linear molecules are sp hybridised. Each hybrid orbital is composed of a combination of an s and a p orbital on the central atom. The other geometries are produced by the proper mixture of atomic orbitals. Molecules based on a triangle are sp^2 hybridised. Tetrahedrally based molecules are sp^3 hybridised. Trigonal bipyramidally based molecules are dsp^3 hybridised. Octahedrally based molecules are d^2sp^3 hybridised. To illustrate how hybrid orbitals are used to describe the bonding in polyatomic molecules, we will examine the bonds that form water, H_2O. Water is AB_2e_2, therefore, its geometry is based on a tetrahedron, and it is sp^3 hybridised. Two sp^3 hybrid orbitals on oxygen with one electron each can form a bond with the singly occupied 1s orbitals on the hydrogen atoms. The remaining two sp^3 hybrid orbitals on oxygen each have two electrons in them and are, therefore, lone pairs.

To produce hybrid bonding descriptions of any compound, first decide what is the hybridisation of the central atom based on its geometry. Next, form bonds between the hybrid or atomic orbitals on terminal atoms and the central atom. Finally, check to make sure that your bonding description agrees with the Lewis structure in the number of bonds formed and the number of lone pairs.

FORMATION OF MOLECULAR ORBITALS

Molecular orbitals arise from allowed interactions between atomic orbitals, which are allowed if the symmetries (determined from group theory) of the atomic orbitals are compatible with each other. Efficiency of atomic orbital interactions is determined from the overlap (a measure of how well two orbitals constructively interact with one another) between two atomic orbitals, which is significant if the atomic orbitals are close in energy. Finally, the number of molecular orbitals that form must equal the number of atomic orbitals in the atoms being combined to form the molecule.

QUALITATIVE DISCUSSION

For an imprecise, but qualitatively useful, discussion of the molecular structure, the molecular orbitals can be obtained from the 'Linear combination of atomic orbitals molecular orbital method' ansatz. Here, the molecular orbitals are expressed as linear combinations of atomic orbitals.

Bonding, Antibonding, and Non-bonding MOs

When atomic orbitals interact, the resulting molecular orbital can be of three types: bonding, antibonding, or non-bonding.

Bonding MOs:

- Bonding interactions between atomic orbitals are constructive (in-phase) interactions.
- Bonding MOs are lower in energy than the atomic orbitals that combine to produce them.

Antibonding MOs:

- Antibonding interactions between atomic orbitals are destructive (out-of-phase) interactions.
- Antibonding MOs are higher in energy than the atomic orbitals that combine to produce them.

Non-bonding MOs:

- Non-bonding MOs are the result of no interaction between atomic orbitals because of lack of compatible symmetries.
- Non-bonding MOs will have the same energy as the atomic orbitals of one of the atoms in the molecule.

Sigma and pi Labels for MOs

The type of interaction between atomic orbitals can be further categorised by the molecular-orbital symmetry labels σ (sigma), π (pi), etc., paralleling the symmetry of the atomic orbitals s, p, etc.

σ Symmetry

A MO with σ symmetry results from the interaction of either two atomic s-orbitals or two atomic p_z-orbitals. A MO will have σ-symmetry if the orbital is symmetrical with respect to the axis joining the two nuclear centers, the internuclear axis. This means that rotation of the MO about the internuclear axis does not result in a phase change. A σ* orbital, sigma antibonding orbital, also maintains the same phase when rotated about the internuclear axis. The σ* orbital has a nodal plane that is between the nuclei and perpendicular to the internuclear axis.

π Symmetry

A MO with π symmetry results from the interaction of either two atomic p_x orbitals or py orbitals. A MO will have π symmetry if the orbital is asymmetrical with respect to rotation about the internuclear axis. This means that rotation of the MO about the internuclear axis will result in a phase change. A π* orbital, pi antibonding orbital, will also produce a phase change when rotated about the internuclear axis. The π* orbital also has a nodal plane between the nuclei.

δ Symmetry

A MO with δ symmetry results from the interaction of two atomic d_{xy} or dx^2-y^2 orbitals. Because these molecular orbitals involve low-energy d atomic orbitals, they are seen in transition-metal complexes.

ϕ Symmetry

Suitably aligned f atomic orbitals overlap to form phi molecular orbital (a phi bond)

Theoretical chemists have conjectured that higher-order bonds, such as phi bonds corresponding to overlap of f atomic orbitals, are possible. There is as of 2005 only one known example of a molecule purported to contain a phi bond (a U-U bond, in the molecule U2).

Gerade and Ungerade Symmetry

For molecules that possess a center of inversion (centrosymmetric molecules) there are additional labels of symmetry that can be applied to molecular orbitals. Centrosymmetric molecules include:

- Homonuclear, X_2
- Octahedral, EX_6
- Square planar, EX_4.

Non-centrosymmetric molecules include:

- Heteronuclear, XY
- Tetrahedral, EX_4.

If inversion through the center of symmetry in a molecule results in the same phases for the molecular orbital, then the MO is said to have gerade, g, symmetry. If inversion through the center of symmetry in a molecule results in a phase change for the molecular orbital, then the MO is said to have ungerade, u, symmetry. For a bonding MO with σ-symmetry, the orbital can be labeled σ_g, and for an antibonding MO with σ-symmetry the orbital can be labeled σ_u, because inversion through the center of symmetry would produce a sign change. For a bonding MO with π -symmetry the orbital can be labeled π_u because inversion through the center of symmetry would produce a sign change. However, for an antibonding MO with π-symmetry the orbital can be labeled π_g because inversion through the center of symmetry would not produce a sign change.

8

Molecules in External Fields

INTRODUCTION

Over the past decade investigations of ultracold quantum gases have been revealing a wealth of intriguing phenomena. In particular, ultracold molecular systems represent a paradigm including molecular Bose-Einstein condensates. External fields on the other hand are equally important for the preparation and control of ultracold systems. They are used for cooling and trapping as well as for quantum state preparation or the tuning of atomic/molecular interactions. Due to their permanent electric dipole moments, heteronuclear polar dimers deserve a special focus.

They open up the possibility to create dipolar quantum gases with long-ranged interactions which introduces exceptional properties for the corresponding quantum systems. Electric fields play here an important role due to their immediate impact on polar systems which leads for isolated molecules amongst others to rotational orientation and alignment.

PHOTOASSOCIATION OF MOLECULES IN ELECTRIC FIELDS

The quest for polar molecular quantum gases attracts a lot of attention. One very promising way to achieve such ultracold ground-state heteronuclear molecular gases is the photoassociation scheme, as depicted in the picture below. In our group we investigate this process in the presence of an external electric field. As it turns out, the application of the electric field is favourable since then the direct production of s-wave molecules is possible.

Rovibrational wave functions of oriented polar molecules.

ORIENTATION AND ALIGNMENT IN STATIC AND LASER FIELDS

Orienting polar molecules is of particular interest for exploiting the dipolar interaction between polar molecules. In our group, we investigate the steric properties of heteronuclear dimers exposed to static or laser fields. We go beyond the so-called rigid rotor approximation by solving the full Schrödinger equation including both the rotational and the vibrational degree of freedom.

FIELD IMPACT ON ROVIBRATIONAL DYNAMICS

Highly excited rovibrational levels of polar dimers are particularly susceptible to external fields since they are embedded in a very dense rovibrational spectrum. We study the effect of a strong static homogeneous electric field on such highly excited states and explore the evolution of the states next to the dissociation threshold. The rotational and vibrational dynamics are greatly influenced by the field; effects such as orientation, angular motion hybridisation and squeesing of the vibrational motion are found.

Probability densities of near-threshold rovibrational states at an avoided crossing.

DIATOMIC MOLECULES IN STRONG ELECTRIC FIELDS

During the past decade a variety of experimental techniques have been developed in order to cool and trap neutral atoms. Using combinations of, *e.g.*, laser and evaporative cooling mechanisms the translational motion of atoms can be slowed down to a few cm/s, which corresponds to typical temperatures on the nanokelvin scale. The motion of the atoms can then be controlled using external fields that provide a suitable trapping potential ~*e.g.*, a magneto-optical trap!.

Since the atoms are isolated from the environment, the traprepresents an ideal laboratory to study the physics of a welldefined ensemble of interacting atoms, their number possibly ranging from a few to typically many millions. Due to their complicated level structure the laser cooling approach cannot be applied to provide ultracold molecules. To nevertheless arrive at ensembles of ultracold molecules the following paths are currently pursued. The first one is photoassociation of two laser cooled atoms that provides translationally cold molecules in certain well-defined ~typically highly excited!

Vibrational states. A major experimental challenge is to prepare molecules also in well-defined rotational states. In a second experimental setup, an array of time varying inhomogeneous electric fields has been used to decelerate and trap polar molecules, providing a technique that can be used for a large variety of neutral molecules as a first step in the cooling processes. Finally, the combination of elastic collisions with a cold buffer gas, such as, *e.g.*, helium, with magnetic traps provide an efficient loading technique to cool and trap a large number of paramagnetic molecules. Moreover, it is expected that these already trapped and cooled molecules could be further cooled by an efficient implementation of, *e.g.*, evaporative cooling.

The prospect of obtaining a Bose-Einstein condensate ~BEC! of molecules has become one of the major objectivesin BEC physics. An analysis of the vibrational and rotational states of the molecules involved is essential to pave the way towards preparation of a molecular condensate.

Beyond this, and due to the interaction between the permanent electric dipole moments of polar molecules, a rich variety of physical phenomena have to be expected in cold dipolar gases, including both spectroscopic and collisional physics. Molecular condensates will give rise to applications in areas as diverse as ultracold molecular physics, molecular optics, and potentially also in quantum computing; in particular, cooling and trapping of molecules opens the way to ultrahigh-resolution and high-precision spectroscopy of molecules, to state-selected chemical reactions, to collisions of ultracold molecules, and to study of collective quantum effects in molecular systems.

In this context the influence of external fields on molecules is of utmost importance: cooling, trapping, guiding, and manipulating atoms and molecules is done by applying suitable electric, magnetic, or electromagnetic fields. Even more, external fields play a key role in the control of molecular rotational and vibrational dynamics. However, little is known about how the rovibrational dynamics of molecules is affected by electric fields. Since several of these experimental techniques proceed via highly excited rovibrational states, especial interest arises in the properties of high excitations exposed to the field.

Historically, one motivation to study the effects of electric fields on the molecular motion was the possibility of orienting or aligning molecular systems in fields. Since the chemical reaction dynamics strongly depends on the mutual orientation of the molecules approaching each other, the possibility of defining and changing their orientation is a major step towards a deeper understanding and control of chemical reactions. Molecular orientation has a rich history during which inhomogeneous and homogeneous electric fields, as well as homogeneous magnetic fields and more recently laser fields have been applied.

In all the above theoretical descriptions of the response of a molecule to an external field the coupling of the rotational and vibrational motions was neglected and the rigid rotor approximation was employed, assuming a fixed permanent dipole moment of the molecule. The resulting "pendular Hamiltonian" for diatomic molecules is integrable. The effect of an electric field on a rigid rotator was studied at the beginning of the seventies by von Meyenn. Later on this analysis was extended to describe non-polar molecules. The term "pendular states" characterises the influence of the electric field on the rotational motion of the molecule: with increasing field strength it becomes a librating one which leads to the orientation of the molecular axis. Each pendular state is a coherent superposition of field-free rotational states. The HCCF molecule in a particular excited vibrational state, the rotation of molecules has exclusively been discussed for low vibrational excitations.

The present work goes beyond these approximations and aims at a more realistic approach to the rovibrational motion in molecules in an external homogeneous electric field. In particular, we include the rotation-vibration coupling and the dependence of the dipole moment on the vibrational coordinates. Especially for highly excited rovibrational states, the additional interactions will have a strong impact on the spectrum and the properties of the systems. Consequently, additional phenomena and effects have to be expected. Effects of weak electric fields on molecular spectra were already investigated very early in the past century.

The latter are not the focus of this analysis. We address the situation of strong electric fields for which the intramolecular and field interactions are of comparable strength, thereby excluding a perturbation theory treatment. The field strength regime of interest is such that it strongly influences the heavy particle dynamic of the molecule but does not yet lead to significant ionisation. Since the energy scales associated with the motion of the heavy and light particles are typically separated by orders of magnitude there is a wide range of field strengths for which these requirements are met.

THE ZEEMAN EFFECT

The atomic energy levels, the transitions between these levels, and the associated spectral lines discussed to this point have implicitly assumed that there are no magnetic fields influencing the atom. If there are magnetic fields present, the atomic energy levels are split into a larger number of levels and the spectral lines are also split. This splitting is called the Zeeman Effect. The Zeeman effect is the splitting of a spectral line by a magnetic field. That is, if an atomic spectral line of 400 nm was considered under normal conditions, in a strong magnetic field, because of the Zeeman effect, the spectral line would be split to yield a more energetic line and a less energetic line, in addition to the original line at 400 nm.

The reason for the Zeeman effect is that in a magnetic field, the angular momentum quantum state can undergo a displacement from degeneracy. For example, the p orbital has three possible angular momentum quantum states that are degenerate (of the same energy) under normal circumstances. However, each angular momentum quantum state has a magnetic dipole moment associated with it, so the effect of a magnetic field is to separate the three states into three different energy levels. One state elevates in energy, one lowers in energy, and one remains at the same energy. The separation of these quantum states into three different energy levels results in 3 different excitation states with slightly different energies that give rise to three spectral lines of slightly different energy (one of the same energy as the original spectral line, one more energetic, and one less energetic) upon relaxation of the atom. This is the simplist case of the Zeeman effect, known as the Normal Zeeman effect.

The Zeeman effect is the splitting of the spectral lines of an atom in the presence of a strong magnetic field. The effect is due to the distortion of the electron orbitals because of the magnetic field.

The (normal) Zeeman effect can be understood classically, as Lorentz predicted. Zeeman discovered the effect, but under closer investigation it did not agree with Lorentz. These differences were explained by the quantum mechanics effects of spin. This is the anomalous Zeeman effect.

In fact, it was the anomalous Zeeman effect that led to the discovery of spin. Any book on quantum mechanics will deal with the Zeeman effect. The usual method is to use perturbation theory, the details depend on the strength of the magnetic field. Consider the hydrogen atom. The full Hamiltonian H is split up into 3 pieces.

H = Hcoulomb + Hrelativistic + Hzeeman

Here Hcoulomb is the Coulomb term, Hrelativistic are the relativistic correction terms and Hzeeman is the Zeeman term produced by the magnetic field. To first-order the relativistic terms led to the fine-structure energy shift. If the magnetic field is weak compared to the relativistic corrections then the Zeeman term can be considered a perturbation of the relativistic terms. If the magnetic field is strong then we can diagonalise the coulomb and Zeeman terms and then consider the relativistic correction as a perturbation. This is the Paschen-Back Effect.

For arbitrary magnetic fields degenerate perturbation theory is needed. For arbitrary atoms it becomes difficult, but the same ideas apply. A very similar effect is the Stark effect in which the atom is placed inside a strong electric field. Again, perturbation theory is the usual approach.

ZEEMAN SPECTRAL SPLITTING

The pattern and amount of splitting are a signature that a magnetic field is present, and of its strength. The splitting is associated with what is called the orbital angular momentum quantum number L of the atomic level. This quantum number can take non-negative integer values. The number of split levels in the magnetic field is 2 * L + 1. The following figure illustrates the Zeeman effect.

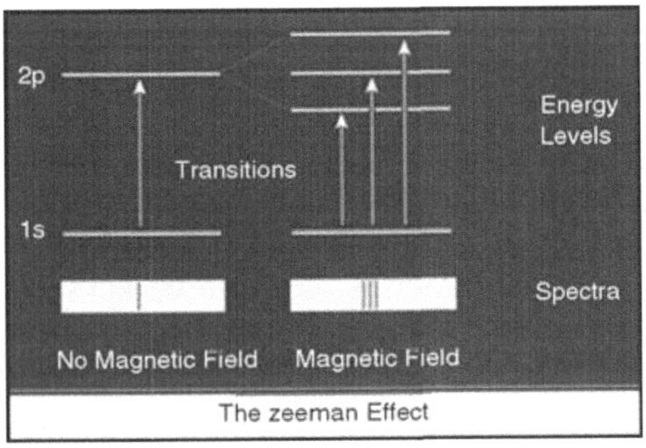

Fig. 8.1

Atomic physicists use the abbreviation 's' for a level with L=0, 'p' for L=1, and 'd' for L=2, and so on (the reasons for these designations are of historical interest only). It is also common to precede this designation with the integer principle quantum number n. Thus, the designation '2p' means a level that has n=2 and L=1.

In the preceding example the lowest level is an 's' level, so it has L=0 and 2L + 1 = 1, so it isn't split in the magnetic field, while the first excited state has L=1 ('p' level), so it is split into 2L + 1 = 3 levels by the magnetic field. Thus, a single transition is split into 3 transitions by the magnetic field in this example.

The Zeeman effect can be interpreted in terms of the precession of the orbital angular momentum vector in the magnetic field, similar to the precession of the axis of a spinning top in a gravitational field.

POLARISATION OF SPECTRAL LINES

The lines corresponding to Zeeman splitting also exhibit polarisation effects. Polarisation has to do with the direction in which the electromagnetic fields are vibrating. This in turn, can have an effect on whether the spectral light can be observed. For example, polarising sunglasses are often effective in suppressing ambiant glare because light reflected from surfaces has a particular polarisation and polarising sunglasses are designed to not pass that polarisation of light.

One practical example in astronomy of such polarisation effects is that in the preceding example the middle transition is polarised such that it cannot be easily be obverved from directly over a surface perpendicular to the magnetic field. As a consequence, when looking directly down on a sunspot (which have strong magnetic fields) typically only two of the three transitions can be seen and the line is observed to split into two rather than three lines (the missing transition could be observed from a different angle where its light would not be suppressed by the polarisation effect, but it is very weak when observed from directly overhead).

ELECTRONIC INTERACTIONS AND SPIN-ORBIT COUPLING

The many capabilities in sample growth and low temperature transport measurement of the experimental component of the Physics of Semiconductors Group at Purdue have been functional to the development of what for me is a new field of research, that of the still unfathomed and exciting physical behaviour of interacting electrons in the presence of spin-orbit coupling.

SPIN-ORBIT COUPLING

One of the most intriguing relativistic effects that manifest themselves in condensed matter systems (the old-fashioned name being solids) is that of the coupling between the orbital motion and the electron intrinsic angular momentum, its spin. This phenomenon is referred to as the spin-orbit coupling. While in most situations "spin space" and "real space" are totally oblivious of each other, this interaction causes the two to become intermingled.

The physical origin of this coupling lies in the fact that in its frame of reference a whirling electron does see as time varying the electric field generated by charges that are stationary in the lab frame. Since a time varying electric field begets a magnetic field, a magnetic coupling to the electron spin ensues.

It is then clear how the magnitude of the effect depends on the local electric field, *i.e.,* on how rapidly the potential energy seen by an electron during its orbital adventures is varying in space. For this reason the phenomenon is usually associated with materials made out of heavy atoms whose nuclei contain a large number of protons which in turn can produce strong local electric fields.

Quite remarkably similar local electric fields can also be produced within the periodic structure of some crystals (this is referred to as an intrinsic coupling) as well as at interfaces both natural and artificial of a chunk of material (the extrinsic variations).

ELECTRONS IN TWO DIMENSIONAL SPACE, SPIN-ORBIT AND CHIRALITY

When the electron motion is confined to a plane (rather interestingly, but this is quite another story, current electronics is based on the dynamics of electrons effectively moving in two dimensional space) it is possible for the confining potential to lead to a sizable extrinsic spin-orbit interaction. In this case the coupling can lead to a puzzling dependence of the orientation of the electron spin on the momentum of the electron.

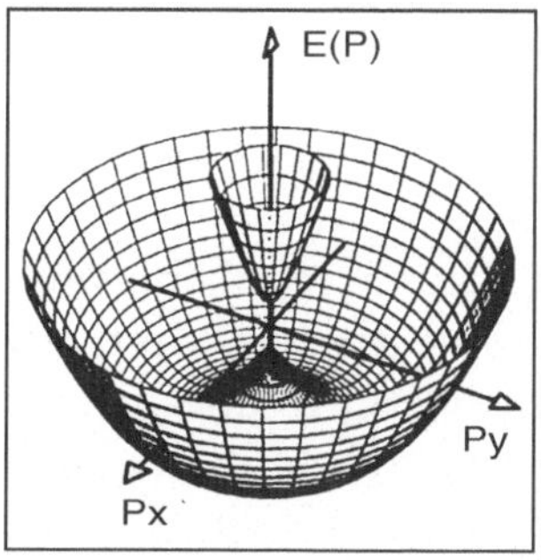

Fig. 8.2

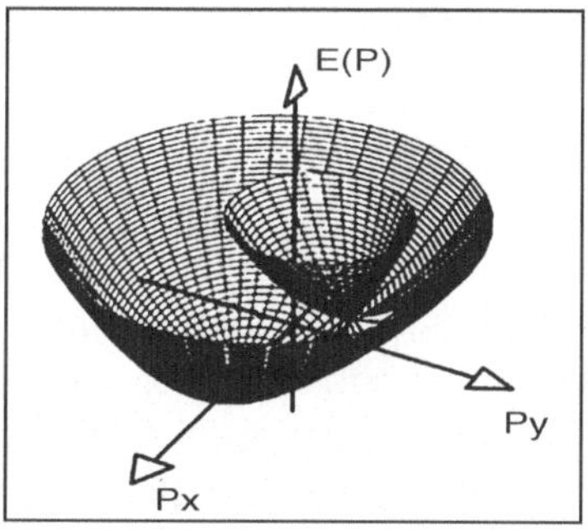

Fig. 8.3

Specifically situations arise in which, rather than being arbitrary (there are no externally applied magnetic fields in this scenario), the electron spin is to a first approximation forced to lie in the plane of motion making a certain specific angle with the direction of its momentum. This peculiar arrangement bestows the electronic states what is referred to as chirality. Furthermore intriguing modifications are induced in the way electrons interact with each other. Energies of electronic chiral states with and without an external magnetic field.

ELECTRON-ELECTRON INTERACTIONS, EXCHANGE AND SPIN-ORBIT

One of the most important ways in which the mutual (repulsive) Coulomb interaction between the electrons manifests itself in the electron liquid roaming the expanse of a metallic system is referred to as the "exchange energy". The phenomenon of exchange is in fact deeply related to fundamental quantum statistical attributes of an electronic system. Simply put, the exchange energy stems in particular from the fact that, due to the Pauli Exclusion Principle, two electrons tend to keep away from each other if they have equal spin orientations.

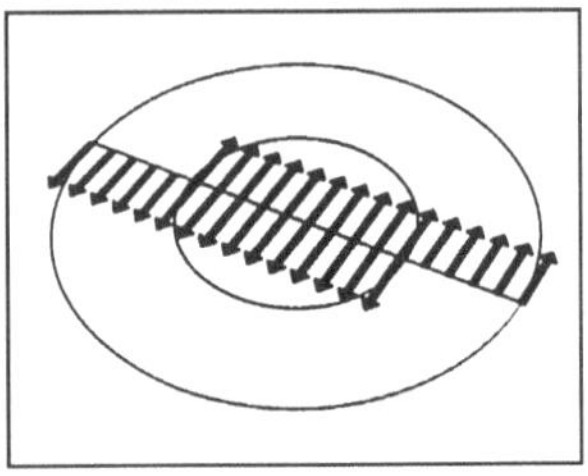

Fig. 8.4

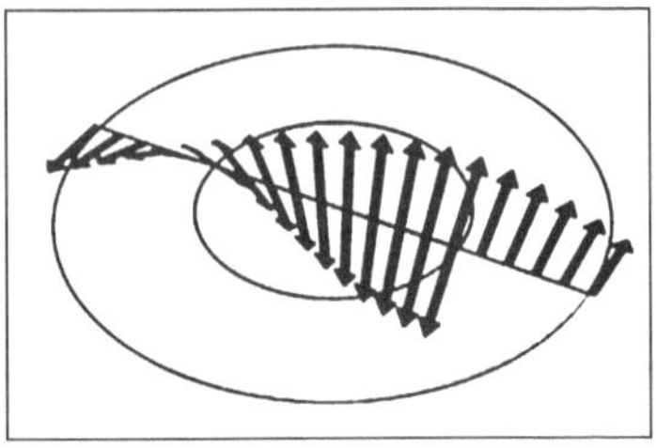

Fig. 8.5

This in turn results in a lower Coulomb repulsion since the average distance between such two electrons is effectively increased. As a consequence the total energy is diminished. Of course this energy gain could be maximized by aligning all or at least a finite fraction of the electronic spins in the same direction. When this happens the system becomes spin polarised, a phenomenon known as ferromagnetism. In general however other quantum mechanical effects play an important role by most often resisting this tendency to polarisation. Of these the most significant is that of the quintessential quantum term of the hamiltonian, the kinetic energy.

Adding to this balance the effect of the spin-orbit interaction scrambles things further and in interesting and to date rather unknown ways. By requiring for the electron spin a precise momentum dependent direction, the spin-orbit coupling in general tends to modify the energy balance and in particular the exchange energy. In this case the whole scenario of the phase diagram of the electron liquid becomes much richer and exciting.

In particular the chirality imposed on the electronic states by spin-orbit leads to the appearance of new states of matter that may one day be studied in systems with electrically controlled spin-orbit coupling. Alongside more mundane unpolarised (so called paramagnetic) states, the list includes a number of exotic chiral polarised states characterised by peculiar spin textures as well as by the surprising emergence of non uniformity in momentum space.

SPIN-ORBIT INTERACTION IN ATOMIC ENERGY LEVELS

Using some semiclassical electrodynamics and non-relativistic quantum mechanics, in this section we present a relatively simple and quantitative description of the spin-orbit interaction for an electron bound to an atom, up to first order in perturbation theory. This gives results that agree reasonably well with observations. A more rigourous derivation of the same result would start with the Dirac equation, and achieving a more precise result would involve calculating small corrections from quantum electrodynamics.

ENERGY OF A MAGNETIC MOMENT

The energy of a magnetic moment in a magnetic field is given by:

$$\Delta H = -\mu.B,$$

where μ is the magnetic moment of the particle and B is the magnetic field it experiences.

Magnetic field

We shall deal with the magnetic field first. Although in the rest frame of the nucleus, there is no magnetic field, there is one in the rest frame of the electron. Ignoring for now that this frame is not inertial, in SI units we end up with the equation,

$$B = -\frac{\upsilon \times E}{c^2},$$

where v is the velocity of the electron and E the electric field it travels through. Now we know that E is radial so we can rewrite $E = \left|\frac{E}{r}r\right|$. Also we know that the momentum of the electron $p = m_e\upsilon$. Substituting this in and changing the order of the cross product gives:

$$B = \frac{r \times p}{m_e c^2}\left|\frac{E}{r}\right|.$$

Next, we express the electric field as the gradient of the electric potential $E = -\nabla V$. Here we make the central field approximation, that is, that the electrostatic potential is spherically symmetric, so is only a function of radius. This approximation is exact for hydrogen, and indeed hydrogen-like systems. Now we can say,

$$|E| = \frac{\partial V}{\partial r} = \frac{1}{e}\frac{\partial U(r)}{\partial r},$$

where U= V is the potential energy of the electron in the central field, and e is the elementary charge. Now we remember from classical mechanics that the angular momentum of a particle L= r × p. Putting it all together we get,

$$B = \frac{1}{m_e ec^2}\frac{1}{r}\frac{\partial U(r)}{\partial r}L.$$

It is important to note at this point that B is a positive number multiplied by L, meaning that the magnetic field is parallel to the orbital angular momentum of the particle.

Magnetic Moment of the Electron

The magnetic moment of the electron is,

$$\mu = -g_s \mu_B S/\hbar,$$

where S is the spin angular momentum vector, μ B is the Bohr magneton and $g_s \approx 2$ is the electron spin g-factor. Here, μ is a negative constant multiplied by the spin, so the magnetic moment is antiparallel to the spin angular momentum.

The spin-orbit potential consists of two parts. The Larmor part is connected to interaction of the magnetic moment of electron with magnetic field of nucleus in the co-moving frame of electron. The second contribution is related to Thomas precession.

Larmor Interaction Energy

The Larmor interaction energy is,

$$\Delta H_L = - \mu . B.$$

Substituting in this equation expressions for the magnetic moment and the magnetic field, one gets,

$$DH_L = \frac{2\mu_B}{\hbar m_e ec^2} \frac{1}{r} \frac{\partial U(r)}{\partial r} L.S.$$

Now, we have to take into account Thomas precession correction for the electron's curved trajectory.

Thomas Interaction Energy

In 1926 Llewellyn Thomas relativistically recomputed the doublet separation in the fine structure of the atom. Thomas precession rate, Ω_T, is related to the angular frequency of the orbital motion, ω, of a spinning particle as follows,

$$\Omega_T = \omega(1-\gamma),$$

where γ s the Lorentz factor of moving particle. The Hamiltonian producing the spin precession Ω_T is given by,

$$\Delta H_T = \Omega_T.S.$$

To the first order in $(\upsilon/c)^2$, we obtain,

$$\Delta H_T = -\frac{\mu_B}{\hbar m_e ec^2} \frac{1}{r} \frac{\partial U(r)}{\partial r} L.S.$$

Total Interaction Energy

The total spin-orbit potential in an external electrostatic potential takes the form,

$$\Delta H \equiv \Delta H_L + \Delta H_T = \frac{\mu_B}{\hbar m_e ec^2} \frac{1}{r} \frac{\partial U(r)}{\partial r} L.S.$$

The net effect of Thomas precession is the reduction of the Larmor interaction energy by factor 1/2 which came to be known as the Thomas half.

Evaluating the Energy Shift

Thanks to all the above approximations, we can now evaluate the detailed energy shift in this model. In particular, we wish to find a basis that diagonalises both H_0 (the non-perturbed Hamiltonian) and ΔH. To find out what basis this is, we first define the total angular momentum operator,

$$J = L + S.$$

Taking the dot product of this with itself, we get,

$$J^2 = L^2 + S^2 + 2L.\,S$$

(since L and S commute), and therefore,

$$L.S = \frac{1}{2}\left(J^2 - L^2 - S^2\right)$$

It can be shown that the five operators H_0, J^2, L^2, S^2, and Jz all commute with each other and with ΔH. Therefore, the basis we were looking for is the simultaneous eigenbasis of these five operators (*i.e.*, the basis where all five are diagonal). Elements of this basis have the five quantum numbers: n (the 'principal quantum number') j (the 'total angular momentum quantum number'), l (the 'orbital angular momentum quantum number'), s (the 'spin quantum number'), and j_z (the 'z-component of total angular momentum').

To evaluate the energies, we note that,

$$\left\langle \frac{1}{r^3} \right\rangle = \frac{2}{\alpha^2 \eta^3 l(l+1)(2l+1)}$$

for hydrogenic wavefunctions (here $\alpha = \hbar / Z\alpha m_e c$ is the Bohr radius divided by the nuclear charge Z); and,

$$\langle L.S. \rangle = \frac{1}{2}\left(\langle J^2 \rangle - \langle L^2 \rangle - \langle S^2 \rangle\right)$$

$$= \frac{\hbar}{2}\left(j(j+1) - l(l+1) - (s+1)\right)$$

Final Energy Shift

We can now say,

$$\Delta E = \frac{\beta}{2}\left(j(j+1) - l(l+1) - s(s+1)\right)$$

where,

$$\beta = \frac{-\mu_B}{m_e e c^2}\left\langle \frac{1}{r} \frac{\partial U(R)}{\partial r} \right\rangle$$

For hydrogen, we can write the explicit result,

$$\beta(\eta, \iota) = \frac{\mu_0}{4\pi} g_s \mu_B^2 \frac{1}{\eta 3 \alpha_0^3 \iota(\iota + 1/2)(\iota + 1)}$$

For any hydrogen-like atom with Z protons,

$$\beta(\eta,\iota)=Z^4\frac{\mu_0}{4\pi}g_s\mu_B^2\frac{1}{\eta 3\alpha_0^3\iota(\iota+1/2)(\iota+1)}$$

EXTERNAL MAGNETIC FIELD ON THE DECOHERENCE OF A CENTRAL SPIN

Maintaining sufficient quantum coherence and quantum superposition properties is one of the most important requirements for applications in quantum information processing, such as quantum computing, quantum teleportation quantum cryptography , quantum dense coding and telecloning . Decoherence is a process by which a quantum superposition state decays into a classical, statistical mixture of states. It arises from the unavoidable interaction and thus entanglement between quantum systems and the environments. When the environmental degrees of freedom are traced out or averaged over, the quantum states of the quantum systems are no longer pure and the quantum systems are said to have decohered.

In recent years, the decoherence behaviour of a small quantum system, particularly a spin system, interacting with a large environment has attracted extensive attention. Different environments result in different decoherence features . In some cases of the problems of a central spin coupled to an environment, a spin environment may be more appropriate to represent the actual localised background spins or magnetic defects than the delocalised oscillator bath that is usually used. The spin environment could be lattice nuclear spins, Ising spin bath, spin-star environment or the device substrates doped with spin impurities.

In the decoherence behaviour of a localised electron spin in the nuclear spin environment is investigated experimentally. The influence of an external magnetic field is also considered. The decoherence factor is shown to be a Gaussian type. By attributing the electron spin decoherence to quantum fluctuations of lattice nuclear spins, Witzel et al attempt to explain the experimental results. There, the significant coupling between the electron spin and nuclear spins is assumed to be the Ising-type interaction and the coupling among nuclear spins is, however, taken to be the dipole–dipole interaction.

Recently, the dynamics of the reduced density matrix for central spin systems in a spin bath described by the transverse Ising model has been analysed using a perturbative expansion method or a mean-field approximation. The interaction between the central spin system and the spin bath for these case was assumed to be a Ising type. It has also been reported recently that the reduced dynamics and for one- and two-spin-qubit systems in a spin-star environment has been analysed. There, the interaction between the system and environment was assumed to be a Heisenberg XY interaction.

Antiferromagnetic materials have been reported recently to have applications in the area of quantum information processing . It was shown that quantum computing is possible with a wide variety of clusters assembled from antiferromagnetically coupled spins .An antiferromagnetic molecular ring was also suggested to be a suitable candidate for the qubit implementation. The decoherence of the cluster-spin degrees of freedom in the antiferromagnetic ring is expected to arise mainly from the hyperfine coupling with the nuclear spins. Meier and Loss investigated the electron spin decoherence rate of the quantum tunnelling of the Néel vector in a ring type antiferromagnetic molecular magnet through the study of a nuclear spin coupled to an electron spin in the ring.

Indeed, the study of the relationship between the pure-mixed state transition of a central spin and the quantum phase transition (QPT) of a bath to which the central spin is coupled has attracted much attention recently. A QPT is driven only by quantum fluctuations (*e.g.*, as happens at zero temperature where the thermal fluctuations vanish) and can be triggered by a change of some of the coupling constants (*e.g.*, external fields) defining the system's Hamiltonian.

In the concept of Loschmidt echo (or equivalently the decoherence factor) has been used to investigate quantum criticality in the XY and anisotropic Heisenberg spin chain models. While the quantum state fidelity approach has also been put forward in to study QPTs in the Dick, BCS-like and XY models. Basically, the signature of QPT (in the case of finite spin number) is the dramatic decay of the asymptotic value of the Loschmidt echo or the quantum state fidelity at the critical point. That is, the closer the bath to the QPT, the smaller the asymptotic value of the Loschmidt echo or the decoherence factor of the central spin.

The extension of the investigations of quantum criticality to finite temperatures has been reported in . We will show in this paper that a similar behaviour of the decoherence factor of the central spin also appears in our antiferromagnetic bath model when the external magnetic field strength is tuned to near the critical field point of the flip–flop transition, a first order QPT.

It is known that the values of the critical magnetic field of the spin–flop transition can be obtained using the spin wave theory. We thus apply, in this paper, the spin wave approximation to deal with the antiferromagnetic environment in a globally applied magnetic field at low temperatures and low energy excitations. We obtain explicitly an analytic expression of the decoherence factor for the central spin. It is found that the external magnetic field affects the decoherence process through its effect on the antiferromagnetic environment.

Our results explicitly show that the decoherence factor which displays a Gaussian decay with time depends on the strength of the external magnetic field and the crystal anisotropy field in the environment. One of the important results of our present paper is that when the magnetic field is increased to the critical field point at which the spin–flop transition happens, the decoherence of the central spin reaches its highest point, consistent with the QPT witness studies in. We also investigate the influence of the environmental temperature on the decoherence of the central spin.

MOLECULES IN STRONG ELECTRIC FIELDS

Over the past decade investigations of ultracold quantum gases have been revealing a wealth of intriguing phenomena.

In particular, ultracold molecular systems represent a paradigm including molecular Bose-Einstein condensates. External fields on the other hand are equally important for the preparation and control of ultracold systems. They are used for cooling and trapping as well as for quantum state preparation or the tuning of atomic/molecular interactions. Due to their permanent electric dipole moments, heteronuclear polar dimers deserve a special focus.

They open up the possibility to create dipolar quantum gases with long-ranged interactions which introduces exceptional properties for the corresponding quantum systems. Electric fields play here an important role due to their immediate impact on polar systems which leads for isolated molecules amongst others to rotational orientation and alignment.

We investigate the steric as well as the radiative properties of heteronuclear dimers exposed to strong static electric fields. We go beyond the so-called rigid rotor approximation by solving the full Schrödinger equation including both the rotational and the vibrational degree of freedom. This allows us to use an electronic dipole moment function depending on the internuclear distance of the molecule, thus coupling the angular and radial motion non-linearly.

By doing so, we calculate the influence of the electric field on the rovibrational spectrum and dynamics as well as on the radiative properties of heteronuclear dimers. Furthermore, by extending the theoretical framework to unbound molecular states, it is possible to describe the advantages of an external electric field for the formation process of ultracold heteronuclear molecules via stimulated photoassociation.

MAGNETIC AND ELECTRIC EFFECTS ON WATER

Due to the partial covalency of water's hydrogen bonding, electrons are not held by individual molecules but are easily distributed amongst water clusters giving rise to coherent regions capable of interacting with local electric and magnetic fields and electromagnetic radiation.

ELECTRIC EFFECTS ON WATER

Water, being dipolar, can be partly aligned by an electric field and this may be easily shown by the movement of a stream of water by an electrostatic source. Very high field strengths (5×10^9 V m^{-1}) are required to reorient water in ice such that freesing is inhibited with lower fields (10^5 V m–1) encouraging ice formation in supercooled water by weakening the hydrogen bonding.

Even partial alignment of the water molecules with the electric field will cause pre-existing hydrogen bonding to become bent or broken. The balance between hydrogen bonding and van der Waals attractions is thus biased towards van der Waals attractions giving rise to less cyclic hydrogen bonded clustering. An electric field also changes the molecular O-H bond lengths (25×10^9 V m–1 causing ~±6 per cent change in a lone water molecule), H-O-H bond angle (25×109 V m–1 causing ~+1 per cent/–0.2 per cent change in a lone water molecule), vibrational frequencies and dissociation energy, depending on the relative orientation of the molecule to the field. This will affect the hydrogen bonded network in an anisotropic manner

High interfacial fields ($E > 10^9$ V m–1, > thermal energy) at electrode (or charged) surfaces can cause a phase transition with an ordered layering of water at high densities similar to ice X. Depending on the value of the field, the restriction pressures may cause melting or freesing as corresponding to the normal phase behaviour. High fields (E ~109 V m^{-1}) might also be found (perhaps surprisingly) at the surface of hydrophilic molecules where caused by the partial charges on the atoms and the small distances between the surface and first hydration layer.

High fields affect hydrogen bonding in an anisotropic manner, hydrogen bonds being strengthened along the field but weakened orthogonal to the field. At low fields, however, both translational and rotational motions may be reduced. Electric fields are expected to increase the differences in the properties between the ortho and para forms of water. Electric fields also lower the dielectric constant of the water due to the resultant partial or complete destruction of the hydrogen-bonded network.

Pure water is a poor conductor of electricity but is not a perfect insulator as it always contains ions due to self-ionisation. Passage of an electric current causes electrolysis, producing O_2 at the anode and H_2 at the cathode with the resulting water storing the charge separation for extensive periods of time (hours).

At metallic electrodes, even quite low voltages can have impressive effects on the orientation of the water molecules and the positioning of ions. A negative potential of –0.23 V orients water hydrogen atoms towards the electrode whereas +0.52 V reverses this; both causing some hydrogen bond breakage and localised density increase. Ions are attracted or repelled dependent on their charge. Similar orientations may take place at the surface of minerals containing alternating positive and negative charges such that a solid (static and non-exchangeable) water layer has been reported at the surface of highly polar metal oxides, (for example, TiO_2). Also, an ambient temperature single layer ice (with all the donor hydrogen bonds oriented towards each other or the silica surface oxygen atoms) is found, using modeling, on the surface of hydrophilic fully hydroxylated silica called ice tessellation), which may explain the many layers of structured water found at the surfaces of complex silicates.

Thus, a high-voltage electric field (333 kV m-1) has been shown to raise the water activity in bread dough, so ensuring a more efficient hydration of the gluten. Rather unexpectedly, such electric fields (~1 MV m-1) apparently increase water's surface tension by about 2 per cent.

MAGNETIC EFFECTS ON WATER

Liquid water is affected by magnetic fields and such fields can assist its purification. Water is diamagnetic and may be levitated in very high magnetic fields (10 T, compare Earth's magnetic field 50 μT). Lower, but still powerful, magnetic fields (0.2 T) have been shown, in simulations, to increase the number of monomer water molecules but, rather surprisingly, they increase the tetrahedrality at the same time.

Other studies show an increase in cluster size in liquid water is caused by a magnetic field. Salt mobility is enhanced in strong magnetic fields (1-10 T) causing some disruption to the hydrogen bonding. However this only causes a net reduction in hydrogen bonding at high salt concentrations (for example 5 M NaCl), whereas at lower concentrations (1 M NaCl) the increase in water hydrogen bonding in the presence of such high magnetic fields more than compensates for this effect. They may also assist clathrate formation. The increase in refractive index with magnetic field has been attributed to increased hydrogen bond strength. Weak magnetic fields (15 mT) have also been shown to increase the evaporation rate. These effects are consistent with the magnetic fields weakening the van der Waals bonding between the water moleculesa and the water molecules being more tightly bound, due to the magnetic field reducing the thermal motion of the inherent charges by generating dampening forces.

Due to the fine balance between the conflicting hydrogen bonding and non-bonded interactions in water clusters, any such weakening of the van der Waals attraction leads to a further strengthening of the hydrogen bonding and greater cyclic hydrogen bonded clustering. This effect of the magnetic field on the hydrogen bonding has been further supported by the increased ease of supercooling (5 mT lowering about 1°C, the rise in the melting point of H_2O (5.6 mK at 6 T) and D_2O (21.8 mK at 6 T) and the 3°C lowering of the sol-gel transition (at 0.3 T) in methylcellulose both indicating a weakening of the van der Waals bonding of the water molecules within a magnetic field.

Far greater effects on contact angle and Raman bands have been shown to occur using strong magnetic fields (6 T) when the water contains dissolved oxygen (but not without the paramagnetic oxygen), indicating effects due to greater clathrate-type water formation.

The magnetic susceptibility of water increases from negative towards positive with magnetic frequency and is reported to be positive (*i.e.*, it is slightly paramagnetic) in the range of 0.4-1 MHz for ambient water.

Static magnetic effects have been shown to cause strengthened hydrogen bonding and an increase in the ordered structure of water formed around hydrophobic molecules and colloids as shown by the increase in fluorescence of dissolved probes. Also, magnetic fields affect the infrared spectrum of water (showing its effect on water clustering) and these effects remain for considerable time after the magnetic field is removed. Surprisingly, even very small magnetic fields may affect the solubility of gasses in seawater (solubility increasing with magnetic field (20-50 μT) probably by their effect on the clathrate stability. This reinforces the view that it is the movement through a magnetic field, and it associated electromagnetic effect, that is important for disrupting the hydrogen bonding.

Such fields can also increase the evaporation rate of water and the dissolution rate of oxygen (due to its paramagnetic nature) but cannot, despite claims by certain expensive water preparations, increase the equilibrium amount of oxygen dissolved in water above its established, and rather low, equilibrium concentration. Magnetic fields can also increase proton spin relaxation which may speed up some reactions dependent on proton transfer. Treatment of water with magnetic fields of about one Tesla increases the strength of mortar due to its greater hydration.

ELECTROMAGNETIC EFFECTS ON WATER

Thus, it appears that electric and magnetic fields have opposite effects on water clustering.. Unstructured water with fewer hydrogen bonds is a more reactive environment as exemplified by the enhanced reactivity of supercritical water. An open, more hydrogen-bonded network structure slows reactions due to its increased viscosity, reduced diffusivities and the less active participation of water molecules. Any factors that reduce hydrogen bonding and hydrogen bond strength, such as electric fields, should encourage reactivity. Water clusters (even with random arrangements) have equal hydrogen bonding in all directions.

As such, electric or electromagnetic fields that attempt to reorient the water molecules should necessitate the breakage of some hydrogen bonds; for example, electric fields have been reported to halve the mean water cluster size as measured by ^{17}O-NMR and increase reaction rates hydration and solubility. Electromagnetic radiation (for example, microwave) has been shown to exert its effect primarily through the electrical rather than magnetic effect. The increased hydration ability of water in electromagnetic fields has been shown by the dissociation of an enzyme dimer (electric eel acetylcholinesterase), leading to gel formation, due to the microwave radiation from a mobile phone. The resultant aqueous restructuring caused by such processes may be kinetically stable.

The solubility properties of the water will change in the presence of such fields and may result in the concentration of dissolved gases and hydrophobic molecules at surfaces followed by reaction (for example, due to reactive singlet oxygen ($^1O_2$) or free radical formation such as OH·) or phase changes (for example, formation of flattish surface nanocavities, termed nanobubbles). It is also possible that these processes may result in the production of low concentrations of hydrogen peroxide in a similar manner to mechanical vibrations. Such changes can clearly result in effects lasting for a considerable time, giving rise to claims for 'memory' effects.

One of the curious facts, concerning reports of the effects of magnets and electromagnetic radiation on the properties of water, is the long lifetime these effects seem to have (for example,). This should not be so surprising, however, as it can take several days for the effects, of the addition of salts to water, to finally stop oscillating and several months where such solutions are still changing.

Also, there is evidence that water structuring in still deaerated pure water increases over a period of a day or two changes in dilute ethanol solution over a period of days and in homeopathic preparations over hundreds of days clathrates may persist metastably in water restructuring after infrared radiation persists for more than a day and water photoluminescence (possibly due to impurities at gas/liquid interfaces) changes over a period of days.

In addition to the breakage of hydrogen bonds electromagnetic fields may perturb in the gas/liquid interface and produce reactive oxygen species. Changes in hydrogen bonding may effect carbon dioxide hydration resulting in pH changes. Thus the role of dissolved gas in water chemistry is likely to be more important than commonly realised particularly as the formation of nanobubbles (that is, nanocavities) containing just a few hundred or less molecules of gas, the stability of larger bubbles (~300 nm diameter) detected by light scattering and nanobubble coating of hydrophobic surfaces have all been recently described. Reinforcement of this view comes from the effect of magnetised water on ceramic manufacture and out-gassing experiments that apparently result in the loss of magnetic and electromagnetic effects or photoluminescent effects. Gas accumulating at hydrophobic surfaces promotes the hydrophobic effect and low-density water formation.

The accumulated gas molecules at such hydrophobic surfaces becomes supersaturating when electromagnetic effects disrupt this surface low-density water. An interesting (and possibly related) 'memory of water' phenomenon is the effect of water, previously exposed to weak electromagnetic signals, on the distinctive patterns and handedness of colonies of certain bacteria. Here, the water retains the effect for at least 20 minutes after exposure to the field.

Extremely low frequency electromagnetic fields (ELF-EMF) have significant and lasting effects on liquid water. Using a weak field, adjusted to give a magnetic field of 45 μT, on glutamic acid solutions causes changes in the pH shifting towards the de-protonated species.

Using just water, FTIR-ATR spectroscopy showed that the lower energy part of the stretching absorbtion band (~3250 cm-1), which is related to the coherent fully-hydrogen bonded population, decreases. Stronger ELF-EMF fields (~0.15 T) were applied to water and its dielectric constant measured and compared with that of untreated water. It was found that the dielectric constant of the ELF-EMF field-treated water was 3.7 per cent higher than the control over the frequency range of 1-10 GHz, which may indicate a higher molecular polarisation in the treated water.

If electromagnetic effects do indeed influence the degree of structuring in water then it is clear that they may have an effect on health.

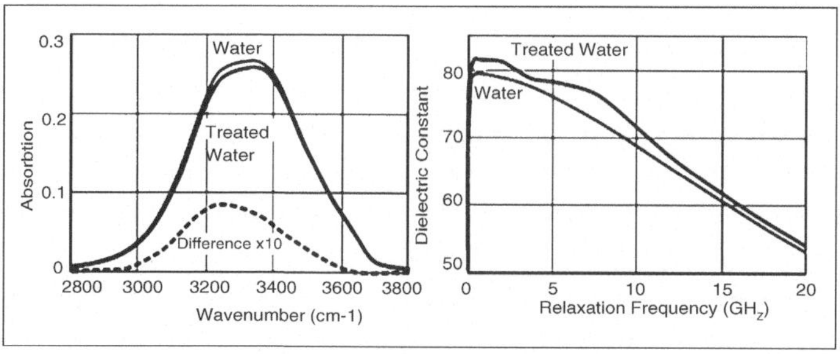

Fig. 8.6

The biological effects of microwaves, for example, have generally been analysed in terms of their very small heating effects. However, it should be recognised that there might be significant non-thermal effects (for example, due to the imposed re-orientation of water at the surfaces of biomolecular structures such as membranes. Similar effects on membranes have been proposed to occur due to magnetic and electric fields. Additionally as low-frequency, low level alternating electric fields have been found to affect the electrical conductivity of pure water the effects of living near power cables and microwave towers should, perhaps, not be thought harmless just because no theory for harm has been formally recognised. Even variations in the geomagnetic field may have some long-term exposure effects.

Other Related Effects

Recently, there has been some debate over 'digital biology'; a proposal from Jacques Benveniste (leader of the team that produced the controversial homeopathy paper) that 'specific molecular signals in the audio range' (hypothetically the 'beat' frequencies of water's infrared vibrations) may be heard, collected, transmitted (for example, by phone) and amplified to similarly affect other water molecules at a receiver. This unlikely idea is generally thought highly implausible. The data has, however, reportedly been independently confirmed but this has not yet been published (which may be rather problematic in the present skeptical climate). Note that experimental confirmation of the phenomenon may not necessarily confirm the proposed mechanism. Rather interestingly, however, electromagnetic emission has been detected during the freesing of supercooled water due to negative charging of the solid surface at the interface caused by surface ionisation of water molecules followed by preferential loss of hydrogen ions a consequence, perhaps, of the Costa Ribeiro effect.

It is not unreasonable, therefore, that similar effects may occur during changes in the structuring of liquid water. Also, it has been reported that microwave frequencies can also give rise to signals audible to radar operators. Possible confirmation of the important effects of electromagnetic fields may be found in a recent paper from Nobel prize-winning Luc Montagnier, who declared that quite dilute solutions (of DNA) show entirely different properties from the less diluted solutions, that seem to depend on interactions with the ambient electromagnetic field. This research, importantly, also appears to show that such effects can be transmitted through space from one container to another.

Belief in whether or not magnetic or electromagnetic fields can have any more permanent effect on water, and solutions, depends on the presence of a working hypothesis for their mode of action. Such hypotheses are emerging. On a cautionary note however, many studies either do not treat results with proper statistical rigour or do not use relevant 'untreated' material for comparison. Permanent changes to the structure of water are reported following exposure to resonant RLC (resistance inductance capacitance) circuits. The effects, however, are small and poorly reproducible and, as with some of the other studies mentioned here, should be viewed with the possibility that pathological science is at work.

CE Procedures

Samples were vacuum injected into a 100-μm diameter, 98-cm length capillary tube (volume 7.7 μl) for 2 s (injection volume 8.6 nl/s). The capillary tube had a detection window 66 cm from the injection site in an ISCO (Lincoln, NE) model 3850 electropherograph with an absorbance detector at 195 nm, absorbance maximum from 0.02–0.2 absorbance units, and a rise time of 3.2 s. The driving voltage was varied between 5 and 25 kV, corresponding to electric fields of 51 and 255 V/cm. The peaks were recorded on a chart recorder (The Recorder Company, Houston, TX) at 1 cm/min and 1 V full scale.

Molecular Radius

Estimates of molecular radius are based on the model of the NE-Asc complex (7) and the CPK molecular model system (8) of 1.25 cm/Å. For the 345 g/mol NE-Asc complex, the complex volume is estimated to be 0.63 nm3. The relationship between molecular weight (MW) and volume is therefore 0.00183 (MW) = nm3. For a sphere of volume $4\pi r^3/3$, this corresponds to a radius of 0.53 nm for the NE-Asc complex. The radii for the other molecules and complexes are calculated in the same way.

STARK EFFECT

the splitting of spectral lines in electric fields. The effect was discovered in 1913 by J. Stark while studying the spectrum of the hydrogen atom. Observed in the spectra of atoms and of other quantum systems, it results from a shift of a quantum system's energy levels and the splitting of the energy levels into sublevéis under the influence of an electric field. The splitting and the sublevéis are referred to as Stark splitting and Stark sublevéis. The term "Stark effect" is applied not only to the splitting of spectral lines in electric fields but also to the shift and splitting of energy levels in such fields.

The Stark effect has been explained on the basis of quantum mechanics. An atom (or some other quantum system) in a state with a given energy ε acquires additional energy Δε in an applied electric field E as a result of the polarizability of the atom's electron shell and the appearance of an induced dipole moment. A non-degenerate energy level, or an energy level to which one possible state of an atom corresponds, will have an energy of $\varepsilon + \Delta\varepsilon$ in a field E; that is, the level will shift. The various states of a degenerate energy level may acquire different additional energies $\Delta\varepsilon_a$; here, $\alpha = 1, 2..., g$, where g is the degree of degeneracy of the level. As a result, a degenerate level is split into Stark sublevéis, the number of which is equal to the number of different values of $\Delta\varepsilon_a$.

Thus, in an electric field, an energy level of an atom with a given angular momentum $M = (h/2\pi)\sqrt{J(J+1)}$ – where h is Planck's constant and J = 1, 2... is the quantum number of total angular momentum—is split into sublevéis characterised by different values of the magnetic quantum number mj, which represents the projection of M in the direction of the electric field. The same additional energy $\Delta\varepsilon$ corresponds to the values $+m_j$ and $+ m_j$. Therefore, all the Stark sublevéis except the sublevel with m = 0 turn out to have a twofold degeneracy, in contrast to the case of splitting in a magnetic field, where all the sublevéis are not degenerate.

A distinction is made between the linear Stark effect, where $\Delta\varepsilon$ is proportional to E, and the quadratic Stark effect, where $\Delta\varepsilon$ is proportional to E^2. In the linear effect, the pattern of the energy-level splitting and of the spectral lines produced upon transitions between the levels is symmetric. In the quadratic effect, the pattern is asymmetric.

The linear Stark effect is characteristic of hydrogen in electric fields that are not too strong. For example, in fields of $\sim 10^4$ volts per cm (V/cm), the effect amounts to a few thousandths of an electron volt. An energy level of a hydrogen atom with a given principal quantum number n is split symmetrically into $2n - 1$ equidistant sublevéis. The components of a spectral line that is split in a field E are polarised.

If the direction of E is perpendicular to an observer, some of the components—called the π components—are polarised parallel to the field, while the remaining components— known as the σ components—are polarised perpendicular to the field.

When observed in the direction longitudinal to the field, the π components do not appear and the cr components are replaced by unpolarised components. The intensities of the various components differ. The splitting of the H_a spectral line of hydrogen (the first line of the Balmer series) as a result of the Stark effect.

The linear Stark effect is also observed in hydrogen-like atoms (He^{+}, Li^{2+}, Be^{3+}...) and for highly excited states of other atoms; in a number of cases, the effect results in the appearance of forbidden lines. The quadratic Stark effect, which exhibits an asymmetric splitting pattern, is typical of many-electron atoms. The magnitude of the quadratic effect is small. For example, in fields of ~10^5 V/cm, the splitting amounts to a few ten-thousandths of an electron volt. The linear Stark effect is characteristic of molecules that are sufficiently symmetric and have a constant dipole moment. In other cases, the quadratic Stark effect is usually observed.

An important case of the Stark effect is the splitting of the electronic energy levels of an ion in a crystal lattice under the influence of the crystalline field E_{cr}, which is generated by surrounding ions. Such splitting may be as high as a few hundredths of an electron volt, is taken into account in crystal spectroscopy, and is essential for the operation of quantum mechanical amplifiers.

The Stark effect is also observed in variable electric fields. The change in the position of the Stark sublevéis in a variable field Emay be used to vary the frequency of a quantum transition in quantum-mechanical devices. An example is Stark modulation.

In particular, the influence of a rapidly varying electric field on the energy levels of atoms or ions determines the Stark broadening of spectral lines in a plasma.

The motion of plasma particles and the associated change in the distances between the particles lead to rapid changes in the electric field around each radiating particle.

As a result, the energy levels of atoms or ions shift by differing amounts when they are split, leading to the broadening of spectral lines in the emission spectra of a plasma. Stark broadening makes it possible to estimate the concentration of charged particles in a plasma, for example, in a stellar atmosphere.

9

Molecular Symmetry and Group Theory

A systematic treatment of symmetry in chemical systems within the mathematical framework known as group theory (the reason for the name will become apparent later on). Once we have classified the symmetry of a molecule, group theory provides a powerful set of tools that provide us with considerable insight into many of its chemical and physical properties. Some applications of group theory that will be covered in this course include:

- Predicting whether a given molecule will be chiral, or polar.
- Examining chemical bonding and visualising molecular orbitals.
- Predicting whether a molecule may absorb light of a given polarisation, and which spectroscopic transitions may be excited if it does.
- Investigating the vibrational motions of the molecule.

Some of these topics again, possibly in more detail, in later courses (notably Symmetry II, and for the more mathematically inclined amongst you, Supplementary Quantum Mechanics).

However, they will be introduced here to give you a fairly broad introduction to the capabilities and applications of group theory once we have worked through the basic principles and 'machinery' of the theory.

SYMMETRY OPERATIONS AND SYMMETRY ELEMENTS

A symmetry operation is an action that leaves an object looking the same after it has been carried out. For example, if we take a molecule of water and rotate it by 180° about an axis passing through the central O atom (between the two H atoms) it will look the same as before. It will also look the same if we reflect it through either of two mirror planes, as shown in the figure below:

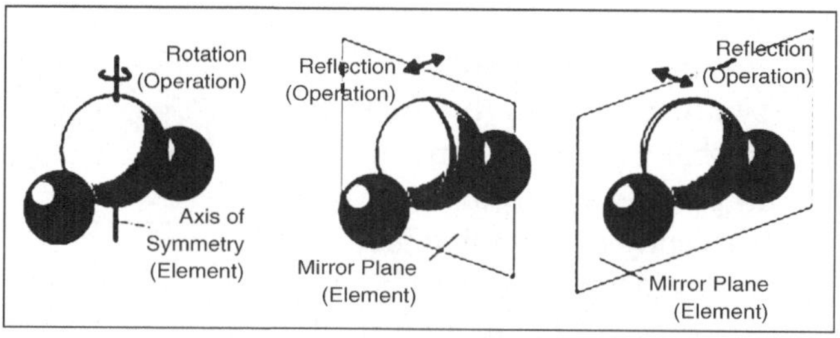

Fig. 9.1

Each symmetry operation has a corresponding symmetry element, which is the axis, plane, line or point with respect to which the symmetry operation is carried out. The symmetry element consists of all the points that stay in the same place when the symmetry operation is performed. In a rotation, the line of points that stay in the same place constitute a symmetry axis; in a reflection the points that remain unchanged make up a plane of symmetry.

The symmetry elements that a molecule may possess are:

- E - the identity. The identity operation consists of doing nothing, and the corresponding symmetry element is the entire molecule. Every molecule has at least this element.
- Cn - an n-fold axis of rotation. Rotation by 360°/n leaves the molecule unchanged. The H_2O molecule above has a C_2 axis. Some molecules have more than one Cn axis, in which case the one with the highest value of n is called the principal axis. Note that by convention rotations are counterclockwise about the axis.

- σ - a plane of symmetry. Reflection in the plane leaves the molecule looking the same. In a molecule that also has an axis of symmetry, a mirror plane that includes the axis is called a vertical mirror plane and is labelled σ_v, while one perpendicular to the axis is called a horizontal mirror plane and is labelled σ h. A vertical mirror plane that bisects the angle between two C2 axes is called a dihedral mirror plane, σ d.
- i - a centre of symmetry. Inversion through the centre of symmetry leaves the molecule unchanged. Inversion consists of passing each point through the centre of inversion and out to the same distance on the other side of the molecule. An example of a molecule with a centre of inversion is shown in fig.9.2.

Fig. 9.2

- Sn - an n-fold improper rotation axis (also called a rotary-reflection axis). The rotary reflection operation consists of rotating through an angle 360°/n about the axis, followed by reflecting in a plane perpendicular to the axis. Note that S_1 is the same as reflection and S_2 is the same as inversion. The molecule shown above has two S_2 axes. The identity E and rotations Cn are symmetry operations that could actually be carried out on a molecule. For this reason they are called proper symmetry operations. Reflections, inversions and improper rotations can only be imagined (it is not actually possible to turn a molecule into its mirror image or to invert it without some fairly drastic rearrangement of chemical bonds) and as such, are termed improper symmetry operations.

Chirality

One example of symmetry in chemistry that you will already have come across is found in the isomeric pairs of molecules called enantiomers. Enantiomers are non-superimposable mirror images of each other, and one consequence of this symmetrical relationship is that they rotate the plane of polarised light passing through them in opposite directions. Such molecules are said to be chiral2, meaning that they cannot be superimposed on their mirror image.

Formally, the symmetry element that precludes a molecule from being chiral is a rotation-reflection axis Sn. Such an axis is often implied by other symmetry elements present in a group. For example, a point group that has Cn and sh as elements will also have Sn. Similarly, a centre of inversion is equivalent to $S_{2.}$ As a rule of thumb, a molecule definitely cannot have be chiral if it has a centre of inversion or a mirror plane of any type (σ_h, σ_v or σ_d), but if these symmetry elements are absent the molecule should be checked carefully for an Sn axis before it is assumed to be chiral.

MOLECULAR SYMMETRY

Group Theory, which is the systematic treatment of symmetry is an extremely powerful tool which simplifies the process of obtaining a variety of information about molecules. Molecules are classified according to their symmetry properties. Once the properties are identified, the molecule is assigned its point group. The physical properties of the molecules, such as molecular orbitals, vibrational modes, hybridisation of atomic orbitals, etc., must all have the same symmetry properties as the point group to which the molecule belongs.

Symmetry elements are properties which are related to the structure of the molecule. They include mirror planes, axes of rotation, centers of inversion and improper axes of rotation. (An improper axis of rotation is a rotation followed by a reflection perpendicular to the rotational axis.) Symmetry operations are actions which places the molecule in an orientation which appears to be identical to its initial orientation. Symmetry operations include rotation, reflection, inversion, rotation followed by reflection, and identity. The identity operation simply leaves the molecule where it is. All molecules have the identity operation. This information is summarised in Table 9.1.

Table 9.1

Symmetry Element	Operation	Symbol
	identity	E
n-fold axis of symmetry	rotation by $2\pi/n$	C_n
mirror plane	reflection	σ
center of inversion	inversion	i
n-fold axis of improper rotation	rotation by $2\pi/n$ followed by reflection perpendicular to the rotational axis	S_n

Molecules are assigned to point groups based on the number and orientation of their symmetry elements. A scheme for determining the correct point group is provided in your text. Highly symmetrical molecules (octahedrons or tetrahedrons) have their own point groups (O_h and Td respectively). Square planar molecules or octahedrons with different atoms on one axis are in the group D_{4h}. Trigonal planar and trigonal bipyramidal molecules are D_{3h}.

SYMMETRY CLASSIFICATION OF MOLECULES

It is only possible for certain combinations of symmetry elements to be present in a molecule (or any other object). As a result, we may group together molecules that possess the same symmetry elements and classify molecules according to their symmetry. These groups of symmetry elements are called point groups (due to the fact that there is at least one point in space that remains unchanged no matter which symmetry operation from the group is applied). There are two systems of notation for labelling symmetry groups, called the Schoenflies and Hermann-Mauguin (or International) systems. The symmetry of individual molecules is usually described using the Schoenflies notation, and we shall be using this notation for the remainder of the course1.

SYMMETRY AND PHYSICAL PROPERTIES

Carrying out a symmetry operation on a molecule must not change any of its physical properties. It turns out that this has some interesting consequences, allowing us to predict whether or not a molecule may be chiral or polar on the basis of its point group.

Polarity

For a molecule to have a permanent dipole moment, it must have an asymmetric charge distribution. The point group of the molecule not only determines whether the molecule may have a dipole moment, but also in which direction(s) it may point. If a molecule has a C_n axis with n>1, it cannot have a dipole moment perpendicular to the axis of rotation (for example, a C_2 rotation would interchange the ends of such a dipole moment and reverse the polarity, which is not allowed – rotations with higher values of n would also change the direction in which the dipole points). Any dipole must lie parallel to a Cn axis. Also, if the point group of the molecule contains any symmetry operation that would interchange the two ends of the molecule, such as a sh mirror plane or a C_2 rotation perpendicular to the principal axis, then there cannot be a dipole moment along the axis. The only groups compatible with a dipole moment are C_n, Cnv and C_s. In molecules belonging to Cn or Cnv the dipolemust lie along the axis of rotation.

APPLICATIONS OF SYMMETRY

Certain physical properties of molecules are clearly linked to molecular symmetry. Molecules which are symmetrically bonded to the same elements will not be polar, due to the canceling dipole moments. Likewise, chirality (left or right handedness) is clearly a symmetry property. Chirality can only be present in molecules which lack an improper axis or rotation. Molecules with a center of inversion or a mirror plane cannot be chiral.

The symmetry properties of molecules are tabulated on character tables. A character table lists the symmetry elements of the point group, along with characters which are consistent with the different symmetry operations of the group. The table characterises how various atomic properties (the symmetry of atomic orbitals, rotations about axes, etc.) are transformed by the symmetry operations of the group. The table for the C_{3v} group is provided below. This group includes molecules such as ammonia, where there is a three-fold axis of rotation which also includes mirror planes (called vertical planes since they include the axis of rotation).

Table 9.2

C_{3v}	E	$2C_3$	$3_{\sigma v}$		
A_1	1	1	1	z $x^2 + y^2$, z^2	
A_2	1	1	−1	R_z	
E	2	−1	0	(x,y) (x^2-y^2,xy), (zx,yz)	(R_x,R_y)

There are many important features to the character table. The standard convention is to specify the major (if there is more than one) axis of rotation as the z axis. You'll note that the table says there are $2C_3$ axis. These represent rotation by 120° and rotation by 240° (or by -120°). There are 3 vertical planes of symmetry, each going through the central atom and one of the other atoms. The symmetry properties of each of these planes is the same, so they are grouped together. The characters (usually integers and zeros) represent how various orbitals or rotations are transformed by the various symmetry operations of the group.

The set of characters in the A_1 set show that the p_z orbital on the central atom is unchanged by all of the symmetry operations. When the orbital is unchanged, a character of +1 is used. Note that s orbitals, which are totally symmetrical always transform as the A_1 set and are usually omitted from the list on the right. The list to the right of the table also indicates that the functions $x^2 + y^2$ and z^2 also remain unchanged by all the symmetry operations of the group, and thus are represented by the A_1 character set. If an orbital is unchanged, it will have a character of +1, if it changes sign, the character will be -1. If a more complicated change occurs, the character will be 0.

The second set of characters, A_2, has the same symmetry properties as rotation about the z axis. That is, rotation will remain the same under the operations of identity or rotation about the principal axis of rotation, but will be reversed by the mirror plane which runs through the z axis. The last set of characters, E, has a few interesting features. The character of 2 in the first column indicates that it is double degenerate. This means that pairs of orbitals or rotations will be represented in this character set. The use of parenthesis in the column to the right of the table indicates that the x and y axes, together, are represented by this set of characters. (Likewise for the other orbitals and rotations paired within the parenthesis.)

Determination of Hybridisation

Symmetry considerations can be used to determine the hybridisation of the central atom. The process involves obtaining a set of characters which transform as vectors representing the sigma bonds in the molecule. The set of characters, called a reducible set, is a linear combination of the irreducible representations found in the character table for the molecule.

The method can be outlines as follows:

- Determine the point group of the molecule.
- Consider the bonds as vectors, and determine how they are transformed by the symmetry operations of the group. The character for each operation will simply be the number of vectors which remain in position while each symmetry operation is performed. This set of characters is called a reducible set.
- Reduce the representation obtained into a linear combination of sets which appear in the character table for the group.

Reduction of Representations

The process outlined above will yield a set of characters which can be reduced to combinations of the sets of characters in the table for the appropriate point group. In simple point groups, the reduction can sometimes be done by inspection. In any case, the process of reducing representations is quite simple. It is determined using the following formula.

$$ni = \frac{1}{h}\sum_{c} g_c x_i x_r$$

where:

ni is the number of times an irreducible representation i occurs in the reducible representation

h is the order of the group (h= total number of operations in the group)
c = the class of operations
g_c is the number of operations in the class
c_i is the character of the irreducible representation for the operations of the class
cr is the character for the reducible representation for the operations of the class

- *Problem:* Determine the characters for the reducible character set which represents the hybrid orbitals of of the molecule BF_3 (point group D_{3h}). Reduce the representation to obtain the hybridisation of boron in the molecule.

D_{3h}	E	$2C_3$	$3C_2$	σ_h	$2S_3$	$3\sigma_v$		
A_1'	1	1	1	1	1	1		x^2+y^2, z^2
A_2'	1	1	−1	1	1	−1	R_z	
E'	2	−1	0	2	−1	0	(x, y)	(x^2-y^2, xy)
A_1''	1	1	1	−1	−1	−1		
A_2''	1	1	−1	−1	−1	1	z	
E''	2	−1	0	−2	1	0	(R_x, R_y)	(xz, yz)

The character table for the D_{3h} point group has an order (h) of 12, because there are a total of 12 symmetry operations for the group. The above table and the worksheet below can be used to reduce the representation for the hybrid orbitals into the linear combination of some of the irreducible representations on the table above. The orbitals corresponding to these irreducible representations will be listed on the right side of the character table.

Table 9.3

D_{3h}	E	$2C_3$	$3C_2$	σ_h	$2S_3$	$3\sigma_v$	h=12	
T_r							Σ	Σ/12
A_1'								
A_2'								
E'								
A_1''								
A_2''								
E''								

A similar treatment can be performed to consider the orbitals used in π bonding in the molecule BF_3. Since the z axis is the one perpendicular to the plane of the molecule, we can consider how the p_z orbitals on each of the fluorine atoms are transformed by the symmetry operations of the group. A character of +1 indicates that the orbital is unchanged by the operation. A character of -1 indicates that the orbital has been inverted, and a character of 0 indicates that the orbitals on different atoms have been interchanged. This produces the reducible set below (Table 9.4).

Table 9.4

D_{3h}	E	$2C_3$	$3C_2$	σh	$2S_3$	$3\sigma_v$
Tr	3	0	–1	–3	0	1

The negative sign for the s_h element indicates that this representation will reduce to double primed (') reducible representations. The set reduces to: $A_{2'}$ + E′. Since the pz orbital on boron belongs to the $A_{2'}$ set, this represents a p bonding molecular orbital. Since the E′ set does not have any boron orbitals as its basis (the d orbitals are much to high in energy), the E′ set represents non-bonding molecular orbitals. A close examination of the characters of the $A_{2'}$ set shows that the changes sign upon rotation about the C_2 axis, upon reflection within the plane of the molecule, and improper rotation. This represents all of the p_z orbitals overlapping on all four atoms to produce a bonding p orbital, or all fluorines having the positive lobe upward and the boron having the positive lobe downward to form an antibonding p orbital. Determining the appearance and relative energies of molecular orbitals is a bit more complicated, and will not be covered further in this course.

DETERMINING MOLECULAR VIBRATIONS

Group theory can also be used to determine the types of vibrations present in a molecule, and whether they will be observed in the UV or Raman spectra of the molecule. A reducible representation which represents all of the types of molecular motion is produced. This representation includes translations, rotations and vibrations. It is obtained by examining how the cartesian coordinates (x, y, and z axes) are transformed by the symmetry operations of the group. For any molecule, the total number of degrees of freedom (rotations, translations and vibrations) is equal to 3N, where N is the number of atoms in the molecule. For linear molecules, 3 of these degrees of freedom arise from translations along the x, y and z axes, and two are the result of molecular rotations. For non-linear molecules, there are three degrees of translational freedom and three degrees of rotational freedom.

The results are summarised below.

- Linear Molecules: modes of vibrations = 3N-5
- Non-linear Molecules: modes of vibrations = 3N-6

These normal modes of molecular vibration are collective motions of the atoms that are independent of each other. They must be consistent with the symmetry for the point group of the molecule, and they can often be reduced to bond stretches or bends.

Using Group Theory to Determine Molecular Vibrations

The symmetry of all molecular motion is obtained by viewing each atom as the center of 3 intersecting axes (x, y and z). The characters of the reducible representation will be related to the changes in these axes as each symmetry operation is performed. If an atom is shifted by a symmetry operation, its contribution to the character is 0. If an axis on an atom is shifted to its negative, that atom contributes a -1 towards the character for that operation.

If an axis is unchanged by a symmetry operation, its contribution towards the character for that operations is +1. Once the characters are obtained, they are reduced by the previously described method. A total of 3N representations are obtained. From this set of irreducible representations, the sets relating to molecular translations and rotations are eliminated, leaving only representations due to molecular vibrations.

The method will be illustrated using water, or any molecule belonging to the C_{2v} point group. The character table for the group is provided below. The orientation of the molecule is such that the molecule lies in the xz plane. The C_2 axis of rotation is along the z axis of the oxygen atom.

Table 9.5

C_{2v}	E	C_2	$\sigma_{(xz)}$	$\sigma_{(yz)}$	
A_1	1	1	1	1	z; x^2, y^2, z^2
A_2	1	1	–1	–1	R_z; xy
B_1	1	–1	1	–1	x, R_y; xz
B_2	1	–1	–1	1	y, R_x; yz

If each atom is considered as the center of a set of cartesian coordinates, the identity element will leave all 9 axes unchanged, so the character will be 9. The C_2 axis passes through the O atom along the z axis. It exchanges both hydrogens, and reverses the x and y axes on the oxygen while leaving the z axis unchanged. As a result, the character for this operations will be –1 (+1 for the z axis, and –1 for the y axis and the x axis).

The xz mirror plane in which the entire molecule lies will cause each atom to have a reversed x axis while maintaining the x and z axes. Each atom contributes +1 towards the character, or a total of +3 for the three atoms. The mirror plane which lies in the yz plane passes through the oxygen atom and interchanges the hydrogen atoms. The y and z axes on the oxygen atom are left unchanged, while the y axis is reversed. Thus the character for σ_{yz} is +1. The reducible representation for all modes of molecular motion is summarised on the worksheet below.

Table 9.6

C_{2v}	E	C_2	$\sigma_{(xz)}$	$\sigma_{(yz)}$	h=4	
T_{3N}	9	–1	3	1	Σ	Σ/4
A_1						
A_2						
B_1						
B_2						

The set reduces to: 3 A_1 + 1 A_2 + 3 B_1 + 2 B_2. These representations include molecular translations and rotations. Translations transform as x, y and z, so A_1, B_1 and B_2 representations can be subtracted. Likewise, rotations transform as R_x, R_y and R_z, so the representations A_2, B_1 and B2 can be subtracted. The resulting molecular vibrations have the following symmetry: 2 A_1 and B_1.

The vibrations consistent with the A_1 symmetry are the symmetrical stretch and the symmetrical bend. These are illustrated below and labeled as n1 and n2. The vibration mode with B_1 symmetry is the third representation. The wave numbers for each vibration can only be determined experimentally.

Predicting Infrared and Raman Activity

Once the symmetry of the molecular vibrations has been obtained, predicting whether the vibrations can be seen in the infrared and/or Raman spectra is quite simple. Vibrations which are infrared active much involve a change in the dipole moment of the molecule. The dipole vector transforms as x, y or z.

Since the symmetry representations for the vibrations in water has either z (for the 2 A_1 modes) or x (for the B_1 mode) as a basis, all three bands will infrared active. For vibrations to appear in Raman spectra, the polarizability of the molecule must change. Polarizability transforms as x^2, y^2, z^2, xy, yz, or xz.

Examination of the basis functions for each of the vibrations in water show that each vibration will also be Raman active. Thus, both the IR and Raman spectra will show the same three bands relating to vibration of the water molecule.

For molecules with a center of inversion, there is an exclusion rule. For molecules with a center of inversion, none of its modes can be both IR and Raman active. As a result, the coincidence (or lack thereof) of vibration frequencies in the IR and Raman spectra can easily be used to determine if certain molecules are cis or trans. For example, a square planar molecule of the general formula MX_2Y_2, can exist with cis or trans symmetry.

If the molecule exists as the trans isomer, it will posses a center of inversion, and hence bands which are seen in the IR spectrum of the molecule will not appear in the Raman spectrum.

SYMMETRY OPERATIONS AND SYMMETRY ELEMENTS

SYMMETRY ELEMENTS AND OPERATIONS

All molecules can be described in terms of their symmetry. Molecules may contain symmetry elements (point, line, plane). Reflection, rotation, and inversion are symmetry operations (movement of the molecules such that after the movement, all the atoms of the molecules is coincidental with equivalent atom of the molecule in original).

Table 9.9 Elements and Operations

Element	Operation	Symbol
Identity	Identity	E
Symmetry plane	Reflection in the plane	σ
Inversion center	Inversion of a point x,y,z to -x,-y,-z	i
Proper axis	Rotation by (360/n)°	C_n
Improper axis	1. Rotation by (360/n)° 2. Reflection in plane perpendicular to	S_n
⊥ rotation axis		

Symmetry operations are geometrical operations applied to molecules (or better, molecular models). The application of a symmetry operation to a particular molecular geometry produces a spatial orientation which is indistinguishable from the initial orientation. For example, rotating a water (H_2O) molecule by 180° about an axis bisecting the H-O-H bond angle will produce a orientation of that molecule which looks the same as its original orientation. In fact, this rotation leads to an exchange of both protons H_a and H_b, but as these two protons may not be distinguished from each other, the resulting orientation of the water molecule is equivalent to the initial one. Another rotation of 180° about this axis leads to an orientation which is identical to the starting geometry.

The five basic symmetry operations that need to be considered are identity, rotation, reflection (mirroring), inversion, and rotary reflection. The symmetry properties of molecules are described as the set (combination) of valid symmetry operations for its molecular geometry. For each symmetry operation there is a corresponding symmetry element, with respect to which the symmetry operation is applied.

For example, the rotation (a symmetry operation) is carried out around an axis which is the corresponding symmetry element. Other symmetry elements are planes (for reflections) and points (for inversions). All spatial points along these symmetry elements (*i.e.,* the symmetry plane, axis, or center of inversion) do not change their positions during the corresponding symmetry operation.

Common to all symmetry operations is that the geometrical center of a molecule does not change its position, all symmetry elements must intersect in this center. In fact, out of the five symmetry operations only two (rotation and rotary reflection) are sufficient to describe all symmetry properties of molecules.

Different (valid) combinations of symmetry operations that leave at least a single common point (the molecular center) unchanged give rise to the so called point groups. When considering crystals, additional symmetries arising from translations through three-dimensional space need to be considered, giving rise to the more extensive space groups.

The basic symmetry operations are:

- **Identity Operation E**

The identity operation does nothing and leaves any molecule unchanged, the corresponding symmetry element is the entire object (molecule) itself. The reason for including this symmetry operation is that some molecules have only this symmetry element and no other symmetry properties. Another reason is the logical completeness of the mathematical description of group theory.

All molecules which do not have any other symmetry element than the identity operation must belong to the C_1 point group, and thus must be chiral. Many natural compounds like carbohydrates and a-amino acids belong to this group.

However, we will see, that all molecules belonging to the C_1 point group must be chiral, but the reverse conclusion is not true. Chiral molecules may not necessarily be a member of the C_1 point group family.

- **Inversion i**

The inversion (the symmetry operation) through a center of inversion (the symmetry element, which must be identical to the center of geometry of the molecule) takes any point in the molecule, moves its to the center, and then moves it out the same distance on the other side again (sometimes called point reflection). The benzene molecule, a cube, and spheres do have a center of inversion, whereas a tetrahedron does not.

At this point, it should be noted, that molecules which contain a center of inversion as the only symmetry element (except for the identity operation, which occurs in all molecules), belong to the Ci point group. However, if a center of inversion is present in a molecular geometry, the corresponding compound must be achiral, irrespective of any other type or number of symmetry elements (mirror planes, rotation or rotary-reflection axes) which may be present in addition.

- **Reflection σ**

The reflection (the symmetry operation) in a plane of symmetry or mirror plane σ (the corresponding symmetry element) produces a mirror image geometry of the molecule. The mirror plane bisects the molecule and must include its center of geometry. If this plane is parallel to the principal axis, it is called a vertical mirror plane denoted σ_v, if it is perpendicular to the principal axis (and bisects it in the molecular center of geometry), it is denoted a horizontal mirror plane σ_h. Vertical mirror planes bisecting the angle between two C_n axes are called dihedral mirror planes σ_d (these mirror planes all include principal axis and intersect in it).

The benzene molecule features all three different types of mirror planes.

Molecules which contain a single mirror plane as the only symmetry element belong to the C_s point group, but any number of mirror planes will automatically result in achiral molecular geometries.

- **n-Fold Rotation C_n**

The n-fold rotation (the symmetry operation) about a n-fold axis of symmetry (the corresponding symmetry element) produces molecular orientations indistinguishable from the initial for each rotation of 360°/n (clockwise and counter-clockwise). A water molecule has a single C_2 axis bisecting the H-O-H bond angle, and benzene has one C_6 axis (amongst one C_3 axis and seven C_2 axes of which the C_3 and one C_2 axis coincide with the C_6 axis). Linear molecules display a C_∞ axis (any infinitely small rotation about this axis produces unchanged orientations), and perfect spheres posses an infinite number of symmetry axes along any diameter with all possible integral values of n.

If a molecule has one (or more) rotation axes C_n or S_n, the axis with the greatest n is called the principal axis.

- **n-Fold Rotary Reflection S_n**

The n-fold rotary reflection (or n-fold improper rotation, the symmetry operation) about an n-fold rotary reflection axis (or n-fold axis of improper rotation) is composed of two successive geometry transformations: first, a rotation through 360°/n about the axis of that rotation, and second, reflection through a plane perpendicular (and through the molecular center of geometry) to that axis. Neither of these two operations (rotation or reflection) alone is a valid symmetry operation, but only the outcome of the combination of both transformations.

For example, a methane molecule has three S_4 axes (amongst other symmetry elements not shown in the image on the right). Any molecule featuring a S_n axes must be achiral. In fact, the most general description of chirality is the absence of any Sn rotary reflection in a molecular geometry, as we will see at the end of this page, this definition also includes inversion centers (= S_2 axis) and mirror planes (= S_1 axis).

Examples for the different basic symmetry operations and symmetry elements are given in the scheme below:

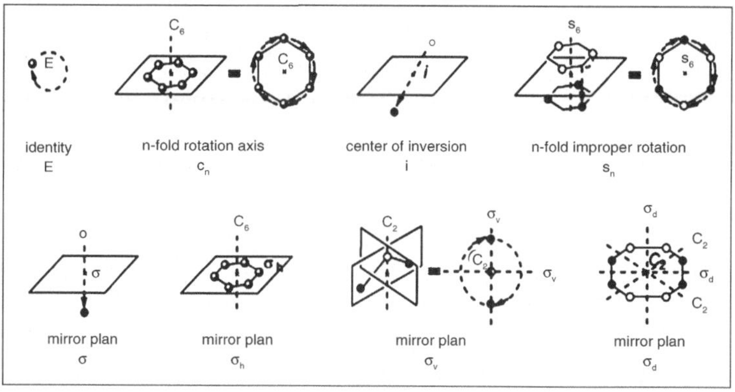

Fig. 9.3

EQUIVALENCE OF SYMMETRY OPERATIONS

Out of the five symmetry operations only two (rotation and rotary reflection) are sufficient to describe all symmetry properties of molecules. The identity operation is equivalent to a C_1 axis of rotation, as rotation of all objects around 360° about any axis produces the initial orientation only. On the other hand, a mirror plane is equivalent to a S_1 axis of rotary-reflection perpendicular to that plane. In addition, a center of inversion can be represented by a S_2 axis of improper rotation with any arbitrary orientation of this axis (all axes must intersect in the inversion center, which also must be the center of geometry for any molecule).

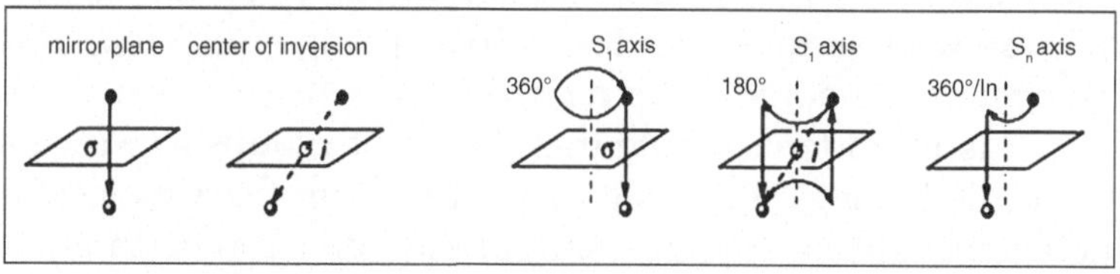

Fig. 9.4

Combination of Symmetry Operations

Symmetry operations may not be combined arbitrarily with each other, but only in a limited number of variations which are the so called point groups. Some symmetry operations implicitly imply others, as for example any S_4 or C_4 axis must be accompanied by a parallel C_2 axis. For example in benzene, the principal C_6 axis simultaneously must be a C_3 and a C_2 axis of symmetry, too. Similarly, any Sn axis with odd n is identical to a C_n axis in conjunction with a horizontal mirror plane σ_h.

However, certain combinations of some symmetry operations implicitly generate other symmetries. For example, the combination of any C_n axis with even n, together with a center of inversion i implicitly generates a horizontal mirror plane σ_h (which is perpendicular to the C_n axis and runs through the inversion center). Similarly, the combination of any C_n axis with a vertical mirror plane sv must imply (n – 1) additional vertical mirror planes σ_v. In addition, combinations of two rotation axes or two rotary-reflection axes must imply a new rotation axis, and combining a rotation axis with a rotary-reflection generates another rotary-reflection axis.

Point Groups

The classification of molecules (better: molecular geometries) is done by collecting all their inherent symmetry properties, and putting together those with identical symmetry elements in a certain point group. The names of these point groups are determined by the symmetry elements they posses. For example, chloroform features a threefold rotational axis (C_3) as well as three vertical mirror planes (σ_v), and thus belongs to the point group named C_{3v}.

It is important to note that the point groups to which a molecule belongs ultimately depends on its exact molecular geometry and its specific configuration and conformation.*) Without knowledge of the exact configuration or conformation, the determination of its point group is impossible. For example the staggered and ecliptic conformations of ethane, or the chair and boat conformations of cyclohexane have different symmetry properties. Similarly, the stereoisomers cis- and trans-1,2-dichlorocyclopropane have different configurations and therefore different symmetry properties belonging to different point groups.

On the other hand, if a molecule is said to belong to a certain point group, we may gain important knowledge on its three-dimensional geometry and its (very often, but not necessarily) low-energy conformation. Transition states are often said to have a certain symmetry, which may imply details on the simultaneity of the bond-breaking and/or bond-forming processes.

For example, the racemisation of the chiral helicene (left- or right-handed helix with point group C_2, respectively) proceeds through an achiral transition state featuring mirror symmetry (point group C_s). Animated examples for this racemisation process can be found on this web site (movies with MPG format or online animations using Jmol):

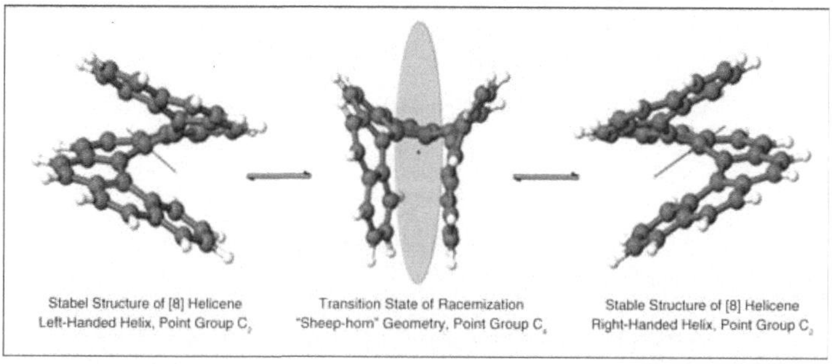

Fig. 9.5

The term configuration describes the three-dimensional connectivity of atoms in molecules and stereoisomers (*e.g.*, *cis*- and *trans*-1,2-dichlorocyclopropane), whereas the conformation describes the exact 3D-arrangment of all atoms in molecules (*e.g.*, the rotameric forms of ethane or chair/boat-conformations of cyclohexane). Below a table of all so called 32 crystallographic point groups is provided, together with a list of their essential symmetry elements. In this symmetry section, there is also a flowchart scheme provided, which allow the determination of the corresponding point group for any arbitrary molecular geometry.

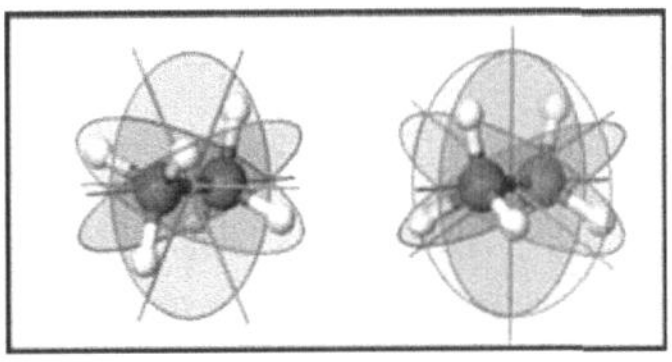

Fig. 9.6 Symmetry Elements of Ethane (Staggered and Ecliptic Conformations)

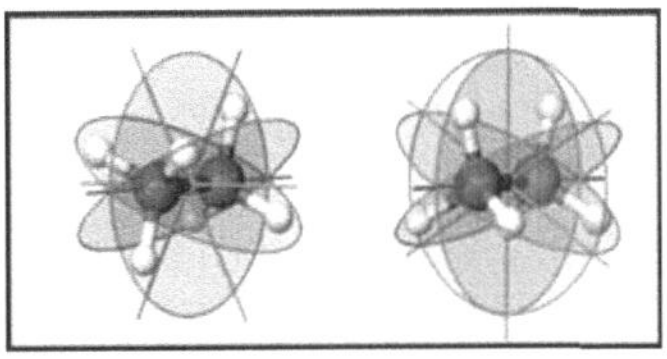

Fig. 9.7 Symmetry Elements of Cyclohexane (Chair and Boat Conformations)

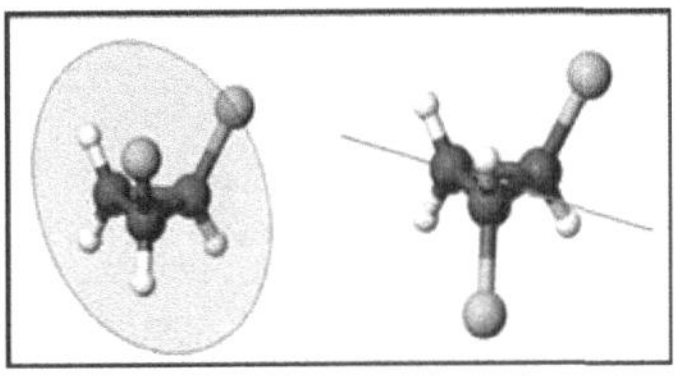

Fig. 9.8 Symmetry Elements of 1,2-dichlorocyclopropane (Cis- and trans-configuration)

SYMMETRY OPERATIONS AND ELEMENTS

A Symmetry operation is an operation that can be performed either physically or imaginatively that results in no change in the appearance of an object. Again it is emphasised that in crystals, the symmetry is internal, that is it is an ordered geometrical arrangement of atoms and molecules on the crystal lattice. But, since the internal symmetry is reflected in the external form of perfect crystals, we are going to concentrate on external symmetry, because this is what we can observe.

There are 3 types of symmetry operations: rotation, reflection, and inversion. We will look at each of these in turn.

ROTATIONAL SYMMETRY

If an object can be rotated about an axis and repeats itself every 90o of rotation then it is said to have an axis of 4-fold rotational symmetry. The axis along which the rotation is performed is an element of symmetry referred to as a rotation axis. The following types of rotational symmetry axes are possible in crystals.

- **1-Fold Rotation Axis** - An object that requires rotation of a full 360° in order to restore it to its original appearance has no rotational symmetry. Since it repeats itself 1 time every 360° it is said to have a 1-fold axis of rotational symmetry.

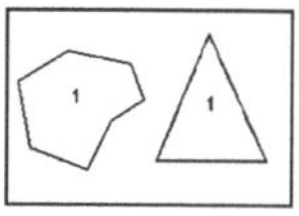

- **2-fold Rotation Axis** - If an object appears identical after a rotation of 180o, that is twice in a 360° rotation, then it is said to have a 2-fold rotation axis (360/180 = 2).

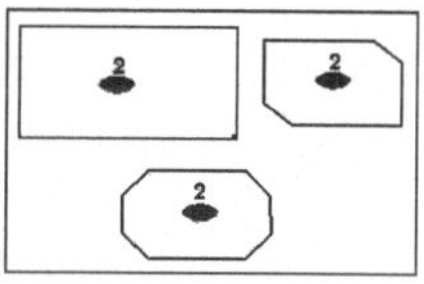

  Note that in these examples the axes we are referring to are imaginary lines that extend towards you perpendicular to the page or blackboard. A filled oval shape represents the point where the 2-fold rotation axis intersects the page.

This symbolism will be used for a 2-fold rotation axis throughout the lectures and in your text.

- **3-Fold Rotation Axis** - Objects that repeat themselves upon rotation of 120° are said to have a 3-fold axis of rotational symmetry (360/120 =3), and they will repeat 3 times in a 360° rotation. A filled triangle is used to symbolise the location of 3-fold rotation axis.

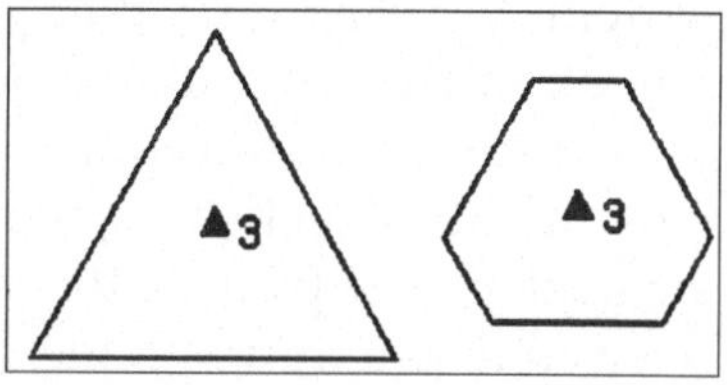

- **4-Fold Rotation Axis** - If an object repeats itself after 90° of rotation, it will repeat 4 times in a 360°

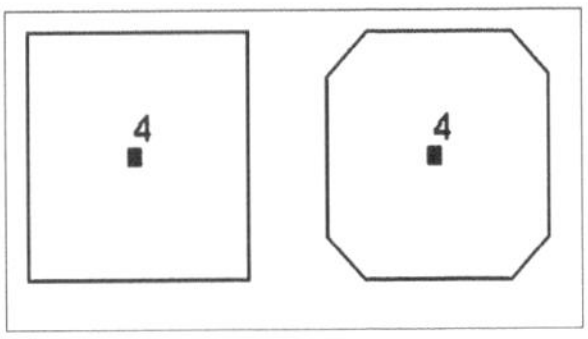

rotation, as illustrated previously. A filled square is used to symbolise the location of 4-fold axis of rotational symmetry.

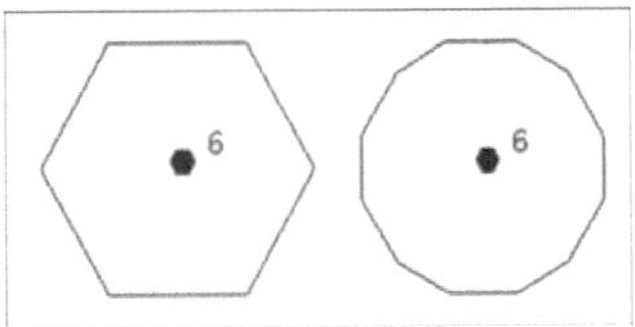

- **6-Fold Rotation Axis** - If rotation of 60° about an axis causes the object to repeat itself, then it has 6-fold axis of rotational symmetry (360/60=6). A filled hexagon is used as the symbol for a 6-fold rotation axis.

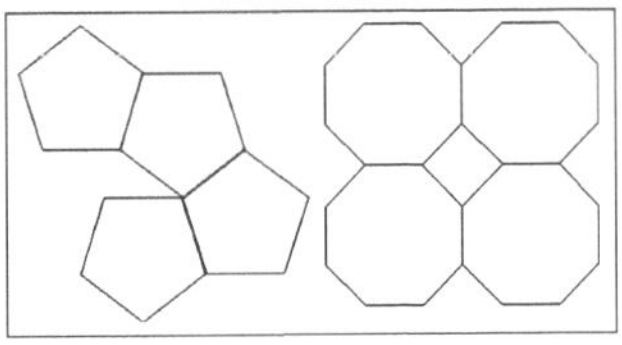

Although objects themselves may appear to have 5-fold, 7-fold, 8-fold, or higher-fold rotation axes, these are not possible in crystals. The reason is that the external shape of a crystal is based on a geometric arrangement of atoms. Note that if we try to combine objects with 5-fold and 8-fold apparent symmetry, that we cannot combine them in such a way that they completely fill space.

MIRROR SYMMETRY

A mirror symmetry operation is an imaginary operation that can be performed to reproduce an object. The operation is done by imagining that you cut the object in half, then place a mirror next to one of the halves of the object along the cut. If the reflection in the mirror reproduces the other half of the object, then the object is said to have mirror symmetry. The plane of the mirror is an element of symmetry referred to as a mirror plane, and is symbolised with the letter m. As an example, the human body is an object that approximates mirror symmetry, with the mirror plane cutting through the center of the head, the center of nose and down to the groin.

The rectangles shown below have two planes of mirror symmetry.

The rectangle on the left has a mirror plane that runs vertically on the page and is perpendicular to the page. The rectangle on the right has a mirror plane that runs horizontally and is perpendicular to the page. The dashed parts of the rectangles below show the part the rectangles that would be seen as a reflection in the mirror.

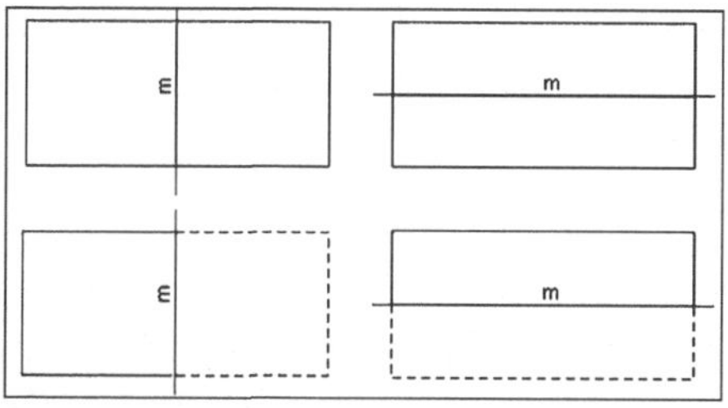

The rectangles shown above have two planes of mirror symmetry. Three dimensional and more complex objects could have more. For example, the hexagon shown above, not only has a 6-fold rotation axis, but has 6 mirror planes.

Center of Symmetry

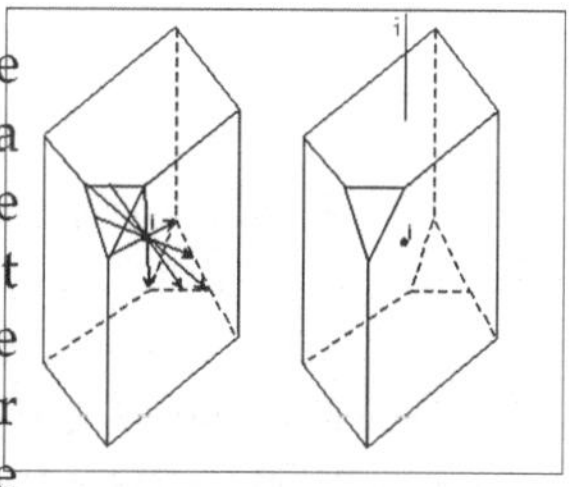

Another operation that can be performed is inversion through a point. In this operation lines are drawn from all points on the object through a point in the center of the object, called a symmetry center (symbolised with the letter 'i'). The lines each have lengths that are equidistant from the original points. When the ends of the lines are connected, the original object is reproduced inverted from its original appearance. In the diagram shown here, only a few such lines are drawn for the small triangular face. The right hand diagram shows the object without the imaginary lines that reproduced the object.

If an object has only a center of symmetry, we say that it has a 1 fold rotoinversion axis. Such an axis has the symbol $\bar{1}$, as shown in the right hand diagram above. Note that crystals that have a center of symmetry will exhibit the property that if you place it on a table there will be a face on the top of the crystal that will be parallel to the surface of the table and identical to the face resting on the table.

Rotoinversion

Combinations of rotation with a center of symmetry perform the symmetry operation of rotoinversion. Objects that have rotoinversion symmetry have an element of symmetry called a rotoinversion axis.

A 1-fold rotoinversion axis is the same as a center of symmetry. Other possible rotoinversion are as follows:

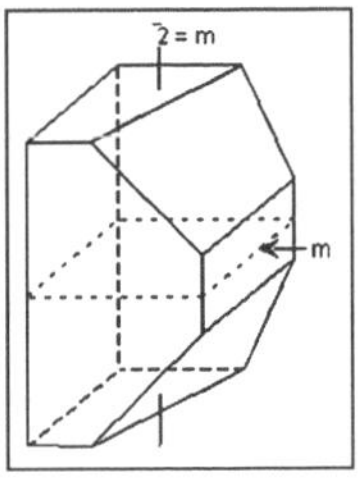

- **2-fold Rotoinversion** - The operation of 2-fold rotoinversion involves first rotating the object by 180° then inverting it through an inversion center. This operation is equivalent to having a mirror plane perpendicular to the 2-fold rotoinversion axis. A 2-fold rotoinversion axis is symbolised as a 2 with a bar over the top, and would be pronounced as 'bar 2'. But, since this the equivalent of a mirror plane, m, the bar 2 is rarely used.

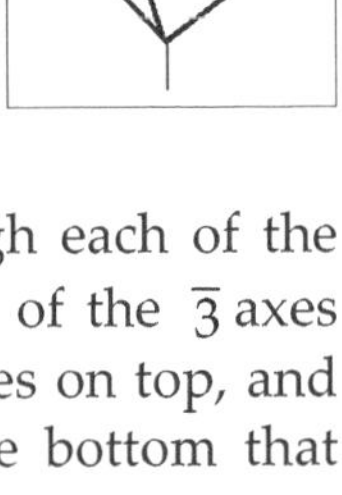

- **3-fold Rotoinversion** - This involves rotating the object by 120° (360/3 = 120), and inverting through a center. A cube is good example of an object that possesses 3-fold rotoinversion axes. A 3-fold rotoinversion axis is denoted as $\bar{3}$ (pronounced 'bar 3'). Note that there are actually four $\bar{3}$ axes in a cube, one running through each of the corners of the cube. If one holds one of the $\bar{3}$ axes vertical, then note that there are 3 faces on top, and 3 identical faces upside down on the bottom that are offset from the top faces by 120°.
- **4-fold Rotoinversion** - This involves rotation of the object by 90° then inverting through a center. A four

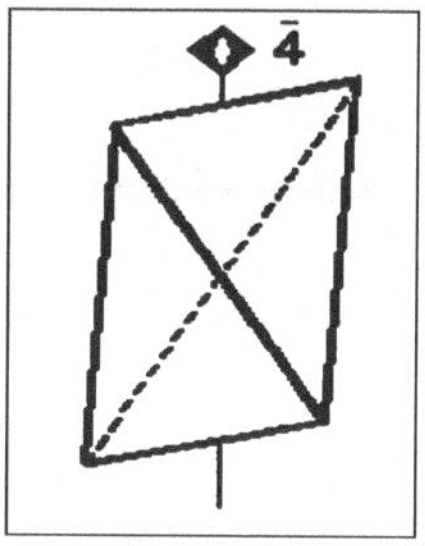

fold rotoinversion axis is symbolised as $\bar{4}$. Note that an object possessing a 4- fold rotoinversion axis will have two faces on top and two identical faces upside down on the bottom, if the $\bar{4}$ axis is held in the vertical position.

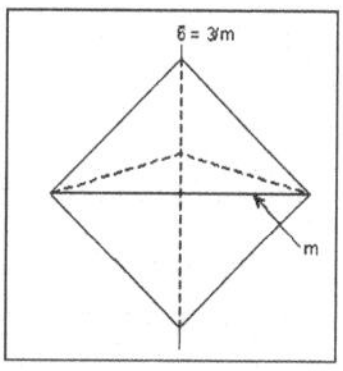

- **6-fold Rotoinversion** - A 6-fold rotoinversion axis ($\bar{6}$) involves rotating the object by 60o and inverting through a center. Note that this operation is identical to having the combination of a 3-fold rotation axis perpendicular to a mirror plane.

Combinations of Symmetry Operations

As should be evident by now, in three dimensional objects, such as crystals, symmetry elements may be present in several different combinations. In fact, in crystals there are 32 possible combinations of symmetry elements. These 32 combinations define the 32 Crystal Classes. Every crystal must belong to one of these 32 crystal classes. In the next lecture we will start to go over each of these crystal classes in detail, but the best way to be able to identify each crystal class is not by listening to me lecture, not necessarily by reading about each class, but actually looking at models of perfect crystals in the lab. In fact, it is my opinion that it is next to impossible to identify symmetry elements and crystal classes without spending a lot of time examining and studying the 3-dimensional models in lab.

Here, we will just give one example of how the various symmetry elements are combined in a somewhat completed crystal. One point that we want to emphasise in this discussion is that if 2 kinds of symmetry elements are present in the same crystal, then they will operate on each other to produce other symmetrical symmetry elements.

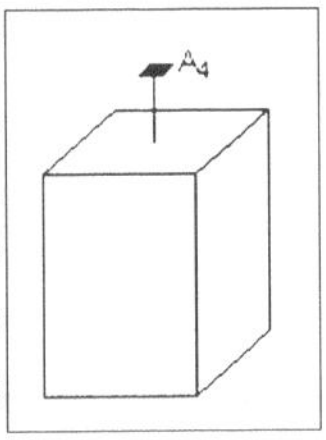

In this example we will start out with the crystal shown here. Note that this crystal has rectangular-shaped sides with a square- shaped top and bottom. The square-shaped top indicates that there must be a 4-fold rotation axis perpendicular to the square shaped face. This is shown in the diagram.

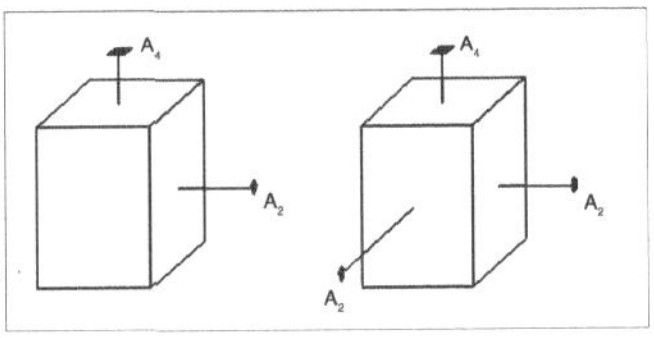

Also note that the rectangular shaped face on the left side of the crystal must have a 2-fold rotation axis that intersects it. Note that the two fold axis runs through the crystal and exits on the left-hand side (not seen in this view), so that both the left and right - hand sides of the crystal are perpendicular to a 2-fold rotation axis.

Since the top face of the crystal has a 4-fold rotation axis, operation of this 4-fold rotation must reproduce the face with the perpendicular 2-fold axis on a 90° rotation. Thus, the front and back faces of the crystal will also have perpendicular 2-fold rotation axes, since these are required by the 4-fold axis.

The square-shaped top of the crystal also suggests that there must be a 2-fold axis that cuts diagonally through the crystal. This 2-fold axis is shown here in the left-hand diagram. But, again operation of the 4-fold axis requires that the other diagonals also have 2-fold axis, as shown in the right-hand diagram.

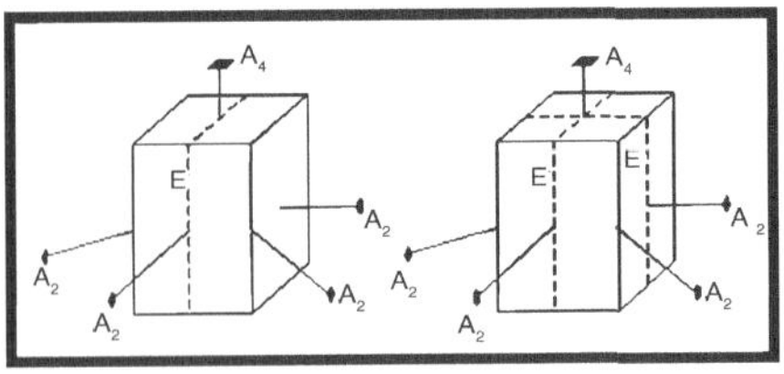

Furthermore, the square-shaped top and rectangular-shaped front of the crystal suggest that a plane of symmetry is present as shown by the left-hand diagram here. But, again, operation of the 4-fold axis requires that a mirror plane is also present that cuts through the side faces, as shown by the diagram on the right.

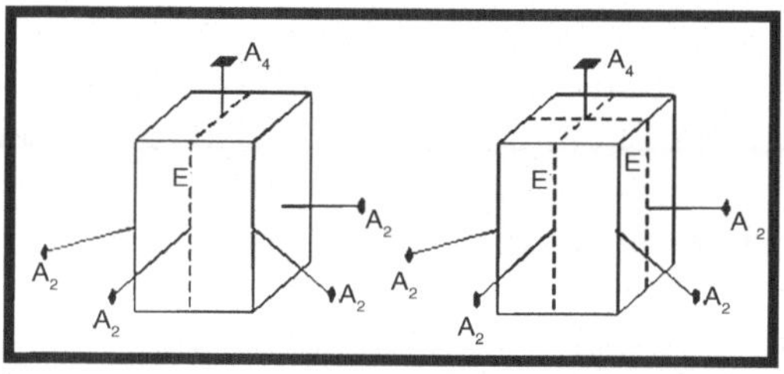

The square top further suggests that there must be a mirror plane cutting the diagonal through the crystal. This mirror plane will be reflected by the other mirror planes cutting the sides of the crystal, or will be reproduced by the 4-fold rotation axis, and thus the crystal will have another mirror plane cutting through the other diagonal, as shown by the diagram on the right.

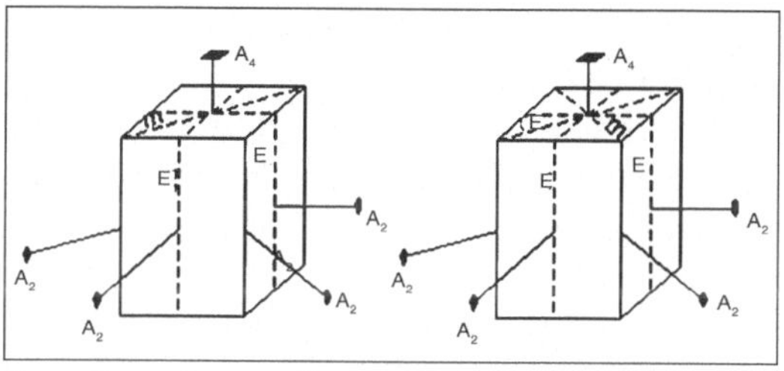

Finally, there is another mirror plane that cuts through the center of the crystal parallel to the top and bottom faces.

Thus, this crystal has the following symmetry elements:

- 1 - 4-fold rotation axis (A_4)
- 4 - 2-fold rotation axes (A_2), 2 cutting the faces and 2 cutting the edges.
- 5 mirror planes (m), 2 cutting across the faces, 2 cutting through the edges, and one cutting horizontally through the center.
- Note also that there is a center of symmetry (i).

The symmetry content of this crystal is thus: i, $1A_4$, $4A_2$, 5m

GLOBAL SYMMETRY

Where the local symmetry determines the environment around a single atom, the global symmetry dictates how the atoms interchange with each other. The first step in determining the global symmetry is to determine the equivalent atoms. First, determine the types of and the relative directions to the nearest neighbour (and second nearest, or higher, if desired) atoms. Two atoms are then equivalent, if their neighbours have the same spatial arrangements. This is straightforward to calculate.

The second step is roughly the same as that found in the local symmetry case, except that the center of mass of the molecule is likely the symmetry center. At this point, if the local symmetries have been determined, only a few unique operations may need to be found to generate the entire group. For example, in the B20 crystal structure, each atom has a local C3 symmetry, and the full point group is generated by including a 2-fold (180? rotation) screw axis which transforms one atom into another. In benzene, two operations are required: a 6-fold (60?) rotation through the central axis and a reflection plane bisecting a bond.

Edit: For the B20 structure, you can use two of the C3 axes, instead, to generate the full group. This should allow you to avoid having to figure out a way to automatically determine the screw axis.

Caution: A caution on using the ideas in the local symmetry section in the global section, to be a symmetry operation, the environment must also be transformed. So, that if you find A, from above, it will only give a candidate symmetry as the transformation may not similarly change the environment appropriately, and further checks are needed. For instance, if the benzene ring had hydrogen atoms sticking out of the plane of the ring along one side, then the reflection plane bisecting the carbon-carbon bond would be fine, but a 180? rotation similarly bisecting the bond would not because it would not reproduce the local environment.

Edit - Translations: There is one other complication that the above discussion on local symmetry ignores: translations. Formally, the correct symmetry operation is,

$$A(x^{\rightarrow}\, i^{-}x^{\rightarrow}\, c) + t^{\rightarrow} = x^{\rightarrow}\, j^{-}x^{\rightarrow}\, c$$

where A and $x^{\rightarrow}$ k, as above, and $t^{\rightarrow}$ is an arbitrary translation. In a symmorphic crystal,

$$\vec{t} = n1\vec{a}1 + n2\vec{a}2 + n3\vec{a}3$$

where $\vec{a}$ i is a primitive lattice translation and ni∈Z, so the point group and translations are completely separable. In a non-symmorphic crystal, $\vec{t}$ can consist of non-primitive translations. The difference between the two is simply that for a symmorphic crystal, a single center of rotation can be found, but for non-symmorphic crystals, this is not true. A molecular system is likely to be 'non-symmorphic' in this latter sense, and require the addition of translations to fully realise the group.

USE OF POINT GROUPS

Group Theory and Point Groups can help us understand and predict important properties of molecules. Three that are described here are:

1. Optical Activity
2. Dipole Moments
3. IR and Raman Spectroscopy.

Optical Activity

Optically active organic molecules (chiral molecules) contain at least one asymmetric carbon atom known as a chiral center. Many inorganic molecules have no chiral centers and yet are optically active. These molecules are called dissymmetric, because they do have some symmetry.

Which molecules are expected to be optically active?

Molecules with no improper axis of rotation are optically active. Note that S1 = σ and S2 = i.

Which point groups have no mirror planes, centers of inversion or other improper rotations?

C1, Cn, and Dn all fit this requirement. C1 is, of course, asymmetric. It has no symmetry and is the familiar situation from organic chemistry.

L-(+)-Lactic acid($C_3H_6O_3$)is a chiral molecule. it is organic and small.

Octahedral metal ion complexes can be optically active, particularly when they are chelated. For example,

$[Co(ethylenediamine)_3]^{3-}$ has two enantiomeric forms with D_3 symmetry.

If one of the ethylenediamine chelates is replaced with two chloride ions, the cis-dichlorobis(ethylenediamine)cobalt(III) ion has C_2 symmetry and is optically active.

Dipole Moments

A molecule will have a dipole moment (that is, it will be polar) if the bond dipole moments do not cancel each other out. So a linear molecule like CO_2 has two polar bonds facing in opposite directions with the result that the molecule itself is not polar. In fact, any molecule with a center of inversion, i, cannot be polar because the bond dipole moments will cancel each other.

Likewise, a molecule with more than one C_n axis $(n>1)$ cannot have a dipole moment. You can realise this logically because the dipole moment of the molecule cannot lie in more than one direction. PF_5 is a good example where the bond dipole moments all cancel. Although it has one C_3 axis, it also has 3 C_2 axes.

All molecules in D point groups all have multiple C axes and therefore cannot be polar. Also, molecules with a horizontal mirror plane cannot have a dipole moment. So, what's left? Polar molecules can be in one of these four point groups: C_1, C_s, C_n, and C_{nv}.

IR and Raman Spectroscopy

One of the most practical uses of point groups and group theory for the inorganic chemist in is predicting the number of infrared and Raman bands that may be expected from a molecule. Alternatively, given the IR or Raman spectrum, the symmetry of a molecule may be inferred. In both IR and Raman spectroscopy the molecule is viewed as containing moving vectors. How these vectors are affected by symmetry will provide a means to determine how many bands would be expected in these spectra.

- IR spectroscopy
- Raman spectroscopy.

IR spectroscopy

For IR spectroscopy, it is the vibrational motions of the atoms that are important. Actually, it is the change in the molecular dipole moment when the atoms vibrate that determines whether the vibration is or is not IR active. The question is: Does the dipole moment change in a way that corresponds with the x-, y-, or z-axis? The mathematically-rigourous way to answer this question is to draw the vectors and then see how these transform against the several symmetry operations in the molecule's point group. The result is called the reducible representation. One can separate this into irreducible representations and compare these to the irreducible representations on a character table to determine the normal modes for the vibrations. If the normal modes correspond with the x-, y-, or z-axis then the vibration will be IR active.

Alternatively, we can stick with pictures and use some logic to realise how many IR bands a molecule will have. Let's use water, H_2O, as our example. Water has three vibrational modes: a symmetric stretch, a bending mode, and an asymmetrical stretch.

Symmetrical Stretch

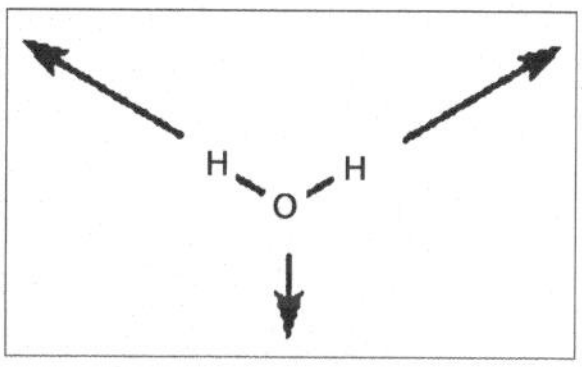

In this mode the dipole moment for the molecule does not change in direction, but it does change in magnitude. As the molecule stretches, the dipole moment increases. So the dipole moment changes and it does so along the z-axis. This vibration is IR active.

Bending mode

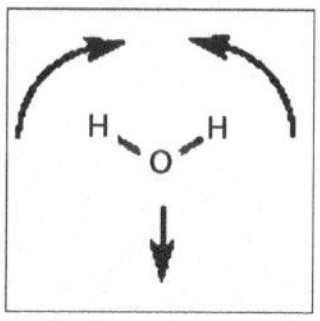

In this bending (scissoring) mode, the dipole does not change direction. It is still pointed along the z-axis, but it does change in magnitude (increasing with the bend). Thus, this mode is also IR active.

Asymmetric stretch

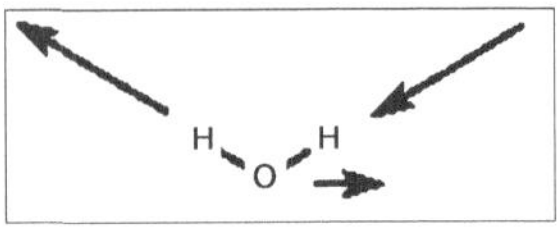

In this mode, both the direction and magnitude of the dipole moment are changing. The dipole moment switches from left to right rather like a windshield wiper. Unlike a windshield wiper, however, the size of the dipole moment increase to each side and decreases when in the middle.

The movement is restricted to the yz-plane of the molecule. There is no change in the x-axis. If you consider the animation closely, you will realise that there is no change in the z-axis component of the dipole. This always has the same magnitude and direction. It is the y-axis component that is changing first to the negative, then the positive direction. Thus, this vibrational mode corresponds to the y-axis (B_2 on the character table) and will be IR active.

10

Rotations and Vibrations of Polyatomic Molecules

When more than one polar bond is present in the same molecule, the polarity of one bond may cancel that of another. Thus the presence of polar bonds in a polyatomic molecule does not guarantee that the molecule as a whole will have a dipole moment. In such a case it is necessary to treat each polar bond mathematically as a vector and represent it with an arrow. The length of such an arrow shows how large the bond dipole moment is, while the direction of the arrow is a line drawn from the positive to the negative end of the bond. Adding the individual bond dipole moments as vectors will give the overall molecular dipole moment.

As an example of this vector addition, consider the BF3 molecule. The dipole moments of the three B—F bonds are represented by the arrows BF′ (pointing straight left), BF″ (pointing down to the right), and BF′″ (pointing up to the right). The sum of vectors BF″ and BF′″ may be obtained by the parallelogram law-a line from F′″ drawn parallel to BF″ intersects a line from F″ drawn parallel to BF′″ at point E. Thus the resultant vector BE (the diagonal of the parallelogram BF′″EF″) is the sum of BF″ and BF′″. The resultant BE is exactly equal in length and exactly opposite in direction to bond dipole BF″. Therefore the net result is zero dipole moment.

Those arrangements of equivalent bonds that give zero dipole moment in this way. In addition to the trigonal arrangement just discussed, there is the obvious case of two equal bonds 180° apart. The other is much less obvious, namely, a tetrahedral arrangement of equal bonds. Any combination of these arrangements will also be non-polar. The molecule PF5 for example, is non-polar since the bonds are arranged in a trigonal bipyramid, as discussed in 'The Shapes of Molecules.' Since three of the five bonds constitute a trigonal arrangement, they will have no resultant dipole moment. The remaining two bonds have equal but opposite dipoles which will likewise cancel.

If we replace any of the bonds with a different bond, or with a lone pair, the vectors will no longer cancel and the molecule will have a resultant dipole moment.

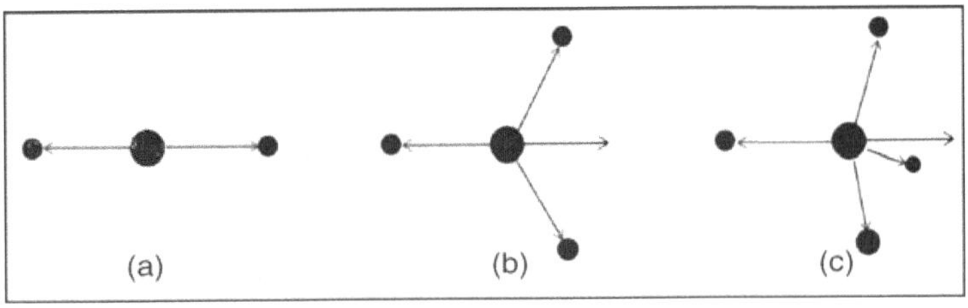

Fig. 10.1

The simplest arrangements of equivalent bonds around a central atom which produce a resultant dipole moment of zero: (a) linear; (b) trigonal. The two right-hand bonds (black resultant) cancel the left-hand bond. (c) Tetrahedral. The three right-hand bonds (black resultant) cancel the left-hand bond.

MOLECULAR STRUCTURE: VIBRATION AND ROTATION

Molecular lasers function differently than atomic lasers because they have vibrational and rotational energies as well as electronic energy. These molecular vibrations occur because the relative positions and orientations of the atomic nuclei are not absolutely fixed within the molecule. The molecular rotations occur because the individual molecules are free to spin and rotate in space since they are in a gaseous state. The energies associated with molecular vibrations and rotations are quantised just like the electronic energy. Transitions between vibrational energy levels emit photons with wavelengths in the infrared region, while transitions between rotational energy levels emit photons in the microwave region.

The CO_2 laser is based on the vibrational and rotational transitions of the CO_2 molecule. This molecule consists of two oxygen atoms covalently bonded with a central carbon atom. Arranged in sp^2 hybrid orbitals, each oxygen atom forms a sigma and a pi bond with the carbon atom and leaves two free electron pairs:

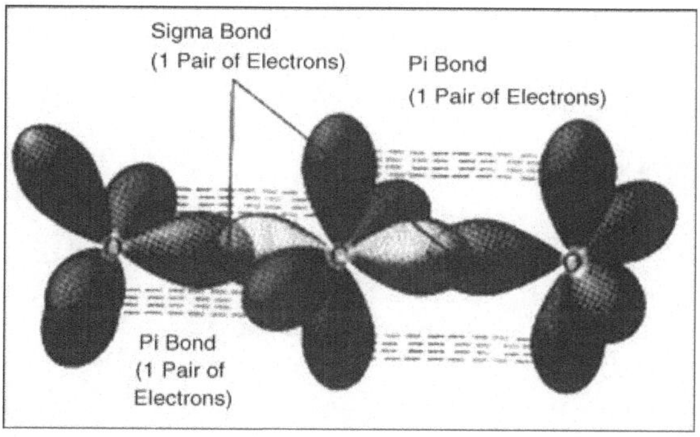

Fig. 10.2

The dynamics of the carbon dioxide molecule are very similar to the dynamics of diatomic molecules such as CO or HCl.

MOLECULAR VIBRATION

In a diatomic molecule such as O_2, N_2 or CO, the individual atoms are bound by a molecular binding force that functions much like the spring constant k of a linear harmonic oscillator. When excited, the two nuclei will vibrate much like two masses connected by a spring. While real diatomic molecules are not perfect harmonic oscillators, their potential energy functions approximate those of a harmonic oscillator for a certain value of inter-nuclear separation. Although Carbon Dioxide is a triatomic molecule, it behaves much like a simple diatomic molecule because its structure is linear. Such a linear triatomic molecule has three normal modes of vibration, described as the asymmetric stretch mode, the bending mode and the symmetric stretch mode.

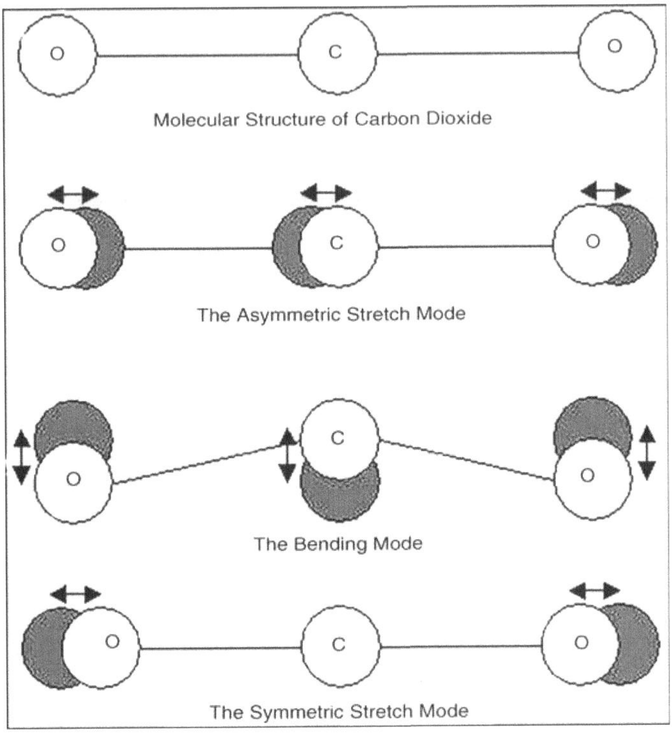

Fig. 10.3

Each one of these normal modes of vibration for the CO_2 molecule is associated with a characteristic frequency of vibration (w) as well as a ladder of allowed energy levels. Therefore we label the three vibrational modes n_1, n_2, and n_3, with their vibrational energy levels being quantised (n = 0, 1, 2, 3...). To describe the vibrational modes we use the notation (n_1, n_2, n3). We can approximate the vibrational energy levels as the quantum mechanical simple harmonic oscillator (h_b = h/(2pi)):

$E_v = h_b w_0$*(n+1/2), where v0 is the classical vibration frequency,

$$w_0 = (k/u)^\wedge 1/2$$

Notice that there will be a ground state vibrational level (corresponding to n=0) with some positive energy $E_0 = h_b w/2$

While in reality each normal mode is slightly anharmonic, the specific equation for the vibrational energy of CO_2 can still be described by:

$$E(n_1, n_2, n_3) = hcw_1 (n_1+1/2) + hcw_2 (n_2+1/2) + hcw_3 (n_3+1/2)$$

RELATION OF ENERGY AND VIBRATION

Newtonian Mechanics

Using Newtonian mechanics the vibrations of a molecule can be calculated by treating the bonds like springs. This is useful because like a spring, a bond requires energy to stretch it out and it also takes energy to squeeze it together. The energy needed to stretch or squeeze the bond is dependent on the stiffness of the bond, which is represented by the spring constant k, and the reduced mass, or 'center of mass' of the two atoms attached to either end denoted by μ. The formula used to relate the energy needed to cause a vibration in the bond is:

$$E = h\nu = \frac{h}{2\pi}\sqrt{\frac{k}{\mu}}.$$

h: is planck's constant

ν: is frequency and represents the rate at which the bond is squished together and pulled apart again. The larger ? the faster this rate becomes.

E: is the energy required to push and pull the bond together.

μ: The reduce mass is the two masses of the atoms multiplied together and divided by their addition:

$$\mu = \frac{m_1 m_2}{m_1 + m_2}.$$

Quantum Mechanics

Using quantum mechanics, the formula that describes the spring is exactly the same as the Newtonian mechanics version except only certain energies or energy levels are allowed. Think of the energy levels as steps on a ladder where a person can only go up or down one rung at a time. Just as that person can't stand on the space between rungs so the bond can not have an energy between energy levels. This new formula becomes:

$$E_n = h\nu = h\left(n + \frac{1}{2}\right)\frac{1}{2\pi}\sqrt{\frac{k}{m}},$$

where n is a quantum number or 'energy level' that can take values of 0, 1, 2... The statement that energy levels can only go up or down one level at a time is known as a selection rule which states that the only allowed transitions between energy levels are:

$$\Delta n = \pm 1$$

where Δn is the energy transition.

MOLECULAR ROTATION:

Again because CO_2 is a linear triatomic molecule and thus behaves very much like a diatomic molecule, it is considerably simple to understand the dynamics of its rotation. To start, picture the molecule as a classical dumbbell with masses on the ends connected by a rod. When the dumbbell then rotates about its center of mass (carbon atom) it has a kinetic energy that is a function of its moment of inertia and the length of the rod.

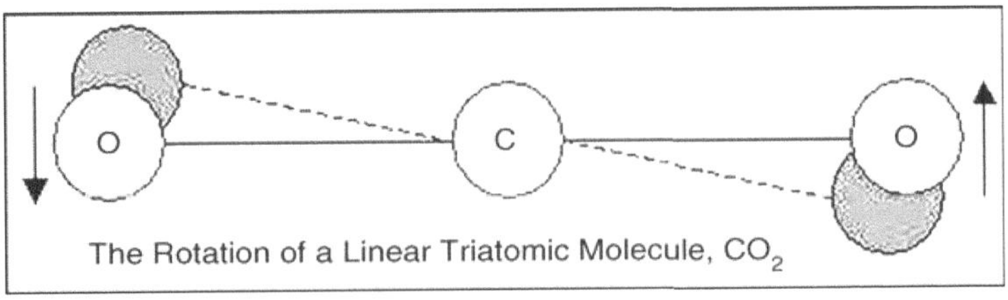

Fig. 10.4

This model must be adjusted somewhat to describe a diatomic molecule because the separation of the masses is not fixed. As the molecule rotates the oxygen atoms are pulled farther apart by the centrifugal force, therefore increasing the moment of inertia. It is even more complicated if the molecule is experiencing a molecular vibration.

Fortunately, for our purposes the rigid dumbbell approximation will suffice for describing the rotational energy of a diatomic molecule. When the classical equation for rotational energy is put into a quantum mechanical form, with the quantum number J describing the rotational states, we then have an expression for the rotational energy of a diatomic molecule. Thanks to its linear structure, the rotational energy spectrum of CO_2 has the same character as that for diatomic molecules and the rotational energy levels are thus approximated by:

$$EJ = hcBeJ(J+1),\ J = 0, 1, 2, 3...$$

$$E = \frac{J(J+1)\hbar^2}{2I},\ J = 0, 1, 2, 3, \ldots$$

where the rotational constant Be for the CO_2 molecule is Be =.39 cm-1. The difference between energy levels is:

$$\Delta E = \frac{J\hbar^2}{I}$$

MOLECULAR SPECTRA

The plasma of the CO_2 laser contains He, CO_2, and N_2. When a potential of 18,000 Volts is placed across the plasma, electrons collide with the N_2 molecules and excite them to their lowest vibrational levels. These vibrational levels of the N_2 molecule are metastable and represent an energy very close to the energy of the asymmetric vibrational states in the CO_2 molecule. This is because the forcing constant for the asymmetric vibration is very near the forcing constant for a stretching of the N_2 molecule. Through collisional excitation transfer, these excited N_2 molecules populate the asymmetric vibrational states in the CO_2 molecule.

The n=1 vibrational levels of the N_2 molecule transfers energy to the (001) states in CO_2, the n=2 levels of N2 populate the (002) states in CO_2, and so forth. The laser's infrared output comes from the CO_2 molecular transitions from rotational states of the first asymmetric vibrational mode (001) to rotational states of both the first symmetric stretch mode (100) and the second bending mode (010). The following is an energy diagram for the lasing process in the CO_2 laser:

The (100) and (020) vibrational levels depopulate when they relax rather quickly into lower vibrational levels, particularly the (010) mode. The CO_2 molecule transfers energy from these lower vibrational levels to the He atoms through collisions. Since the infrared laser transitions are relatively slower than this depopulation mechanism, a population inversion results.

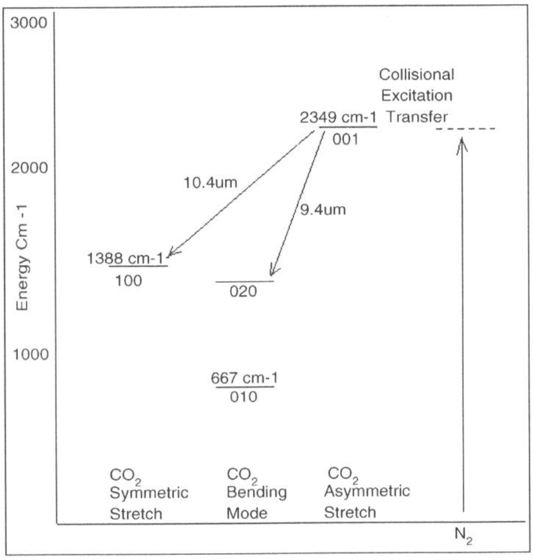

Fig. 10.5

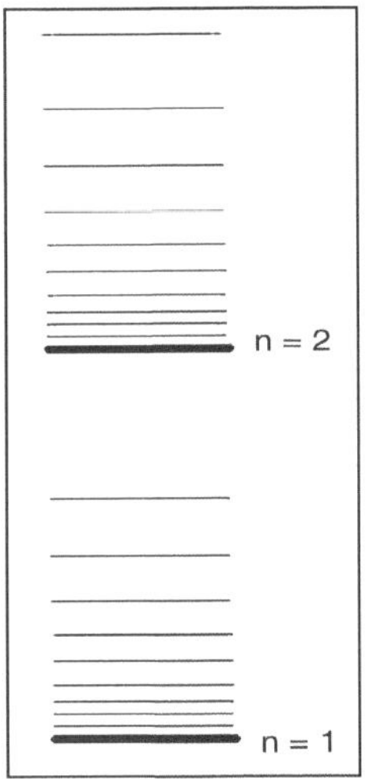

Fig. 10.6

As discussed in the Molecular Structure page, a molecule in a particular vibrational mode may also be in one of several rotational states.

These rotational states have a degeneracy of (2J+1) and differ by energy E= J(J+1)h^2/I. Because the photon resulting from any transition must have angular momentum and because angular momentum must be conserved, molecules in a particular vibrational and rotational state may transition to another rotational state only if the change in J is +1 or -1.

(Likewise in electronic transitions, electrons may transition to other levels such that the change in quantum number 'l' equals +-1.) A molecule in the (001) mode and the J(7) rotational state may transition to either the J(6) or J(8) in either the (100) or the (010) vibrational mode. It may not transition to another J(7) state.

If the energy difference between the lowest (001) state and the lowest (100) state is E0, then the energy of the transition between the J=7 (001) state and the J=6 (100) state will be of energy:

$$E = E_0 + \frac{(J)\hbar^2}{I} \Rightarrow E = E_0 + \frac{(7)\hbar^2}{I}$$

Likewise, transitions where the change in J is +1, the energy released will be:

$$E = E_0 + \frac{(J)\hbar^2}{I}$$

So, we should see two types of transitions in the laser output: those with energy just greater than E0, and those with energy just below E0. This will form a branched structure in the emission spectrum.

Transitions corresponding to a change of -1 in J are said to belong to the 'R' branch, while transitions corresponding to a change of +1 in J are said to belong to the 'P' branch. R(6) refers to the transition from the J=7 rotational state of the (001) vibrational mode to the J=6 state of the (100) mode.

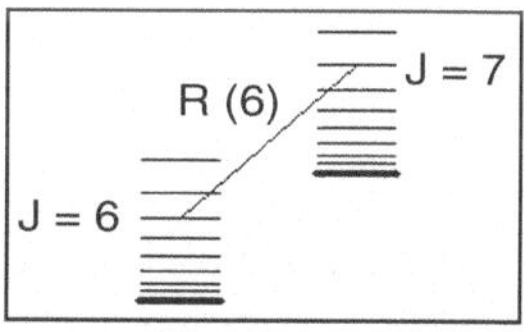

Fig. 10.7

Moreover, we should see in the laser emission two distinct bands, each having P and R branches, corresponding to the series of transitions from the (001) to the (100) and from the (001) to the (020) vibrational modes. Because the difference between adjacent rotational levels increases as J increases, the separation between emission lines in the P and R branch will increase as J increases. The branches will be centered around frequency v0 (corresponding to E0).

According to Maxwell-Boltzmann statistics, the distribution of molecules in rotational states should follow the relation:

$$N(E) = G(J)e^{-E/kT}$$

where G(j) is the degeneracy of each state, which happens to be 2J+1. So, the population of molecules in the Jth rotational state should be proportional to:

$$N(E) = (2J+1)e^{-E/kT}$$

This will give a distribution that looks like this:

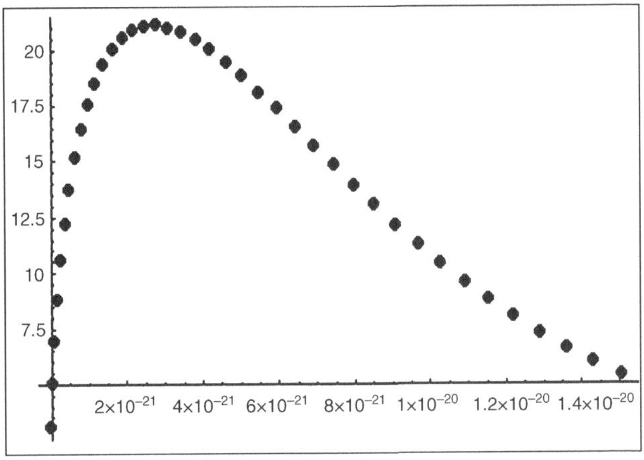

Fig. 10.8

When the excited CO_2 levels are populated by collisions with N_2 the levels will be populated according to this relation. Laser transitions will be most probable from the rotational states that have maximum population (*i.e.,* the maximum on the Boltzmann curve) As a result, each branch in the emission will be curved similarly to the Boltzmann curve.

APPLICATIONS OF VIBRATIONAL MOTIONS

When light of a certain frequency hits a molecule that has a vibration whose motion corresponds to the same frequency then the light gets absorbed into the molecule and the energy from the light causes the bonds to move in that specific vibrational motion. By checking for light that gets absorbed, scientists can tell if a certain kind of molecular bond is there and match it against a list of molecules that have that bond.

However, some molecules like helium and argon have only one atom and don't have any bonds. This means that they won't absorb any light in the same way a molecule with more than one molecule can.

The specific fields of chemistry that use molecular vibrations in their studies include infrared spectroscopy (IR) and Raman spectroscopy (Raman) with IR being more widely used and having three subfields of its own. These subfields are known as Near IR, Mid IR and Far IR spectroscopy. The following is a general list of these fields and real world applications

Near IR: quantitative determination of species such as proteins, fats, low low-molecular-weight hydrocarbons and water. Further use is obtained in the agricultural products, food, petroleum and chemical industries

Mid IR:The most popular of the IR fields, is used in determining structure of organic and biochemical compounds.

Far IR: this field is less popular though it has found uses in inorganic studies

Raman: Is used for the qualitative and quantitative study of inorganic, organic and biological systems often as a complimentary technique to IR.

ANHARMONICITY

In classical mechanics, anharmonicity is the deviation of a system from being a harmonic oscillator. An oscillator that is not oscillating in simple harmonic motion is known as an anharmonic oscillator where the system can be approximated to a harmonic oscillator and the anharmonicity can be calculated using perturbation theory. If the anharmonicity is large then other numerical techniques have to be used.

As a result, oscillations with frequencies 2ω and 3ω, etc., where ω is the fundamental frequency of the oscillator, appear. Furthermore, the frequency ω_0 deviates from the frequency ω_0 of the harmonic oscillations. As a first approximation, the frequency shift $\Delta\omega = \omega - \omega_0$is proportional to the square of the oscillation amplitude A:

$$\Delta\omega \propto A^2$$

In a system of oscillators with natural frequencies ω_α, ω_β... anharmonicity results in additional oscillations with frequencies $\omega_\alpha \pm \omega_\beta$.

Anharmonicity also modifies the profile of the resonance curve, leading to interesting phenomena such as the foldover effect and superharmonic resonance.

GENERAL PRINCIPLE

A generalised version of harmonic oscillator in which the relationship between force and displacement is linear. The harmonic oscillator is a highly idealised system that oscillates with a single frequency, irrespective of the amount of pumping or energy injected into the system. Consequently, the harmonic oscillator's fundamental frequency of vibration is independent of the amplitude of the vibrations.

Applications of the harmonic oscillator model abound in various fields, but perhaps the most commonly studied system is the Hooke's law mass-spring system. In the Hooke's law system the restoring force exerted on the mass is proportional to the displacement of the mass from its equilibrium position. This linear relationship between force and displacement mandates that the oscillation frequency of the mass will be independent of the amplitude of the displacement.

In a mechanical anharmonic oscillator, the relationship between force and displacement is not linear but depends upon the amplitude of the displacement. The non-linearity arises from the fact that the spring is not capable of exerting a restoring force that is proportional to its displacement because of, for example, stretching in the material comprising the spring. As a result of the non-linearity, the vibration frequency can change, depending upon the system's displacement. These changes in the vibration frequency result in energy being coupled from the fundamental vibration frequency to other frequencies through a process known as parametric coupling.

Examples in Physics

There are many systems throughout the physical world that can be modeled as anharmonic oscillators in addition to the non-linear mass-spring system. For example, an atom, which consists of a positively charged nucleus surrounded by a negatively charged electronic cloud, experiences a displacement between the center of mass of the nucleus and the electronic cloud when an electric field is present. The amount of that displacement, called the electric dipole moment, is related linearly to the applied field for small fields, but as the magnitude of the field is increased, the field-dipole moment relationship becomes non-linear, just as in the mechanical system.

Further examples of anharmonic oscillators include the large-angle pendulum, which exhibits chaotic behaviour as a result of its anharmonicity; non-equilibrium semiconductors that possess a large hot carrier population, which exhibit non-linear behaviours of various types related to the effective mass of the carriers; and ionospheric plasmas, which also exhibit non-linear behaviour based on the anharmonicity of the plasma. In fact, virtually all oscillators become anharmonic when their pump amplitude increases beyond some threshold, and as a result it is necessary to use non-linear equations of motion to describe their behaviour.

Bibliography

Skoog, D. A.; Holler, F. J.: *Crouch, S. R. Principles of Instrumental Analysis,* Thomson Brooks/Cole: Belmont, CA, 2007.

McQuarrie, D. A.; Simon, J. D.: *Physical Chemistry A Molecular Approach,*Anne McGuire, University Science Books, 2001.

Grasselli, J. G.; Bulkins, B. J.: *Analytical Raman Spectroscopy,* New York: Wiley, 2003.

Atkins, P. W.: *Molecular Quantum Mechanics,* New York, Oxford University Press, 2004.

Guillory, William.: *Introduction to Molecular Structure and Spectroscopy,* Boston, MA: Allyn and Bacon, Inc., 2003.

Struve, Walter.: *Fundamentals of Molecular Spectroscopy.* Wiley, University Press, 2005.

Harris, Daniel, and Michael Bertolucci.: *Symmetry and Spectroscopy,* Oxford University Press, 2002.

Cotton, F. Albert.: *Chemical Applications of Group Theory,* Wiley, University Press, 1990.

Horak, M., and Antonin Vitek.: *Interpretations and Processing of Vibrational Specta,* University Press, Wiley, 1978.

Diem, M.: *Introduction to Modern Vibrational Spectroscopy.* Wiley, 2004.

Kondratyuk, P.: *Spectrochimica Acta Part A: Molecular and Biomolecular Spectroscopy, Cambridge Bridge,* New York, 2001.

Christopher J. : *Atomic Physics,* Oxford University Press, 2008.

Conway, A.: *Orbital Mechanics,* Oxford Univ. Press, London, 1993.

Datta, S. : *Electronic Transport in Mesoscopic Systems*,Cambridge University Press, Cambridge, 1995.

Dayal, Deepak : *Modern Methods of Teaching Physics*, APH Pub, Delhi, 2007.

Edwards, S. F. : *The Theory of Polymer Dynamics*, Oxford University Inc NY, 1986.

Flensberg, K. : *Many-Body Quantum Theory in Condensed Matter Physics*, Oxford University Press, Oxford, 2004.

Gedde, U.W.: *Polymer Physics*, Chapman & Hall, 1995

Ghoshal, S. N. : *Atomic Physics Modern Physics*, S. Chand Publisher, Delhi, 2008.

Herzberg, G. : *Molecular Spectra and Molecular Structure*, Van Nostrand Reinhold Company, New York, 1979.

Herzberg, G.: *Molecular Spectra and Molecular Structure*, Van Nostrand Reinhold Company, New York, 1979.

Index